BUMPING & SNACKING

DISCOVERING A WORLDVIEW

ROBERT B. HAFEY

Published by:

Robert B. Hafey
13915 Lemont Road
Homer Glen, Illinois 60491
rbhafey@gmail.com
www.roberthafey.com

First Edition

ISBN 978-0-9991032-2-7 (e-book)
ISBN 978-0-9991032-3-4 (paperback)

Cover design by Kristen Gurnitz Bernier
Inside artwork by Larkin McPhearson
Editing by Denise M. Baron-Unland
Photographs by Robert B. Hafey

To all the people of the world.
May you find acceptance and understanding.

Visit www.roberthafey.com and the *Bumping & Snacking* Facebook page to view photographs that link to the stories in each chapter.

https://www.facebook.com/bumpingandsnacking

CONTENTS

PREFACE

My friend, Dusty, who has spent his adult life living overseas, encouraged my wife Sandy and I to travel to Europe. To give us comfort, and reduce any anxiety, he offered to plan a rough itinerary and then travel with us, acting as our personal guide. How could we say no?

A few months later, our flight landed in Shannon, Ireland. After retrieving our luggage and clearing customs, we left the secure portion of the airport to be greeted by Dusty and his partner Ulla.

After cramming our luggage into the rear of their small European hatchback car, we squeezed into the back seat to begin our adventure. Then this childhood friend asked Sandy and I the question that became the inspiration for the title of this book. "Are you two ready to go bumping and snacking?"

"Bumping and Snacking" implies touring around in a car (local bus, train, or urban hiking) with few firm plans, and then stopping for something to eat when hungry. Intentionally loosely planned, relaxed and semi-structured travel, which allows the culture of the place visited to rub off on the traveler a bit. This type of travel allows time for the culture to come to the traveler, instead of running from one tourist site to the next.

That trip set the standard for our future travel. We decided we did not have to see all the tourist sites in the places we visited. Taking time to sit and enjoy a cup of coffee at a sidewalk café, became as important as seeing another site.

Travel has altered my view of the world and the people who occupy it. I hope reading this book will inspire others to strike off on their own, or with a few friends, to expand their worldview.

ACKNOWLEDGMENTS

Most of the stories in *Bumping & Snacking* are shared experience travel stories. My wife Sandra is my traveling companion. For me, traveling together has been one of the joys of my life. Our shared travel experiences have helped to cement my relationship with the one I love.

She gets total credit for taking on the responsibility of planning our trips. She enjoys digging into the details required to make travel arrangements and plan our itinerary.

A dear friend and inspiration, Dennis (Dusty) Luke Golobitsh, has influenced me in many ways. He had wanderlust early in life and shared his stories of travel to places I only dreamt of. I think it rubbed off on me. He is also a skilled photographer and became my informal mentor. He helped me both understand what having a worldview means, and how to artistically capture images during my travels.

I would also like to recognize the members of a local writer's group, WriteOn Joliet, who have helped me to become a better writer and enjoy the process of writing. They are included in my ever-expanding circle of creative friends who inspire me to create.

Denise M. Baron-Unland edited *Bumping & Snacking*. She is a gifted and prolific writer, as well as a talented editor. She gently pushed and prodded me to improve my skillset as a writer, and by doing so helped me grow as a person.

Laurie Mayfield proofread the manuscript twice during the writing process. Her attention to detail is evident in the finished book.

Kristen Gurnitz-Bernier, a talented and creative graphic artist, designed the cover for *Bumping & Snacking*. After sending her a conceptual sketch, she took over and created a fun cover that graphically tells the reader what to expect between the front and back covers.

Larkin McPhearson, a creative artist, contributed a piece of art that is inside the front cover and then accepted the challenge to create the unique chapter ornaments that sit below each chapter heading title.

INTRODUCTION

I think Mark Twain said it best. This quote, from his book "The Innocents Abroad," which was published in 1869, is as applicable today as it was then. "Travel is fatal to prejudice, bigotry, and narrow-mindedness, and many of our people need it sorely on these accounts. Broad, wholesome, charitable views of men and things cannot be acquired by vegetating in one little corner of the earth all one's lifetime."

During childhood, we are as malleable as a lump of bread dough and become less so, like a crusty two-day old baguette, as we age. Our environment and upbringing help to define our beliefs, customs, prejudices, and the foods we are comfortable eating. As life unfolds, we interact with countless people and visit new places. We experience joy, wonder, love, heartbreak, and sadness. Those combined experiences, with people and places, determine and constantly reconfigure our view of the world. This worldview not only determines how we view the world, but how the world views us. Quantity matters. The more frequently we are exposed to people different from ourselves, and the places they live, the broader our worldview.

Bumping & Snacking contains self-planned travel experiences. Planning and then traveling on your own, helps travelers begin to understand the beliefs, customs, prejudices, and foods of a wide variety of people. It will put the traveler in touch, literally, with new people and places.

Food is a universal language with many dialects. To gain an understanding of this language one must be open to eating what is unfamiliar. Self-planned travel forces one to decide, multiple times a day, what to eat. Partaking in food that is local and different opens doors to cultural understanding and acceptance.

Consider this entry-level opportunity to learn about different cultures. With friends, plan and visit restaurants and grocery stores owned and operated by people who emigrated from other countries. This takes courage because it draws people out of their comfort zone. But doing so can begin to expand one's worldview.

Independent self-planned travel is a form of risk-taking. Traveling in a country where you are the minority and cannot speak the local language is both humbling and anxiety-inducing. Many people are averse to risk, which is why cruises and bus tours are popular with tourists. Risk-averse tourists feel comfortable when someone else does the planning. They simply show up to be transported, fed, and shepherded from one tourist site to the next. Tourism has one big drawback. It eliminates the opportunity for the happenstance, chance encounters with local people that could provide cultural insights.

Self-planned travel is also an opportunity for self-discovery and personal growth. It is a chance to be brave, to get past the fear of cultures, people and food that differ from the norm. It pushes individuals outside of their isolated and insulated little worlds.

Pack your bags. To see the world differently, go experience it.

1

ITALY

THE WHOLE COUNTRY IS A MUSEUM

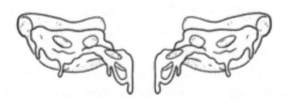

My wife Sandy and I had watched the Rick Steves PBS programs featuring Italy and knew about the pickpockets targeting visitors to Rome. This, and other preconceived notions of a country, often change while visiting.

Flights to Europe, from our home base near Chicago, generally depart in the early evening. When the trip flight time is combined with the destination local time, arrival in Europe can be from early to late morning, depending on the arrival city.

We arrived in Madrid around 9:00 am and then had to endure a four-hour layover before our flight to Rome departed. It was late afternoon when we arrived in Rome and we were both tired and hungry. Sleep on an airplane, for me, is as elusive as the mythological Big Foot. It just does not exist. That is why our arrival day is a zombie day. During zombie day we attempt to stay awake as long as possible, like college students at an all-night frat party, before going to bed.

Even though I had been awake for over twenty-four hours, as I departed the plane, I felt the adrenaline-driven excitement caused by visiting someplace new. Our travels would take us to Rome, Florence, Siena, Tuscany, Venice, and Milan and we had finally arrived.

After retrieving our luggage and clearing passport control, we searched for signage, or someone, who could direct us to the railway platform and the train that would take us to the main transportation hub, Termini Station, located in central Rome. Eventually a sign, with a graphic symbol of a train, guided us to the ticket office and train platform. Once we arrived at Termini Station, we planned to catch a taxi to our hotel where we would collapse onto our bed.

Using trains for travel is foreign (pun intended) to most people from the United States. The percentage of people in the United States who use train transportation, other than daily commuters, is low because the United States sees no value in investing in rail infrastructure. Therefore Americans, who rarely consider train travel when planning domestic trips, have no experience when they arrive in Europe. For them, walking into a train station with twenty-five different arrival and departure platforms, while throngs of people are rushing to and from all of them, can be daunting. Fortunately for us, this and most airports have only a single train line that shuttles passengers to and from city-center.

With our tickets and luggage in hand we climbed aboard the next train for Termini Station. As we looked for seats, we scanned the passengers to determine which one might be the pickpocket. Could it be that teenager in the T-shirt, or that middle-aged man who seemed a bit shifty and nervous? We anxiously watched as the train pulled into each stop to drop off and pick up new passengers. Every new passenger was a possible threat and if anyone came near, we used a death grip on our luggage.

When we exited the train at the final stop, Rome's Termini Station, it was late in the afternoon. As we walked from the arrival platform and then through the low-light cavernous station, we stopped to get our bearings. We acknowledged that everything had gone to plan so far, but to complete our long and tiring day of travel, we had to locate a taxi to transport us to our hotel.

Most travel guidebooks contain a list of key words in the local language. Therefore, prior to any visit to a non-English speaking country, I will reference that list to try and learn a few words, like taxi, that might be required upon arrival. Guess what the word for taxi is in Italian? Taxi!

As we moved toward the terminal exit an overhead directory, containing the word "taxi" and an arrow, directed us to the taxi stand located outside. The sun had already set and in the dim early evening light we walked to the back of an exceedingly long line of people with their luggage. It was disheartening to see the line for we were both tired, and the bed was calling.

Wishing and hoping for a taxi quickly replaced my thoughts and concerns about pickpockets. In the fifteen minutes we patiently waited in line, not even one appeared. Could they be on strike? I mumbled one of the choice Italian swear words I had memorized (Porca miseria!) before we began a conversation about our other transportation options like buses or the Metro subway system.

While planning our trip, we had researched and written down the name of the Rome Metro stop located in our hotel's neighborhood. After a bit of angst, we agreed to the challenge of taking the Metro to our hotel. It could be accessed directly below Termini Station. As we rolled our luggage toward the stairs that led down to two different platform levels, we observed six young children walking by. At the top of the stairs stood a policeman. He said something while pointing at the children. Because I did not understand what he had said, I asked, "What?"

He repeated, "Pick-pockets," while pointing directly at the pack of young children.

I blurted out, "WHAT! Bambinos, pick-pockets?"

While keeping an eye on the youth gang walking away from us, we headed down the Metro stairs where we found, and then stood staring at, a metro map. When you take a plane, the destination is clearly understood for there is only one. When you board a train, the destination is clearly listed, but very often that is not your destination. Your stop is more than likely one of the many stops the train makes on its way to its final destination. So, we stood there scanning all the stops on each of the Metro lines trying to find the name of the Metro stop for our hotel's neighborhood. Once located, we then decided on which Metro platform to wait to board the correct line. We purchased tickets from a vending machine and crossed our fingers as we climbed aboard the next train.

We kept our weary eyes glued to the stop chart located in our rail car and counted down the stops until we had reached ours and confidently bounded off. Metro stops do not just have one exit to the streets above. So, we stood gawking at four different exist signs not knowing which one might get us close to our hotel. We made a joint decision to just take any exit and began to walk up an extremely long sloping ramp.

I had expected to come out on a street where I could fire up my Garmin GPS unit, plug in the hotel address, and then be guided to our hotel. Instead the exit ramp led to an underground parking garage. Due to the length of time we had already spent underground I began to wonder if we might catch a glimpse of the catacombs.

As we stood there staring at a map, first one, and then another local walked up and offered to help. We did not speak Italian and they did not speak English, but we used map finger-pointing, grimaces, and moans to communicate that we were lost, tired and hungry. As we pointed to our hotel's location on the map they conversed in Italian as they worked on our escape plan.

Suddenly, and quite unexpectedly, a miracle occurred. Out of the corner of my eye, I observed a taxi pulling up to a stairway, right below where we stood, to drop off a passenger. Because my Termini station experience had led me to believe no taxis existed in Rome, you can imagine my excitement.

After racing down the stairs I used my body as a roadblock so he could not depart and then using a combination of hand signals and words he clearly had difficulty understanding, I asked, no begged, the driver to take us to our hotel.

"Hotel, per favore?" I pleaded.

Finally, he nodded an approval. I ran back up the stairs to claim our baggage and Sandy, and then stopped in front of the two strangers who had offered to help, grabbed our map, shook their hands, and repeatedly said, "Grazie, grazie, grazie." As the taxi pulled away, I looked back at them and observed large beaming smiles that mirrored the one on my face.

Within a few minutes we had been dropped off at our hotel, walked in, and approached the hotel proprietor who sat behind the counter. I walked up to him and proudly used my Italian language skills to say, "Buongiorno."

He looked up and said, "Hello."

Like most people who deal with tourists on a regular basis, he spoke some English.

After he checked us in, we asked, "Could you recommend someplace to get something light to eat?"

He responded, "Would you like some fresh fruit, so you don't have to go out?"

"Per favore," I responded.

He departed and returned with two purplish red plums and some crisp almond cookies. He then showed us to our small spartan room that contained a double bed. We quickly ate our snacks and unpacked while staring longingly at the small bed. We soon said "Buonanotte" to each other and collapsed in bed. As I lay there, I thought about the fact that Rome was full of kind and helpful people, despite the gangs of young children waiting to fleece the next unsuspecting tourist.

Because of our long layover in Madrid, and the transportation snafu in Rome, we had already been in a zombie state for some hours when we hit the bed about 7:00 pm. Sleep came easy for both of us and twelve hours later we were ready for the breakfast included in the cost of our room. To go up two floors, we climbed aboard a minuscule elevator that had a capacity of two. If riding with a stranger, your hands should be kept above your head to ensure you are not accused of inappropriate behavior. As the doors opened to release us from our confinement the alluring smell of coffee greeted us like an old friend.

The small dining area, located on the top floor, provided a view of the surrounding roof tops and St. Peter's Basilica, our first day destination, off in the distance. My dream that the hotel owner's grandmother awoke at 4:00 am to bake local specialties for the hotel breakfast buffet proved to be just that, a dream. Instead, there was a plate of purchased food factory made cornettos, the Italian version of a French croissant, fresh fruit, and strong coffee. Sipping my second cup of coffee, I felt happy that zombie day was behind us and Rome lay ahead.

During our trip planning we had listed some of the well-known tourist sites we hoped to visit. They included Trevi Fountain, the Colosseum, Roman ruins, and the Vatican. Rome has a variety of public transportation options to get around the city. The Metro, buses, and yes, even taxis, can all be used, but my preferred method is walking, or urban hiking, as I like to call it.

Walking is a slow process that allows me to view the city differently. The historical sites might be the destination, but the walk between those sites provides views, sounds, smells, and the opportunity to interact with local people.

I learned on previous trips that the shops and restaurants near the historical sites in any city are not a true reflection of the city. They are there to serve the tourists. As an example, a waiter at a restaurant near the Spanish steps in Rome once berated me in English because he felt I did not tip him sufficiently. The restaurant had already added a cover charge, and we tipped beyond that. Yet, he knew we were Americans and expected American-style tipping. Because of that experience, when it is mealtime, I like to move away from the tourist sites and find a restaurant where the locals are dining.

Another reason for urban hiking is the opportunity for artistic expression. A camera is always in my hand, at the ready to record images that stay burned into my memory for years after the trip. The photos I take are a form of visual journaling. My goal is to tell a story about the place and the people who live there. Pictures of the historical sites, like the Coliseum, are certainly included in my collection of photographs, but the photographs I appreciate most contain people.

Following breakfast, we started our Rome adventure by visiting the Vatican. Since we had both been raised in the Catholic faith, and Sandy is a Catholic chaplain, she added it to our Rome itinerary. After consulting both a map and our GPS unit, we determined our urban hiking route. The selected path offered just what I wanted, views of day-to-day life in Rome.

As we walked, we passed Romans on their way to work. No one carried a disposable coffee cup. The Italians stop at small cafes, order a shot of expresso, and quickly drink it while standing at the counter. A few people walked by with their dogs and had hopeful facial expressions, just like people all over the world who wish their dog would take a shit quickly. We soon crossed over the Tiber river and it surprised me that the unkempt river's banks had not been cleaned up and developed like the Seine in Paris. We then turned onto a wide street and could see the Vatican far up ahead. Our excitement grew with each step forward. Soon we could clearly see St. Peter's Basilica which stood centered at the back of a huge piazza. A semi-circle of massive columns radiated out from the Basilica in both directions. Topping the horizontal stonework that capped the columns stood large statues. Soon we stood at the far edge of St. Peter's Square, taking in the vastness of what stood before us. I just love the feeling of wonder and joy I experience when I first view something grand and beautiful.

Then as we walked forward, I stopped to take a photograph of a large ornate water fountain, the Maderno fountain. We stood there in the bright sunlight, watching the water shoot from the pointed top before being collected in a raised bowl from which it would cascade to the large pool at the fountain base. Just after I had framed and taken a photograph, a group of seven nuns approached the fountain. Based on their identical religious habits, they all belonged to the same religious order and yet their wide variety of skin tones validated the worldwide appeal of the Catholic church. I watched as six of them lined up in front of the fountain for a photo, while the seventh held the camera, ready to take the picture.

Shouting out, "Un minuto sister," to interrupt, I used sign language to offer to take the photo that would include all of them. The camera was handed over and after I had taken the shot they started to disperse. I quickly shouted, "Ancora uno," as I raised my own camera to record the moment. They all smiled and laughed for they understood my act of kindness came with an ulterior motive. The image I captured, shows seven nuns dressed in black and white while both the fountain's falling water droplets and their smiles are frozen in time. It is the type of photograph that I treasure for it contains people. It still makes me smile and chuckle when I view it. To me their smiles represent the happiness they felt while visiting the Vatican, a place to which they had a strong bond.

As we walked through the Vatican museum and St. Peter's Basilica, the items on display caused words like opulent, gaudy, empire building, and over-the-top to creep into my mind. Just before we exited the basilica, I snapped a photograph that to me represents what the catholic church, and all churches, have to offer. Hope. The photo frames a side altar set far back from a heavy iron fence and gate. Streaming in from above is bright sunlight that illuminates the altar and the area in front of it. Peering through the gate's vertical bars are nine people, including two nuns. The photo, shot from their rear, shows them craning to see something inside the gate. Symbolically, they are looking for answers that they cannot get to, for the gate separates them from what they seek. All churches offer hope to those who are seeking answers.

We soon departed through massive fifteen feet tall cast metal doors, trading the darkness of the massive basilica for the bright sunlit piazza. A walk through the Vatican had influenced me. I made a commitment to give my charitable contributions directly to people in need, rather than organized religions.

Memorable photos ask questions of the viewer. As we walked to the outer edge of St. Peter's Square, we passed the gigantic six-foot-wide marble columns that circle the square on two sides. There I observed a bald man, sitting on a corner of the square base of the last column. Two rows of lighter colored paving stones created an arrow shape that pointed at and drew my eyes toward him. A large white shopping bag sat on the ground to his right. He wore a green and white plaid shirt, gray trousers, and a green jacket. The low seat on the column base elevated his knees above his waist. He rested both hands, knuckles down, on his knees while burying his face in the palms of his hands. All the visible details I have described are easy to understand, yet the question, "What was he thinking?" as he sat there, with his face buried in his hands, still haunts me years later.

As we walked away from the Vatican, we allowed a small meandering street to guide us. Soon we had to dodge small metal tables, set with plates, silverware, napkins, and wine glasses, occupying a portion of our walkway. Then the smell of sautéed garlic, drifting from restaurant kitchens, triggered our appetites. We selected a small place, sat down, and ordered glasses of Chianti wine.

When they arrived, I raised my glass to Sandy and said, "Salute, thanks for all you did to plan this trip."

"I love to do the planning," she responded.

"I know you do, and that is one of the reasons why I love you."

We toasted our good fortune, sipped the wine, and perused the menu. I am always looking for new food experiences when I travel. This restaurant's lunch menu contained familiar pasta dishes but one of them, spaghetti carbonara, is what I ordered. Back home this dish is often bastardised with the addition of cream. I was hoping for an authentic version. What arrived was a bowl of perfectly cooked spaghetti tossed with a sauce made of only raw eggs, Pecorino cheese, and crispy pieces of cured pork. I lowered my face down to the steaming hot dish and breathed in the aroma of the meat and pecorino.

"Umm, that smells good," I mumbled.

Soon I sat gazing into my empty bowl, wondering if licking up the remaining sauce is culturally acceptable in Italy. Then the waiter's hand swooped in and took the bowl to prevent my embarrassment. After looking longingly at the disappearing bowl, I turned my attention to the salad that quickly followed. Eating a salad at the end of a meal, which is the tradition in Italy, makes sense to me. The simple salad of crisp bright green lettuce and deep red tomatoes, dressed with olive oil and acidic red wine vinegar, became the perfect foil to the rich carbonara dish. When finished, we felt recharged and ready to continue exploring Rome.

Following the same street, we came to the unsightly and dirty Tiber River and turned right to get to a crossing bridge. The Bridge of the Angels, first constructed during the reign of emperor Hadrian, is for pedestrians only. Knowing this, the hawkers of goods and pickpockets congregate there waiting for tourists to pass. As we turned onto the bridge, displays of knock-off designer purses, laid out on blankets, lined the walkway. The salesmen, all black men of African descent, relied on hustling tourists to make a living. Blankets had become their preferred method of displaying the rainbow assortment of shining purses because if the police appeared, they would gather the four corners, sling the merchandise over their shoulder, and bolt down the street.

I bypassed the purses and headed directly to a man with a boombox radio blaring techno dance club music. In front of the radio, as if floating in air, two small hand-colored paper figures of Mickey and Minnie Mouse danced to the beat. My head moved to the beat and I began to enter a trance-like state. Soon I realized this huckster, just like the Vatican, had based his business on selling a mystery. Mickey and Minnie, suspended by only small strings, danced to the beat. It seemed illogical that paper figures could dance to music, yet I became a believer, forked over two euros, and walked away feeling good with Mickey and Minnie safely stowed in my backpack.

Spoiler alert! No matter how much I encouraged them, or what music I played, Mickey and Minnie refused to dance when I returned home. Reflecting on my purchase, it became clear I had been sold more than two paper figures. For only two euros, I had purchased a travel story. As the dance club music faded into the background, we danced our way toward our next destination, Trevi Fountain.

Passing an ATM on the way, we decided to withdraw some cash. We quickly learned you must notify your bank of your travel plans, before attempting transactions in foreign countries. "Transaction denied" flashed on the screen with each attempt. Cursing in Italian did nothing to solve the issue, so I called the 1-800 number on the back of the credit card and in fifteen minutes we had gelato money in our pockets.

We walked a short distance before we encountered a crowd of people. Looking beyond the crowd we could see Trevi Fountain, a massive wall of bright white marble carved into enough columns, human figures, and horses to fill the Vatican museum. Crystal clear water spewed from the marble structure before being captured in the fountain's coin littered pool. Smiling people stood and sat all around the perimeter of the fountain. I watched as they took turns photographing each other, while tossing a coin over their shoulder and into the fountain. I could sense the joy all around me. Joy is infectious. I rummaged through my backpack and found two coins. Then we attempted, without knowing all the words, to sing "Three Coins in the Fountain," as we performed the cliché coin toss.

With smiling faces, we departed for the Colosseum. Passing a small storefront our eyes drifted toward a muted rainbow of colors. Gelato! Small stainless-steel containers of this cold refreshing treat stood lined up, side by side, in a glass front case. This milk-based style of ice cream featured the flavors of fresh fruits, citrus, nuts, and chocolate. After ordering, the shop attendant handed us our selections. Our icy cold treats sat in tiny paper cups with the smallest plastic spoons imaginable standing upright in the gelato. The first taste of any cold dessert, like gelato, is always the best. Continuing to eat a cold dessert mutes your taste buds so using this diminutive spoon to take small bites limited that chilling effect. I am not sure if the culinary world has given the Italians enough credit for this stroke of genius. I was so intrigued by the long lingering taste of this freshly made cold treat that we stopped for a gelato break every afternoon for two weeks. I considered it a scientific experiment and accepted the fact that a bulging waistline might be one of the results.

We talked about hosting dinner parties back home at which we would serve gelato and surprise our guests with those cute little spoons. So, after finishing our gelato, we would dispose of the cups and toss the little spoons into the side pocket of my backpack. Departing Italy, at the end of our trip, a customs agent manning the scanning machine called me over.

"Sir, are you planning to open a gelato shop?" He asked. "You have a pouch full of spoons."

For the next day and a half, we continued to explore Rome and its historical sites. Then we packed up and moved on to Florence by train. As the Italian countryside flashed by the train window, I contrasted it with the flat landscape back home, which made the hilly Italian countryside even more inviting.

Pulling into the Florence train station, or as I later learned, any train station in Italy and much of Europe, will expose you to new and unusual artwork, graffiti. Almost all flat vertical surfaces like walls, fences and buildings facing the tracks are covered in brightly colored graffiti. The graffiti is not visual images like murals. It is instead highly stylized letters and words, or tags. The first response is one of shock. This type of illegal art, especially in a country full of historical sites, seems to despoil the view and taints one's perception of place. This form of rebellious art is a symptom of deeper societal issues. Italy's fairytale world of ancient tourist sites when juxtaposed with the graffiti helped me better understand the countries struggles with immigration and immigrants. People who are not accepted, or who do not fit neatly into an existing culture, find ways to express their frustration. Independent travelers get multiple views of the counties and cities visited, and therefore leave with a deeper understanding of the culture.

As we prepared to depart the train in Florence, I looked at the wheels on our luggage. They are one of the reasons traveling has become so easy. Credit goes to Mr. Sadow, who in 1970 mounted casters to some luggage, and a few years later filed for and received the patent for "rolling luggage." Thank-you, Mr. Sadow. Because of your genius, we hauled our wheeled luggage off the train and easily walked several blocks to our Florence hotel.

Our GPS unit guided us to our hotel by taking us down a busy street and past the Duomo, the large cathedral that dominates the Florence skyline. I complimented Sandy on the hotel's location.

"Seems like the perfect spot," I said.

"Ricky (Rick Steves) recommended the place," she said, and laughed.

After checking in, the hotel clerk guided us to our room. The second-floor room was dated, but it faced the street and bright sunlight streamed into the space. I opened a window, leaned out, and could see the Duomo just a few blocks back up the street that we had walked down. We quickly unpacked so we could get out and see Florence. Just before leaving, I noticed ear plugs on both nightstands and pointed them out to Sandy.

"The hotel is watching out for you. They must have known I am a snorer," I jokingly commented to my wife.

She just gave me a look.

After a few hours of urban hiking and then stopping to enjoy a basil pesto fettuccine dinner, we walked back to our hotel. As we approach the entrance, we noted the business across the street, the English Bar, had a large busy outdoor seating area. Entering our room Sandy commented that it was warm, so I opened the windows. The real reason for the earplugs on our nightstands quickly became clear. It appeared that every British tourist, currently in Italy, had made their way to the English Bar to eat fish and chips and meat pies, washed down with pints of Boddingtons. The later it got, the louder it got.

The following day we walked through the architecturally inter-esting Duomo. The multi-colored and patterned exterior and its massive dome made it different from other cathedrals. We also visited the Uffizi Museum to view Michelangelo's statue of David. The size of the statue, seventeen feet tall, along with the pure beauty of the white marble sculpture froze me in my tracks. Despite the signs that read "no photos" I bravely, or illegally, snapped a few. As we toured the upstairs galleries, I noticed an open window. From it there was a great view of the Ponte Vecchio bridge that spanned the Arno River. The walking bridge, opened in 1345, is unique for it has small shops, primarily selling gold jewelry, located on its entire length.

Just before noon, we checked out and rolled our luggage toward a rental car facility. I observed a symbol of the Italian relaxed and laid-back lifestyle as we walked across a large piazza. An exceptionally large, mostly black, long-haired dog slept soundly on the large sun-warmed natural stones that paved the piazza. After having unintentionally joined last night's party at the British Pub, my first inclination was to lay down next to the dog.

Instead, we pushed on to rent a vehicle for the next portion of our trip, a four-day stay in Tuscan wine country. We found the rental facility, entered, and took a seat.

When it was our turn, we approached the counter and said, "Buongiorno." Our customer service agent, based on that one spoken word, determined our country of origin, and began to speak English with a lovely Italian accent.

While completing the required paperwork she asked, "Would you like to rent a GPS unit?"

I replied, "No, I have a Garmin GPS."

With a twinkle in her dark Italian eyes, she responded, "Oh, you already have a marriage saver."

As we drove away in our small gray standard transmission Fiat Punto, we chuckled because we knew, from our past experiences of using only hand-held maps to guide us on vacation road trips, the customer service agent was a wise lady.

We put the address of our Tuscan agritourismo (bed and breakfast) into our GPS unit and drove off toward our countryside lodging.

As the Garmin barked out orders, to turn left or right, we obeyed without emotion.

Our agritourismo was in the middle of Tuscan wine country. Rolling hills covered with vineyards surrounded our accommodations. It was a laid back, quiet and peaceful setting when compared to the hustle and bustle of Rome and Florence. Our room, in an old outbuilding on a family-owned vineyard may have housed cattle or poultry years before. The room was Spartan in size, two cattle would have been comfortable, and minimally furnished with a queen bed, nightstand, a small desk and one chair. Our goal, when traveling, is to find reasonably priced accommodations, around eighty euros, and we had. The amenities like pools, bars, restaurants, and concierge services, provided by resorts and large hotel chains would be wasted on us, for we would be out exploring and not be there to enjoy them.

After unpacking, we walked across the lawn to the common building. Here guests could just sit and relax, eat the breakfast meal provided each morning or purchase bottles of the wine made on site. Vineyards with row after row of vines surrounded the agritourismo. The early spring weather had coaxed light green leaves, tendrils, and tiny grape clusters to explode from the vine stems that had been severely pruned back after the prior year's harvest.

As we sat at some outdoor seating, enjoying the view of the surrounding vineyards and the quiet of the countryside, an unmistakable and familiar cackling sound came from the vineyard. When younger I had lived in a rural area and often heard and viewed cock pheasants calling to attract hens. I grabbed my camera and walked between two rows of vines toward the sound. Cock ring-necked pheasants, unlike the females who are perfectly camouflaged in drab browns, are brilliantly colored. Their red and iridescent green head, along with a breast that shines gold and orange in the sunlight, makes them uniquely beautiful. Pursuing the cackling sound, we played cat and mouse until I finally caught a brief glimpse of the brightly colored cock as he ran between rows. I felt like I had won the game of hide-and-seek, by just seeing the pheasant, and retreated to my seat.

Sitting there in the bright spring sunlight, it felt good to be out of the city and amongst the vineyards and rolling hills of Tuscany.

During our four-day stay, we filled most late afternoons by relaxing at the agritourismo, but each morning, after a light breakfast of pastries and coffee, we excitedly piled into the Punto and drove off to visit and explore a different Tuscan hill town.

Unlike the flat, straight, and monotonous roads at home in the Midwest, the tree and vineyard lined narrow lanes in Tuscany constantly twisted and turned as they directed us to and around the ancient hill towns. I had anticipated driving in Italy knowing the roads would be curvy. Driving here would remind me of when I owned a Triumph Spitfire, a small British two-seat sports car. I fondly recalled the fun I had guiding that car around curves as I now ran through the gears of my Punto, before down shifting at each bend in the road, and then accelerating while coming out of the curve's apex.

Passing another car safely seemed impossible because I rarely encountered a straight section of road. Not that I wanted to pass anyone. But every Italian driver, familiar with the local roadways, wanted desperately to pass me. Looking in my rear-view mirror I could see them twitching, like Formula 1 drivers, as they rode my ass while waiting for the perfect opportunity to pass, which was never going to come. To support their machismo, I became an expert at pulling over and letting them zoom by. At first, I thought they were waving hello as they passed, but soon realized it was some other kind of gesture, involving their fingers.

Our reliance and trust in the GPS unit, during our four days in Tuscany, prevented the, "I told you to turn there, but you never listen to me!" conversations that often occurred during our pre-GPS owner-ship days. Trust can be a fragile thing.

One afternoon, when returning to the agritourismo on a familiar road she, the GPS unit, instructed us to take a right turn onto a ridiculously small road. Since the unit was programmed to always take the quickest route, we extended trust, assumed she knew a shortcut and took the right turn. Quickly the road turned to gravel and then tree branches began to brush both sides of the car. Soon it sounded exactly like our car was going through a waterless automated car wash. I stopped, put the Punto in reverse, and backed off the hiking trail while Sandy yelled at the Garmin.

"What were *you* thinking?" I could tell that was not a good road to turn on. Do I have to give *you* directions?"

As she continued to scold the Garmin, I mumbled to myself, "I am falling in love with that Garmin."

Deciding where to eat lunch, as we walked around the Tuscan hill towns, became one of the highlights of each day. We could order pasta and pizza everywhere. Not just in Italy, everywhere on earth. Seeking out something new and different became my mission. In one town we ordered and ate a mortadella sandwich. If you are familiar with mortadella, I know what you are thinking. What could be so special about a bologna sandwich? Well, buttered crusty fresh Italian bread filled with fatty mortadella seasoned with black pepper, myrtle berries and pistachios far surpassed the bologna sandwiches I ate as a child. It was an amazing sandwich.

Another memorable lunch sandwich that featured pork had a name that is now burned into my memory: the porchetta sandwich. As we strolled through a medieval hill town, we came across a small shop that sold nothing else. The smell of roast pork emanating from that shop drew travelers like me inside. Entering, I immediately noticed something laying in repose behind a glass fronted counter. As I moved closer, I observed two-thirds of a whole roasted pig, with crispy mahogany colored skin, which beckoned me to partake even though I had already eaten lunch. I ordered a sandwich and watched with interest as the proprietress prepared it. She positioned herself at the exposed cut end of the pig. Using a long sharp knife, she cut thin slices of juicy pork and crispy skin that fell directly onto a beautiful piece of crusty Italian bread. To finish the sandwich, she sprinkled the pork with sea salt and topping it with a second piece of bread. Standing in the street, Sandy and I entered pig heaven as we passed the sandwich back and forth until it had disappeared. After licking the salty pork grease from the sandwich wrapper, I moved on while keeping an eye out for a gelato shop.

On another day, in another hill town, we decided to have lunch in a small place filled with locals. Opening the menu, I noticed and then ordered the "coniglio." When it was delivered, the smell of the fragrant rabbit, which had been slowly braised in olive oil along with onion, celery, carrot, fresh rosemary, and parsley, drew me in. The first bite confirmed my ordering decision was a good one. It did not take long to replace the fork, used to eat the tender pieces of meat, with pieces of crusty bread to wipe up the cooked down vegetable and olive oil mixture that resided at the bottom of the serving bowl. After wiping up every bit of that umami flavored sauce, only the rabbit's skeletal remains sat visible in the dish.

I commented to Sandy, "That was not a pretty dish, but it was the best of the trip so far."

"So it was brutta ma delicioso," she confidently stated in Italian.

"Yes, ugly but delicious," I repeated.

Italy is so much more than pasta and pizza.

After returning from a daytrip we walked past an outside seating area at our agritourismo. Sitting there, sharing a bottle of the wine produced by the agritourismo owners, was another couple. After saying hello to break the ice, we discovered they lived in Colorado. As we shared travel stories, they noted they would drive to a new location, a city east of Siena called Cortona, the next morning, while we planned to spend two more nights here at the agritourismo. We wished each other safe travels and headed to our room.

Two days later, we drove to Assisi. After parking, we walked down the main street of town, which led directly to the basilica where St. Francis is buried. Because of the connection to St. Francis, Assisi is a pilgrimage destination as well as a tourist site. Every one of the gift shops we passed had statutes of St. Anthony, in every size imaginable, on display. As our walking route took us out of the commercial area of town and closer to the church, the towns position on a hilltop provided beautiful distant views of the agricultural land-scape far below.

After waiting in line, we entered and walked through the basilica. Other than enjoying some frescoes that depicted life during St. Francis's lifetime, I remained unmoved by the experience and a little pissed because a no photography policy was enforced. We exited through a different door, which led us down a walkway lined with arches. Stepping out into a large stone paved piazza, I turned back toward the basilica to take a photograph. Centered in the frame is the large basilica, and the two arched walkways which angled in toward the church, drew my eyes to it. The piazza, covered in alternating light and dark linear paving stones, provided depth to an interesting architectural photograph.

We continued our walk back to city-center and selected a restaurant for lunch. My light pasta lunch apparently did not fill me, for soon after our meal I found myself standing and staring longingly into the window of a pastry shop. Then surprisingly, that same Colorado couple, Mark, and Kitty, walked up and said, "Hello." As we talked, we discovered we would all be traveling to Venice in two days.

"Then let's meet in front of Saint Mark's Cathedral on Friday night and have dinner together," I proposed.

They looked at each other, and then said, "Okay, what time?"

"How about 6 pm?"

They agreed, we said our goodbyes and went our separate ways. It was exciting to have dinner plans in Venice.

When we first checked into our Tuscan agritourismo, we asked about local restaurant recommendations. The proprietress mentioned a communal meal that would be served later in the week, by a couple who planned to establish a cooking school in their home. It sounded like a unique experience, so we asked her to call and reserve seats for us. So, on our last night in Tuscany, we joined fourteen other people for a delicious meal of local specialties prepared in the home of the cooks.

It was a warm spring night, so we gathered outside and introduced ourselves to the other guests. Soon bruschetta, olives, and a selection of cheeses, along with a selection of local red wines, appeared to begin the feast. The location, overlooking a vineyard, and the warm early spring weather, both added to a beautiful experience. I watched as the owner placed four, three-inch-thick beefsteaks onto a grill positioned over a ground level wood fire glowing with hot embers. Quickly the smell of the grilling meat filled the air and acted as an aperitif.

Thirty minutes later his wife ushered us inside and assigned our seats at large round tables. She segregated the guest by first language. The Italian speakers at one table, while we joined a group of six Americans from Alaska. This group of friends had planned their trip to Italy to celebrate their upcoming fiftieth birthdays. The featured main courses, a wild boar Bolognese sauce served over pappardelle pasta, followed by the grilling beef steak from the local Chianina cattle, were both rich, soul satisfying dishes. Following the entrees, we enjoyed a refreshing crisp green salad while chatting with the other guests. Then, to wrap up the night, our nearly exhausted hosts offered us chocolate biscotti, studded with toasted almonds, accompanied by small glasses of the Italian version of fire water, grappa. As we departed, I shook the hands of the young couple who had worked so hard to prep and then prepare the feast, and said, "Delicioso, grazie." They smiled appreciatively, as if they understood that I knew how much effort they had put forth. And I did, for we entertain dinner guests routinely.

The next morning, we drove back to Florence and dropped off our rental car. As we passed through the rental car office, we smiled and winked in unison at the "marriage saver" lady behind the counter, and then walked to the train station to board a train for Venice.

I like train travel because it puts me in contact with local people. Driving in a rental car causes isolation but does provide a level of freedom to explore and stop anywhere. But after having driven around Tuscany for four days, the uneventful and relaxing train trip to Venice was just what I needed to recharge. It felt good to have someone else drive.

Once we arrived, with luggage in tow, we descended the stairs of the Santa Lucia station and approached the Grand Canal. I looked left, and then right, and wanted to shout, "Oh, Venice!" Did Walt Disney have a hand in this? Under blue skies filled with large puffy clouds stood a city unlike any other. Venice was a city with a different kind of hustle and bustle. Boats provide all transportation, and the canal was filled with vessels of different shapes and sizes going in all directions. The gracefully aged, colorful, and ornate Venetian buildings that fronted the canal, looked like a movie set. Magical is a word that must be used when describing Venice. At least, until you check into your room and immediately notice it smells like shit. But before that happened, we stood awestruck by the beauty of this city built on soggy swampy land. As a water taxi transported us down the canals toward our hotel, the whole city appeared to magically float on water. Then, a few days later the city appeared to be sinking as rainwater flooded part of Saint Mark's Square.

All the buildings in Venice are old, which adds to the charm of this city crisscrossed by canals. Walking into the grand, vaulted ceiling lobby of our hotel impressed both of us. But as soon as we entered our room, the faint smell of sewerage, rather than a lavender room freshener, assaulted our noses. Sandy, whose olfactory senses are like that of a bloodhound, was not happy. We quickly opened the windows and hoped the smell would dissipate while we went urban hiking. If it did not, we prepared ourselves to accept the fact that this might be part of the Venice experience.

During the time between the shitty smell and the flooding, we fell madly in love with Venice. Every twist and turn of the small pedestrian lanes and the intertwining canals offered spectacular views. Gondolas filled with tourists plied the smaller canals. I stood on a small bridge and shot photos of a newlywed Asian couple in their wedding gown and tuxedo, as they passed under the bridge in a gondola. They had their own film crew aboard the gondola filming the special experience. As we strolled along a larger canal, six gondoliers who had tied their gondolas all together, prepared to eat their lunches while talking about life. The main tourist area, around Saint Mark's Square, was overrun with tourists unloaded from large cruise ships during the day. To avoid that mess, we headed off down narrow walkways and over small canal bridges to explore.

Photographs I took captured a newlywed couple, him in a black tuxedo and she in a brilliant white wedding dress, sitting canal side with their feet dangling over the water. Another photograph framed small row boats anchored in a still, reflective canal. The red, green, and blue colors of the boats and buildings just pop out of the photograph. Stopping at an outdoor fish market provided a chance to watch and photograph the locals bargain with the fish mongers. Want a bottle of wine? With an empty water bottle and two euros in hand, the staff in a small shop full of wooden wine casks would fill up your bottle with vino. Venice offered a condensed compact urban hiking experience that we enjoyed.

On Friday night, we walked to Saint Mark's cathedral to meet up with Mark and Kitty from Denver. We wondered if they would show up, and I am sure they had the same concern about us. At the appointed time they appeared, and we greeted each other like old friends, and then walked to a recommended seafood restaurant. The night included a shared bottle of pinot grigio, delicious food, including a fish large enough to feed us all, and wonderful conversation. Talking to strangers has its benefits. That chance encounter at a Tuscan agritourismo just a few days earlier led to not only dinner in Venice, but a decade long friendship. Since that initial encounter, we have traveled together to multiple countries on three different continents. Both the shared travel experiences and our common values have resulted in us becoming good friends in every sense of the word.

With just two days left in Italy, we boarded an outbound train to Milan. The train's path took us through new territory that allowed me to look out the window and observe the vineyards and orchards that dominated the landscape along the tracks. It was late afternoon when we arrived and checked into our hotel. It was modern and the hotel's sparse sleek metallic furnishings reflected the creative spirit of Milan, Italy's center for fashion and design. We quickly unpacked and headed out to visit one of Milan's main attractions, the Milan Duomo, a brick and marble gothic cathedral studded with rooftop spires. As we walked across an expansive piazza toward the cathedral, we could see scaffolding covered most of the exterior. We must have appeared disappointed, for as we passed a group of young people who carried a sign that read, "Free Hugs," they approached us and offered a hug. We both accepted their offer, and I momentarily thought about trying for seconds.

When we walked up to the cathedral entrance, signage listed a series of fees from three to thirteen euros for accessing the roof, using an elevator to get there, and visiting a crypt. By this point on our trip we were churched out. We had visited numerous basilicas, cathedrals and churches and agreed to just say "no." We could spend the euros on something better like, ah, gelato. So, instead we walked toward a large open-air shopping district.

Northern Italy is where the wealth of the country has always resided, and this shopping area reflected that. Stylish Italian fashion was on display both in the store display windows and on the local shoppers. We both felt underdressed, like we had inadvertently walked into a grand wedding reception in our hiking clothes. Our mindset had already started to shift to our trip home the next day, so we decided to force down one more tiny cup of gelato, for scientific reasons of course, and then walked back to the hotel. We ate nearby that evening and flew home the next day.

It had been a great trip. Ancient ruins, old churches, stone walls and walkways had been the backdrop for a trip where we had been the minority. Not knowing the local language causes a kind of tension that made me feel alive. As non-Italian speakers we relied on the help and kindness of others. It was always offered and graciously accepted.

In 2015, a few years after our initial visit to Italy, some generous friends invited my wife and I, along with some of their family and other friends, to stay at an Italian villa just outside of Siena. They had rented an old monastery, now converted into a nine-bedroom villa, for an entire month. It would be our home base for a ten-day stay.

Our plane from the U.S. landed in Rome mid-morning. After clearing customs and retrieving our bags, we made our way to the car rental facility. After twenty minutes, I began mumbling complaints under my breath about the disorganized facility and staff. Only after I noticed someone with a numbered card in their hand, did I realize taking a number and then waiting to be called to the counter was the customer service process. That provided a chance for some self-flagellation using Italian words. "Deficiente, Idiota!"

As I stood there holding my number, I had difficulty keeping my eyes open and maintaining focus. I had already entered the first day of European travel "zombie state" by the time we completed the paperwork, and the clerk escorted us to our Fiat Punto. We climbed into the diminutive car and loaded our first destination, Castglioncello, into our GPS unit. The device noted it would take three and a half hours to get from Rome, to this small seaside town on the Ligurian Sea. We planned to spend two nights in that coastal city before driving almost directly east to Siena, to join our friends at the villa.

As we left the airport, the GPS device directed us to the entrance ramp of a northbound expressway. Within minutes, I had the Punto cruising along at ninety kilometers an hour. Discounting the four and a half minutes of restless sleep I had on the flight, I had now been awake for about twenty-two hours. Not yet dead tired, but getting close, I focused on the drive.

Then about an hour into our trip, when a toll booth appeared ahead, I panicked and swerved back and forth between the electronic pass and cash lanes. My mind started racing like the Punto's engine. Where to go? Did the rental car have a transponder? Do I have enough cash?

I chose a cash lane. Rather than an attendant greeting me with a "buongiorno" and an offer to help, I found myself staring at an ATM machine. Great, I thought. Then I notice the universal symbols of money transactions, the Visa and MasterCard logos, next to a slot. I pulled a credit card from my wallet and inserted it, hoping I was not giving my financial information to the mafia. I pressed several keys, hoping they were the right ones, and waited for the toll gate to open. It did! Feeling confident from the toll paying experience, I headed down the tollway wishing that more toll booths would appear on the horizon so I could demonstrate my talent.

The adrenaline rush resulting from that toll booth experience jolted me into a wide-awake state for at least thirty minutes. But soon after we both hit a wall and agreed we needed caffeine.

I pulled off at the next gas station rest stop area. I wobbled inside and started to say, "Due espresso," but the Italians already knew what I needed. While one took my payment, another cranked up the gleaming stainless-steel steam-driven coffee extraction machine. After a few hisses and puffs of steam, the barista turned to me holding two three-ounce plastic cups. They each contained about an ounce of the blackest of viscous liquids capped by a thin layer of brown foam. Gently gripping each one between a thumb and index finger, I walked back to the car.

Sandy asked, "Where is the coffee?"

I just smiled and handed her a thimble sized container. We toasted our good fortune before drinking the expresso like a petite shot of whiskey. Within minutes, caffeine pulsated through my veins, and we safely continued our Italian road trip.

Our destination, Castiglioncello, was off the tourist path, which meant we might be two of the few Americans in town. The tourist trade focuses on towns with large old buildings and big churches and this town had neither. The small commercial area of town contained small businesses all intended to serve the townspeople. Just walking through a city without the gift shops that dominant larger tourist centered locations was refreshingly different. We next walked toward the sea and found a small harbor containing some anchored boats, and a few restaurants on its perimeter. We looked over and liked the menu featuring seafood, posted in front of one of the restaurants and decided to reserve a table for that evening. Before entering we agreed we would dine later in the evening, as is the custom in much of Europe, and asked for a 7:00 pm reservation. The restaurateur who greeted us responded to our query with a knowing smile (Oh, you Americans!), and made it clear that opening time was 8:00 pm. I quickly said, "Molto bene, grazie."

The setting sun still illuminated the harbor as we arrived for our 8:00 pm reservation. Along with branzino, a local sea bass, we shared a green salad and a bottle of local wine for our meal. After dessert and complimentary glasses of Limoncello, we departed and walked inland to a small park where we discovered a small night market. Each booth in the market, illuminated with bare light bulbs, created pockets of light in the tranquil evening darkness. As we passed the vendors looked up or stood to look longingly as we passed. We nodded or said, "Buonanotte," and continued on our way.

We left for Siena the following morning. The sixty-six-mile drive east to Siena took two hours. The time to travel any distance in Italy, if not on a four-lane expressway, is always double the time it takes in the flat Midwest. The reason is simple. Italian secondary roadways are never straight.

As we neared Siena our GPS routed us onto an expressway. When we approached our destination's exit, I could see the terrain was made up of large, plowed hills. We exited and followed the small twisting roads through this hilly terrain to get to the villa entrance. From the car window, I could see a sharp left followed by a climb up a long steeply angled hill would take us up to the buildings located far above. I put the standard transmission in first gear, gunned it, and up we went. I felt pretty cocky about my manual transmission skills as the engine raced, and we continued our ascent. Then an automatic gate, blocking our entrance, appeared just before we crested the hill. While swearing in Italian, I jammed in the clutch and stood on the brake pedal to keep us from rolling backwards down the hill. Sandy, intent on saving her own life, exited the vehicle to open the gate. Using the clutch skills, I had acquired during my late teen years, I raced the engine, popped the clutch, and zoomed to the top.

Pulling up in front of a beautiful old stone villa in Italy and having our good friends from home, Hank and Kathy, walk out to greet us was a heartwarming moment. After we exchanged welcoming hugs and chatted a bit, they offered, and then gave us, a tour of the villa property. Opposite the villa stood the owner's home. Like the villa it was built of large stone blocks and stood on a hillside. We followed a path past two old outbuildings that contained equipment, like a tractor, used to maintain the grounds of the villa. We continued walking until we reached the back of the property where we stood to take in the view of the surrounding rolling hills from our high perch. Our return path took us past a covered brick grilling area and an open-air pavilion paved with large stones. Passing the villa building, I caught a glimpse of a large inviting swimming pool surrounded by lounge chairs.

During our walk, I observed fig, pomegranate, pear, and olive trees that seemed to flourish on the property. One olive tree, thought to be 300 years old, became a subject for my camera throughout my stay. As the light changed throughout the day, I was continually drawn back to this ancient tree with a massive trunk to take another photograph.

During the ten days we spent at the villa, different guest came and went. With them we had many shared experiences that made this trip unique. Occasionally we ventured out on our own, but often with others. That first afternoon, Hank asked, "Do you want to take a ride to pick up some wine?"

"Sure, I'll go to the store with you." I replied.

We headed down the twisting rural roads to a place the owners of the rental villa had recommended. As we turned from the road and into a courtyard, the architectural style and age of the old stone structures it contained, made it clear the wine we planned to purchase would not be from a commercial retail establishment. I quickly envisioned multiple farm families and their cattle, pigs and chickens living in this compound one hundred years earlier. Two story buildings, with living space above and shelter for animals below, surrounded the center courtyard on three sides. A decades old stone wall, with the opening through which we had driven, on the fourth side completed the compound perimeter.

A lady on the second floor, hearing our car doors close, looked out an open window. Hank shouted up to her, "Buy wine!" She mimicked making a phone call by holding her hand up to an ear, to let us know she would make a call. In about ten minutes, an old flatbed truck pulled into the courtyard. Two men, wearing weathered jackets and muddy work boots, exited the vehicle. One of them then used a key to unlock the door to a storeroom containing cases of red and white wine. They did not speak English, so we made our choices by pointing and using our fingers to convey the quantity. The cost was written on a piece of paper, and after Hank paid them with cash, they loaded the wine into our car. We had purchased three cases, two red and one white, of locally produced wine for only sixty euros. Feeling immense guilt, I jumped into the getaway car, looked at Hank and asked, "Did we just pay less than two euros per bottle?"

He let out a joyous laugh and then said, "Yeah, pretty cool, huh?"

As we settled into the villa, I could see the interior had been remodeled. All nine bedrooms, many of them with their own bathrooms, occupied the second floor. The first floor had a large open space with couches and comfortable chairs for sitting and relaxing, and a large dining room. The dining room table easily held sixteen people and when we ate in, it was a joyous wine-infused celebration.

On another day, everyone staying at the villa jumped into one of the available cars, and we all drove into Siena for the weekly morning market. Having driven into Siena earlier in the week, I knew the entire day could be spent driving in circles around the old walled city looking for parking. Today was no different. The town was jammed with cars, so locating a parking spot would be as difficult as finding deep dish pizza in Italy. We decided to follow signs to a parking area adjacent to the local soccer stadium. After parking, we headed to an event akin to a traveling circus, only without the animals.

This outdoor traveling market was set up and taken down in a different city every day. For the next few hours, we split up and wandered past stalls, tents and trailers containing meat, cheese, wine, clothing, shoes, housewares, and souvenirs.

When we had seen enough, we walked to the city-center to meet up with some friends from the villa for lunch. After lunch, as we walked toward the soccer stadium parking area, we noticed the market stalls, trailers, tents, and all the merchandise, had been removed. Only multiple cleaning crews, sweeping up debris and removing trash, remained in the market area.

We located our car, and five of us jumped in. As I drove toward the exit, I commented, "This is a different gate from the one we entered this morning." As soon as I exited, I immediately noticed an absence of cars and then realized I had driven into the market area where no traffic was allowed at this time.

I sped up while frantically looking for a way out. One of the smart-ass passengers located in the back seat kindly pointed out, "That was the wrong exit."

Soon we sighted a gated exit. I pulled up to the gate and nothing happened.

Another passenger suggested, "A few Hail Mary's might help."

"Ha-ha," I responded. "How does that go? Deliver us from this parking lot?"

Moans could be heard in the back seat as I put the car in reverse and parked the car. I instructed my passengers to stay put while I went to ask someone how to get out. Finding a cleaning crew, I did my best to explain the situation using hand gestures and grimaces. In response, I believe they said, "Pulla upa toa agata."

Figuring I had not pulled in far enough to trip the gate sensor, I jogged back, hopped in, and pulled up until the front of the car was in contact with the gate. No luck. I reversed the car and then drove off, seeking another escape route.

On our first trip to the automated gate, to my left, I had viewed parallel vehicle traffic moving on a street a block away. The only problem was the street I had looked down was marked a one-way street. To escape, I would have to break the law. Since the street was devoid of traffic, I made a snap decision while shouting, "Hang on," and raced down the street going the wrong way.

Cleaning crews shouted and made animated hand gestures as we sped past them. While I screamed to my passengers, "Do not make eye contact," to prevent any feelings of guilt, I raced to the end of the street and just barely squeezed the car between two metal posts, intended to block vehicles, in order to enter the flow of traffic. We had escaped.

I asked for silence in the car while listening for the sound of sirens. The only sound heard was the wind whistling through the car windows.

Feeling euphoric I shouted, "How about that for some fun?", which caused joyous laughter that continued until we returned to the villa.

It was revealed, shortly after our return, that someone in the rear seat, young Jon, had videoed the escape sequence using his cell phone. Later as I snuck out the front door of the villa to inspect both sides of the rental car for damage, I heard hearty wine-infused laughter ricocheting through the Tuscan hills as everyone watched the video multiple times.

For the balance of the trip, the now immortalized phrase, "Do not make eye contact," was used even when it was totally inappropriate. This confirmed one of my beliefs regarding travel. Adversity creates lasting travel memories and stories.

Almost every afternoon, after adventuring out somewhere, we would return to the villa to sit and relax with a glass of that local wine. Hank, John, Jerry, and I would congregate under the open-air pavilion to enjoy the silence of each other's company. This Tuscan hilltop perch was our recharging station. We sipped and savored the delicious red wine and nibbled on olives while reading or just staring into the distance. The large green olives, a product of Castelvetrano, Sicily, had a unique mild flavor and a crisp texture. People who do not like olives should taste these. They would become olive lovers.

Eventually the olive bowl contained only gnawed pits and all that remained in the bowl of each wine glass was a small dried purple smudge. We would give each other a knowing nod and walk back to the villa. We had again strengthened our special bond without the use of words.

During our ten days at the villa we either ate in or went out for dinner. Since the villa came equipped with a complete kitchen, I could not wait to cook there. One of the couples staying at the villa, had hired a driver for a few days rather than rent a car. One morning, they invited us to join them, and we accepted. While being driven from one small town to another, I noticed a man selling fresh porcini mushrooms from the back of his parked vehicle. I begged our driver to stop and jumped from the car into the porcini aroma filled air. At home I had purchased and cooked with dried porcini, but I had only dreamt of fresh porcini. I purchased five large mushrooms and imme-diately began to plan a menu, for the next day, which would include porcini risotto.

The other villa guests agreed to the proposed menu, so the next morning we created a shopping list and drove to a food store located in a nearby small village. We had already visited the store three days before. On that trip, we learned about the requirement to put on plastic gloves before touching any of the produce, after we had touched all the produce with our bare hands. We also learned we should have weighed each bagged produce item in the produce department. This lack of understanding caused the checkout clerk to take all our bagged produce back to the scale to weigh each item. This store closed every afternoon for two hours, and our actions came close to delaying the 1:00 pm close. This created tension in the air as we "ugly Americans" said, "Grazie," and departed. It was good that we did not speak Italian, for as we exited, I heard muttered words and observed unusual hand gestures that I had not seen before.

So, on this, our second trip to the same store, we arrived early and felt like regular customers. As we entered, I glanced at the checkout lady and even though she gave me the stink eye, I smiled and said, "Buongiorno!" One of the dishes on the menu, chicken Marsala, required us to buy a bottle of Marsala wine. After searching the liquor section, I asked for help, and eventually they found a bottle in the storeroom. We found everything else on our list and checked out without creating an international incident.

The menu featured two types of risotto, porcini, and asparagus with prosciutto, chicken Marsala, and a fennel orange salad. For dessert two tarts, made with figs and pears picked from the villa property, were featured. And of course, plenty of crusty Italian bread and local wine accompanied the meal. Our host's son, Michael and his girlfriend Katie, stood at the stove making the asparagus risotto while I had the chance to teach a young French lady named Cynthia, who grew up in Provence, how to make porcini risotto. Everyone enjoyed the meal, but not as much as I enjoyed cooking it. Planning and preparing that Italian meal, in an Italian villa, was for me a highlight of the ten-day trip.

When we ventured out for dinner, we picked one of two places. Both were close by in rural Tuscany. The first, a small casual place with outdoor picnic table seating, was in a nearby village. They served good, reasonably priced pizza and pasta dishes much like we could get at home. The second, a full-service restaurant, was just off a four-lane expressway exit. It was much larger, more upscale in their food and drink offerings, and was always full of boisterous fun-loving Italians. While glancing through the menu, I noticed they had fettucine with shaved Tartufo (truffle) for sixteen euros. I began to salivate. When served, the heady earthy aroma of the tartufo made me giddy. As I ate the egg rich fettucine, covered with shaved truffle, and sauced with a butter-infused white wine sauce, I was tempted to order another plate. The earthy, almost musty flavor and aroma, unlike anything else I have ever eaten, created a lasting food memory.

Eventually Sandy and our friends begged me to stop saying, "Delicioso!"

Our ten days at the villa soon came to an end and we drove back to Rome. Before departing Italy, we spent a few days in Rome revisiting some of the tourist sites with friends who were visiting Rome for the first time. On the flight home, I reflected on all the wonderful experiences we had while staying at the villa. Shared travel experiences give you stories, and co-storytellers, that last for decades. We will always be grateful for the generosity of our villa hosts, Hank and Kathy, who had invited us to be part of their Italian cultural immersion experience.

During our ten-day stay we also had the chance to introduce our *Bumping & Snacking* method of travel to another couple named Jerry and Gina. They are both of Italian heritage and this was their first trip to Italy. Together we drove around Tuscany and created lasting memories. It was such a joy watching them experience Italy.

PASTA CARBONARA

Ingredients

1 lb. dried spaghetti
1/3 lb. thick cut bacon cut into ½ inch pieces
3 large room temperature eggs
4 oz. block of Parmigiano-Reggiano finely grated
Salt
Black pepper

Preparation

Bring a large pot of water to a boil. Add a tablespoon of salt and then the pasta. Stir occasionally to keep pasta from sticking and cook until al dente. Before draining the pasta, remove 1 cup of the pasta cooking liquid.

While the pasta is cooking, heat a skillet and then add the bacon and cook over medium-high heat until it is browned but not crispy. Set the skillet aside. In a bowl, whisk together the eggs, cheese and ½ teaspoon of black pepper until combined. Whisk ¼ cup of the hot pasta cooking liquid into the egg and cheese mixture.

Quickly add the drained pasta to the skillet and then pour the egg* and cheese mixture over the pasta while stirring. Continue to stir and toss the pasta, adding more pasta water if required, until a creamy sauce is visible clinging to the pasta. Serve immediately with a cold crisp Italian Pinot Grigio.

*You have permission to lick up any sauce remaining in your bowl.

*Please be forewarned that eating eggs that are not fully cooked could cause sickness.

2

FRANCE

FOOD, FOOD AND FOOD

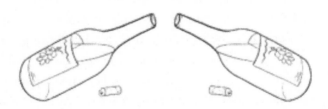

A grade school classmate of mine had a French war-bride mother. When I was in sixth grade, he returned home from a trip to France with his parents and presented me with a small cast metal Eiffel Tower. It triggered childhood dreams of far away and mysterious Paris. Then decades later, Sandy and I planned our first trip to see Paris, the city of lights. Like the Eiffel Tower, many of Paris' other sites such as the Louvre Museum, Notre Dame Cathedral, the Seine River, the Arc de Triomphe and Sacre Coeur church had been burned into my psyche via photographs and French films like *Amélie*. Therefore, seeing those sites for the first time produced a real euphoric buzz.

After landing at Paris Charles de Gaulle Airport, we searched for and found the metro train that would transport us into city-center. We boarded the railcar and sat facing each other with our suitcases occupying the seats alongside both of us. The car was rather empty, so it seemed okay to put our luggage on the seats and out of the aisle. Then, with each stop the car began to fill. Suddenly two ladies in brilliantly colored African print robes and matching head wraps stood staring at me. One of them looked directly into my eyes and then at my suitcase, before pointing to the luggage rack above our seats. I quickly moved our luggage up and then moved over to sit beside Sandy so they could sit together, across from us.

They sat down, talked in an African dialect, and snacked on the pulp covering the seeds they extracted from Tamarind pods. I had used tamarind paste, and its unique sweet-sour taste, to flavor Indian dishes, but I had never tasted tamarind right from the pods. I tried not to stare but wanted to ask them for a seed so I could taste the difference. As I sat there, I mentally framing photographs of them. One shot would feature just their faces surrounded by the bright fabric, and a second would zoom in on one woman's hands holding a tamarind pod. Those images, and many other travel photographs reside only in my memory when I do not have the courage or opportunity to shoot the photograph. As we stood, grabbed our luggage, and prepared to exit the train, I made eye contact and said, "Au revoir." They simply nodded while continuing their conversation.

Our hotel room in the Saint-Germain area of the sixth arrondissement was a little larger than a double closet. The dated furnishings, and floral wallpaper, made it appear the room was last decorated hastily after WWII. The double bed, when perfectly centered in the room, allowed us to shuffle sideways around it to get to the bathroom. I became very adept at this sideways shuffle and found the technique useful in a few crowded museums.

Breakfast, served in a common area, was included in the room price, and featured all beurre (butter) croissants. They looked amazing and tasted even better. With each buttery bite, small brittle shards of the deep brown crispy paper-thin top layers shot across the table like shrapnel. Eating croissants of this pedigree meant I would never again eat from the Costco plastic bin of croissants. After the third one, slathered with raspberry preserves and butter, just in case they did not use enough butter to make the croissant, I accepted the fact that a few extra pounds might be one of my Paris souvenirs.

To stave off some of the expected weight gain, we urban hiked Paris every day. The city is full of grand monuments and museums, which is why it is one of the most visited tourist destinations in the world. As we urban hiked between the Louvre, the Eiffel tower, Le Jardin du Luxembourg and the Arc de Triomphe, I watched for patisseries (pastry shops), boulangeries (bread bakeries), fromageries (cheese shops), and maisons du chocolat (chocolate shops). Finding any one of them caused me to stop and stare, and intensely study the items on display. After a while, I began to use a paper napkin to wipe my nose prints from the display windows before walking away. The easy availability of quality specialty food products tempted us to graze all day rather than sit down for meals. Our daily meal plan, following croissants at the hotel, became a mid-morning break for a coffee and a pastry at a Patisserie, a picnic lunch, featuring items we purchased in specialty shops, and then dinner at a restaurant.

On one occasion, we began our lunch food acquisitions by entering a Boulangerie to purchase a loaf of French bread, or baguette. Buying that loaf of bread was my crowning achievement related to French language conversation. Because of my love for food and cooking, my French vocabulary consisted solely of food words. So, for weeks before our departure date, I studied a few basic French phrases. I had even watched reruns of the Pink Panther movies, starring the English actor Peter Sellers, so I could mimic his mouth half-open and full of cotton balls approach to mumbled French. Standing in line at the bakery, I visualized Peter Sellers while mentally rehearsing the sentence I planned to use, to order a small baguette.

Then it was my turn to order. I could not have been more nervous as I blurted out, "Bonjoir, je voudrai un baguette petit." The clerk turned toward the rack containing the loaves, and I felt ecstatic. She understood me! Then while pointing to the rack containing small baguettes, she asked me a question just to test me. I could see two choices, a plain or seeded baguette. Without missing a beat, I calmly said, "A gouche." She grabbed and bagged the plain baguette located on the left, handed it to me in exchange for the payment, and after I shouted out a joyful "Merci!", I walked out the door feeling like I had just climbed Mount Everest.

Now with the baguette proudly displayed under my arm like a Frenchman, we entered a small grocery looking for lunch meat or something else to put on it for our picnic lunch. In the deli counter display case, we observed three types of pate. The small placard above one contained the words foie gras or goose liver. Using simple sign language, pointing, and using the distance between my thumb and index finger to signify the thickness of the cut, we ordered a slice of foie gras pate. An elderly lady, who stood next to me, closely observed the clerk weighing our pate on the deli scale. Suddenly, she became highly animated and called out the clerk. After some back and forth emotional conversation, it became clear the clerk had entered a higher price per pound into the scale than was listed on the placard. I immediately adopted this lovely caring lady as my French grandmother. As we departed, I turned and said, "Merci," which caused a helpful, knowing smile to spread across her face.

We also stopped at a fruit stand, a cheese shop and finally a wine shop to complete the purchases for our lunch menu. Then we carried the baguette, pate, a small round of ash covered goat cheese, two apples, and a bottle of light fruity Pinot Noir wine to a pedestrian bridge that spans the Seine River. Finding a spot on the bridge we sat in the warm spring sun, with our backs against the railing, and ate like the kings of France. The foie gras pate was so delicious I would have accepted a bout of gout, the "disease of the kings," in exchange.

Because there is so much to see in Paris, planning some down time, to just let Paris come to us, became part of our daily routine. Sidewalk cafes are everywhere. They are the perfect spot to sit and observe a fractional view of Paris life. My preferred time to take a break was about three o'clock in the afternoon. Once seated at a table, I would order a pastis, an anise flavored aperitif. My preferred brand was Ricard. It would be served in a small tumbler filled with ice. A small pitcher of water accompanied the drink. When I poured the water over the light yellow/green liquor, it turned milky. By sipping slowly, and adding water when the level dropped, I could easily spend two hours watching people for the price of one drink.

Eventually we would head back to our hotel and take a short rest before heading back out for our evening meal. Sandy flipped on the 1980's vintage television to check on the world. Although we could not understand the French announcer it was clear that the gravely ill pope might not live much longer. The following afternoon, as we sat in our room with the windows wide-open, church bells all over Paris rang in unison and continued for about thirty minutes to announce his passing. The chorus of bells brought some joy to a sad event.

Prior to our trip, I had been warned by a co-worker that the French were snooty, arrogant and difficult to deal with. Our experiences did not support that view. We found being respectful, rather than demanding, was the best approach when one does not speak the local language. If we worked up the courage to attempt to speak in French, and they knew some English, they would quickly re-direct the conversation to the English language. Or, if we did not want to attempt to use French, I would ask, "Puis-je parler anglais?" (May I speak English?). Asking for their permission, rather than automatically expecting them to understand and speak English, elicited a friendly response. Except for one waiter, in a very touristy area, we found everyone helpful and friendly. He was snooty and arrogant and difficult to deal with because he dealt with demanding tourists, rather than independent travelers, every day.

We so loved the sights, sounds and food of Paris that we talked about returning before leaving. It was everything I thought it would be and more. Our return trip happened sooner than expected. Three years later, in 2010, we were touring Ireland with our friends Mark and Kitty. After a week of traveling together they boarded a bus in Galway, going to Dublin, to catch their flight home the following morning. Sandy and I still had an additional six days booked to explore the area north of Galway. The weather on this trip had been mostly damp and wet. Or, as the Irish might say, "A bit of the soft rain" had fallen almost every day.

Not long after dropping off our friends at the bus station, I turned to Sandy and said, "Let's go someplace else in Europe to get out of the rain."

She was intrigued by the prospect of dry hair and agreed to a visit with a travel agent. Within an hour, we had booked round trip flights to Paris the following morning, along with a hotel room near the Eiffel Tower. We then drove across Ireland, on the new four lane motorway, to Dublin. After we checked into an airport hotel, we called our friends, who had bused across the country just a few hours before.

"Want to join us for dinner tonight?" I asked.

"What did you say?" Mark responded, with a puzzled tone in his voice.

That evening, over an Irish pub dinner we explained what we had done, and early the next morning we flew to Paris. We felt so European.

That is how we found ourselves back in sunny Paris for five days. Since we had departed from Dublin, rather than the U.S., we did not have to suffer through a zombie day.

Our hotel, which the travel agent had selected, turned out to be a Rick Steves-recommended hotel. We figured that out when we noticed a group of guests looking through Rick's Paris guidebooks while sitting in the hotel lobby waiting for a local guide. His hotel recommendation was a good one. We had a comfortable room in a great Paris location. It was in a busy area of the sixth Arrondissement (district) with restaurants and specialty food shops all around.

On our first night, we dined at a bistro that occupied an entire corner just a half block from our hotel. We asked to be seated at a table on the street and under the stars. The hostess then showed us to a small metal table with metal chairs in the tightly packed outside seating area. All around us people talked and laughed with joy in their voices. The warm summer night added to the magic. When our server arrived, we ordered a bottle of Cotes De Rhône red wine. Then I noticed and told Sandy, "Look, you can see the top of the Eiffel Tower from here."

Just then our waiter delivered and poured our wine. At the same time an accordion player, who had taken up residence on the opposite corner, began to play. It was the perfect cliché Paris moment. I opened the voice memo app on my phone and hit the record button. We raised our glasses to toast our good fortune and tapped them together as the music played in the background. Playing that thirty-three second sound bite, and I often do, transports me right back to that magical Parisian moment.

Another memorable moment occurred one afternoon as we urban hiked up the Champs-Elysees toward the Arc de Triomphe. We decided to jump on one of the city buses passing by. We assumed it would go out to some point and return to the same area on the opposite side of the street. You know what they say about assumptions. Well, our joy ride ended at a large bus terminal where everyone had to get off. As we stood gaping at a route map, trying to decide which return bus to catch, a stranger observed us and offered to help. We pointed at the destination we wanted to reach, and she pointed to the correct bus route. Then she guided us to the right boarding location in the terminal. Before she departed, we both said, "Merci." She smiled, knowing she had helped. We have found that there are train and bus angels all over Europe waiting to help independent travelers.

This short spontaneous visit to Paris had gotten us out of rainy Ireland. Paris, for the second time, had been lovely and yet, we wanted to experience more of France. So, a few years later when friends Michael and Lynn suggested we rent a house in Provence, we said, "Oui." They had researched and found the "old stone house" located in the small town of Menerbes. The house did not have an address, but both a clue to its location and the keys for the three-story house had been mailed to them prior to our departure.

After landing in Marseille, the four of us drove north on a modern expressway. Soon we exited onto a small two-lane road and found ourselves in the countryside of Provence where farmland and vineyards dotted the landscape. As we entered Menerbes, one thing was clear. Every house in the village appeared to be an old stone house. The location clue provided with the key stated, "There is an old church across from the old stone house." After driving a circular meandering path through the village's narrow streets multiple times looking for a church, we noticed an unusual archway above a door on a small building. Upon closer inspection, we also observed a worn crucifix in an upper window. A three-story stone house, with closed shutters on all the windows, was across the street. We parked the car, walked up to the front door of the house and knocked. When no one answered, we inserted the key in the door lock, while hoping we were not breaking in, turned the key, and the door opened.

The old stone house became our home base for the next six days. Using the rental car, we explored the cities, Roman ruins, abbeys, and food culture of Provence. In more than one small town, we encountered a weekly open-air market. These markets are like traveling flea markets with food. Because smaller towns do not have the population density to support brick and mortar stores, the portable stores roll into town once a week. The market provides a meeting location for the residents, who not only shop but socialize. These purpose-driven gatherings are wonderful because they get people outside and build a sense of community.

Clothing, kitchenware, shoes, freshly cooked, and preserved foods, filled the market stalls. I started to salivate as we passed a vendor roasting whole chickens on a vertical rotisserie. In a metal tray, directly below the skewered chickens, sat cubed potatoes. They simmered gently in the fatty drippings that fell from the spinning birds. The potatoes looked so good I thought about asking Sandy to be my accomplice and distract the Frenchman tending the chickens, so I could steal a potato or two. Opportunities to graze on local foods existed all over Provence.

One afternoon, we enjoyed a picnic lunch of creamy white Comte cheese, a crusty baguette shaped like a wheat sheaf, strawberries and blueberries while sitting in a wooded spot that overlooked an ancient monastery. After lunch, we walked down to visit the still active abbey. As we followed a well-used path it passed fields of lavender that were not yet in bloom. I breathed in the warm spring air and imagined their fragrance. Entering the abbey, we could hear singing echoing throughout the building. We followed a long hallway until we came to a chapel where the resident monks stood chanting as part of their Mass. Their harmonious and hauntingly beautiful voices filled the church and gave me goose bumps.

On our return trip from the abbey, we stopped at a small roadside place for drinks. While sitting at a small outside table, under some severely pollarded trees, I took a photograph of my glass of Campari and orange juice that contained a unique stirrer: It was topped with the profile of a bare breasted woman. How French I thought.

As we sat and talked we struck up a conversation with some other travelers. They told us about, and then insisted we go to Arles the following day to see a unique annual event, the Arles Guardian Day parade. Arles is in a part of France known as the Camargue. It has long been, and still is, horse and cattle country. As it was only an hour away by car, we decided to take their advice.

We arrived early in downtown Arles on a chilly spring morning. Like cats on a warm windowsill, I photographed a group of people who had gathered on the sunlit stairs leading into an old stone building to warm themselves. We found a café, ordered hot coffees, and waited with anticipation. About thirty minutes later, the distant sound of flutes and drums announced the start of the procession. As the participants came into view and passed our location, we felt as if we had traveled back two centuries in time.

The guardians, or cowboys, along with their female counterparts outfitted in seventeenth century dresses, rode white horses, an ancient Camargue breed unique to the area. The women wore colorful elaborate ankle-length dresses and handmade fine lace shawls, while the men donned black felt-like suits and brimmed hats. I observed most of the parade through my camera's lens, as I shot photo after photo.

One photograph of a young girl sitting behind her father on a twitchy white horse, stands out. She was as pretty as the lily-of-the-valley flowers that spilled from her father's suit coat front pocket. Her proud dad skillfully guided the nervous horse along the parade route to show off his maybe seven-year-old daughter who, because of her shyness, would not make eye contact with the camera and refused to smile.

While driving back from Arles, we passed through a small town. From the car, we noticed people walking toward and entering a small sports arena. To find out what was happening in the arena, we parked the car and walked back to the venue. When asked, the man in the ticket booth said, "Bull games." What that meant was unclear, but we bought tickets, entered the arena, and found seats in the wooden bleachers.

Bull games, it turned out, was a form of bull fighting. In this version, the bull is neither injured nor killed. Teams of bull fighters, tease and taunt the bull until it charges, and then attempt to slip fiber rings onto the horns of charging bulls. Two teams of muscular young men, dressed in white jeans and tight-fitting white T-shirts, competed against each other.

Soon after we had taken our seats the two teams paraded into the bright sunlit bullring. Then one team exited the ring and a bull entered. He charged in, slid to a stop, and then raised his head to survey his surroundings. Immediately, the team that remained in the ring began to taunt the bull by waving, hollering, or running toward it, until it charged one of them. The balance of the team then raced toward the fence that surrounded the bullring.

It was now one man versus the bull. As the bull charged toward and past his target, the young man stepped clear of the horns and attempted to place the fiber ring, he held in his hand, on the closest horn. Then as fast as he could run, he sprinted toward the fence with the bull right on his ass. At the base of the fence was a step about eighteen inches off the ground. He hit that step while running full speed and bound over the fence and out of the ring like an acrobat. The bull put on the brakes and slid toward the fence as gravel flew into the air. We then exhaled.

When the bull tired of the game and refused to charge, a fresh bull replaced him. I imagined the tired bull thinking, "This is bullshit!" Each team continued to take its turn in the bullring until time expired. The team who placed the most rings on a horn won the game.

During our stay at the old stone house, we dined locally in and around Menerbes for most evening meals. These eateries served simple dishes made with fresh local ingredients rather than haute cuisine. On one occasion, I enjoyed a meal of fish served with a white wine, butter, lemon, and caper sauce, fresh green beans, and a crisp lettuce salad dressed with a simple mustard vinaigrette. When the waitress asked if we wanted to order dessert, we all said, "Oui," in unison. I ordered a slice of an almond tart, which is essentially an almond custard made with ground almonds. What made this almond tart so special and unique is that the chef had infused the custard with the zest of a fresh orange. I savored each bite. As the waitress cleared our table, I asked her to compliment the chef. His attention to detail was evident in the balanced flavors and presentation of each course. The waitress went into the kitchen to relay my message and the chef came out to visit our table. When I asked if I could take his photograph, the chef declined until he had retreated into the kitchen to put on a clean chef's jacket. Then, and only then, did he stand proudly in his bright white jacket as I framed and shot the photograph. His slight smile, and his smiling eyes, will always remind me of the pride he had in the food he had prepared for us that night.

Our week at the old stone house passed quickly. Our friends Michael and Lynn bid us adieu and departed for the Marseille's Airport in the rental vehicle. A few hours later, our friends Mark and Kitty, who had just arrived in France, pulled up in their rental. Together we headed to the southern coast of France, the Cote d'Azur, or the French Riviera.

Our first stop was the city of Antibes. Our hotel room in that coastal city was on the second floor. Since the weather was warm and pleasant, the room window, which overlooked the commercial street below, had been left ajar while we slept. Suddenly, around 5 a.m., something jolted me awake. What was that fragrant smell? Jasmine bushes in bloom? Flowering citrus trees? No. It was something much better. The aroma of caramelizing sugar and browning butter wafted from the ovens located in the patisserie directly across the street.

I feigned interest in the simple breakfast of factory-made pastries, sliced cheese and ham provided by the hotel, knowing my calories would be better spent across the street. The curse of this, or any good bakery, is the abundance of choices. Unable to make a quick decision, I stood trancelike, staring at my options. I eventually chose a still warm almond croissant and then walked, with my wife and friends, a short distance and sat on a bench in a small park. Biting into that pastry made from a day-old croissant, which, before baking, had been split horizontally, liberally brushed with a liquor-infused simple syrup, and then spread, inside and on top, with an almond frangipane before being topped with slivered almonds, was amazing.

"Best pastry ever!" I shouted enthusiastically after the first bite.

"You say that every time you eat a pastry," Sandy quickly responded.

Topless beaches, beautiful coastal views, seafood, topless beaches, art museums, topless beaches, and yes, more pastries filled our week. We visited Nice, Monaco, Cannes, and Saint-Tropez before dropping our friends off at a rail station just outside of Aix-en-Provence. They were taking the train to northern France while we were heading home the following day. We arrived in the area a few hours early, so the four of us decided to stop in Aix-en-Provence and urban hike around the city.

Driving was a challenge. In a city with a history going back to 123 BC, most of the one lane city-center streets were built before cars existed. We found a parking spot behind a small hotel and went for our stroll. When we decided to leave for the train station, I put the address into the GPS unit, and we departed. The GPS advice was troublesome. It tried to direct us down one-way lanes or on routes that seemed circular. As we slowly drove down a long narrow one-way street, I thought we might finally escape. Then the road made a slight right turn, and we suddenly found ourselves trapped. A local restaurant had set up their lunchtime tables and chairs blocking one third of the single lane. Backing up was not an option. As I inched forward a Frenchman, who was sitting at one of the tables, got up and quickly began to move tables and chairs out of our way. Sandy still claims our car brushed aside some chairs. I still deny it. Before pulling away we all shouted, "Merci beaucoup!" to our new French friend, and I vowed to never drive in Aix-en-Provence again.

When I dropped off the vehicle at the rental agency the following day, I distracted and annoyed the attendant by trying to converse in French so he would not inspect the sides of the car. Since our post trip credit card statement did not list a charge for rental car repairs, I have the right to tell people, "I almost hit some chairs."

There is much more to see, do and eat in France. Their culinary history is long and recognized globally. They influenced cooking around the world both in the past and still today. Because of my lifetime interest in food and cooking, I am keeping France on my list of places to visit again.

ORANGE ALMOND TART

Ingredients

Crust:
½ cup cane sugar
8 tablespoons softened butter
¼ t salt
1-1/2 cups all-purpose flour
¾ cup toasted almond flour

Filling:
4 T softened butter
1 cup cane sugar
3 large room temperature eggs
1-1/4 cups toasted almond flour
1 t vanilla extract
Zest of one large orange

Preparation

Heat the oven to 350 degrees. Add the two cups of almond flour (divide later) to a skillet and heat over medium heat while stirring until the color changes to a light golden brown. Let cool.

For the crust, in a food processor mix the sugar, butter and salt by pulsing until well combined. Add the flour and ¾ cup of the toasted almond flour. Pulse until the dough starts to come together and will hold its shape if pinched together.

Press the dough into a removable bottom tart pan and then freeze for 15 minutes. Bake for 10-12 minutes or until the edges just begin to brown. Cool in the pan.

For the filling, in the food processor pulse the sugar, butter, and orange zest for 20 seconds. Add the eggs and almond flour and pulse just to combine. Spread the filling in the crust and bake for 20-24 minutes or until the top is lightly browned. Cool the tart.

To serve, cut individual wedge-shaped slices, dust with powdered sugar, and garnish with supremed (citrus segments without the membrane) orange slices.

Or, you can do away with the fuss by cutting a generous piece, laying it on your open hand, and then savor each bite while dreaming of France.

3

SPAIN

A CHANCE TO USE MY HIGH SCHOOL SPANISH

F ood was one of the main reasons I wanted to travel in Spain. A few years before our trip, I watched a travel/food/cooking series on PBS titled, "Road Trip Spain." One of the four people who traveled around Spain in the series was a drop dead gorgeous, black haired and dark-eyed Spanish actress. Whenever she tasted something magically good, she would almost imperceptibly toss her head back while vocalizing, not really a word, a low guttural sound, "Whaah!" I have given a lot of thought to what that meant. A good translation might be, "OMG, that was f**king amazing!" I mention this just in case we are dining together, and you hear me say, "Whaah."

The itinerary for our first trip to Spain consisted of six days in Barcelona. While I planned a business trip to northern Germany, Sandy made the decision to accompany me. So, we decided to add some vacation time, in another European location, following my business. The fact that it was March narrowed our preferred choices to warmer southern Europe. Because a planned trip to Spain had been cancelled due to a family illness a few years before, we decided on Spain, or, more specifically, Barcelona.

When I completed my work in a small town near Dusseldorf, we trained south, where we spent a few days visiting our friends, Dusty and Ulla, in Bonn.

Following our visit, they drove us to a local airport from which we flew onto Barcelona. I was excited about visiting a Spanish speaking country. After all, I had taken three years of Spanish in high school many decades ago. And you know what they say, "If you don't use it, you lose it."

After landing and claiming our luggage, we hired a taxi to drive us to our hotel. The middle-aged driver seemed friendly and tried to engage us in conversation by asking us where we lived, and how long we would be in Barcelona. I immediately began to converse with the driver in Spanish. My portion of the conversation was not in full sentences, but rather individual words combined with sign and body language. He was impressed with my attempt and we talked, if you want to stretch the meaning of that word, continually during the twenty-minute ride to the hotel. We exchanged large smiles and a handshake after he removed our luggage from the trunk. I felt like I had my first friend in Barcelona and was tempted to give him a man hug. I had forgotten to check the Rick Steve's guidebook to see if that was socially acceptable, so I kept my hands to myself.

It was late afternoon when we checked into our modern and newly decorated hotel. Loud, upbeat, and rhythmic dance club music filled the lobby space with youthful energy. Modern design elements like metal and plastic furnishings and abstract wall art made this hotel different. While checking in, the staff, friendly and English speakers, suggested a nearby place for dinner. Most restaurants in Spain serve dinner from 9 - 11 pm. Fortunately, the recommended restaurant opened at 8 pm. Later that evening, we walked three blocks to the restaurant and when the doors opened, we burst in like people who had not eaten in a week.

After our server poured two glasses of deep purple fragrant rioja wine, made from the tempranillo variety of grape, we toasted our good fortune and then began our dinner with the simplest of dishes, tomato bread. Slices of toasted crusty bread had been rubbed with a fresh tomato, drizzled with fragrant olive oil and sprinkled with a finishing salt.

"Delicioso," I exclaimed. If only my high school Spanish teacher, who was from Spain, could see and hear me now.

For my entrée I ordered octopus. A slightly charred grilled arm of octopus had been positioned atop a smear of chickpea hummus on a rectangular plate. Finished with a drizzle of olive oil, it looked beautiful and was delicious. This first meal confirmed what I had been told. Spend a little more, by-pass the countless ordinary tapas bars, and you will love the food in Spain.

The next morning, we headed out on our first urban hike. The cost of breakfast at the hotel convinced us to eat on the street. We found cups of yogurt at a small Middle Eastern grocery. The elderly proprietor warned me, the traveler, about keeping my backpack closed and secure on the streets. With my backpack cinched up, we continued our walk until we came across a bakery where we purchased fresh fried dough pastries, covered in cinnamon and sugar, and coffees with cream. Sitting on a bench, we ate our continental breakfast, while sitting in continental Europe. When finished we continued toward our destination, the Gaudi designed basilica, Segrada Familia.

Europe contains thousands of old crumbling churches, basilicas, and cathedrals. I have overdosed on churches, so I often just wait outside while Sandy goes in for a look. If I do enter, it is only to take photographs. In Spain, I photographed many massive altars completely covered in gold foil. It seemed to me there was a history lesson involving the Incas, Aztecs, religion, and theft, in those unapologetic displays of wealth. In St. Peter's Square, I captured four people, including a priest standing on a chair, looking in different directions, searching for something. The church has always sold hope, and still does, for those who are looking. No matter what country I visit, when I enter old churches, I will invariably encounter a few elderly people sitting or kneeling and staring toward the altar. Before I leave, I always wish their hopes are fulfilled.

As we approached the Sagrada Familia basilica, our eyes were automatically drawn upward toward the multiple pointy spires that crown the massive structure. That is the engagement power of architecture. The groundbreaking ceremony for this basilica took place in 1882, and its expected completion date is around 2032. That is crazy! We paid our admission fee, the new form of tithing, and walked into a cavernous space lined with massive brightly colored stained-glass windows that flooded everything and everyone with a kaleidoscope of colored light. As organ music filled the immense space, we stood staring up in awe while spinning in circles to absorb it all.

A bit dizzy and rubbing our sore necks, we continued our Gaudi architecture tour by walking to a modernist apartment building he designed before he began work on the basilica. When you approach the outside of this structure, completed in 1910, you begin to understand his genius and once inside, it is confirmed. It appeared Gaudi had an aversion to straight lines. His modernist organic style of architecture used both unusual shapes, forms, and materials, to create one-of-a-kind buildings, unlike anything else constructed at that time. Because I am a child of the sixties, I believe drugs or heavy alcohol use had to be part of the design process.

We ended our Gaudi tour and headed back toward our hotel by following Las Ramblas, a wide pedestrian only street. We stopped at the Mercat de la Boqueria, a large market featuring local seafood and jamon, to grab some lunch. The cup of fresh cantaloupe, strawberries and raspberries we shared, paired nicely with some salty shaved jamon Iberico, the famous Spanish ham. We could have continued to graze on the food offering at the market but held back, because we knew we would be eating tapas at Quimet & Quimet that evening.

The hotel staff, who had recommended Quimet & Quimet, noted it was small and would be crowded. We arrived at 7:15, fifteen minutes prior to opening time, and joined two couples cued up at the entrance. When the roll-up door opened, we took seats at the bar. Within ten minutes, people started queuing up outside because all the seat had been occupied.

To say the place was miniscule would be descriptively generous. It had eight to ten seats at the bar and three small round high tables, without chairs, behind us. Directly in front of us, just past the narrow rectangular bar surface, was the tapas prep station. Standing there, ready to fill the tapas orders, were the two proprietors, a man, and a woman. Behind them, on three tiers of horizontal shelving, stood the wine and liquor inventory.

I felt like I was in a sushi bar watching food performance artists. As they grabbed a small plate from a tall stack of clean plates, and then prepared and plated the item ordered, they flowed like running water. Every motion was intentional, well-practiced and fluid. I watched as he prepared one of my favorites. He set down a plate with one hand while the other hand grabbed five large freshly cooked pink shrimp and arranged them in a spiral on the plate. The hand that had set down the plate, already held a decanter of fragrant Spanish olive oil and began to drizzle a small amount on the shrimp. His free hand then grabbed a pepper mill, and he used both hands to season the shrimp with freshly ground black pepper. Each item we ordered was created directly in front of us, just like the shrimp dish I described, and then served immediately. Each carefully crafted and beautifully presented tapa received almost instantaneous feedback, as we moaned and groaned in pleasure while savoring them. The fresh ingredients, and simple flavor combinations, made this a food experience to remember.

Our six days in Spain was like eating the first order of tapas. We left still hungry for more.

So the following fall we returned to travel in southern Spain. Our trip began and ended in Madrid and included visits to Ronda, Seville, Granada, and Cordoba.

We chose not to rent a car and traveled by train and bus. Why? Because the anxiety of dealing with all of the hubbub at the bus and rail stations, like having to purchase tickets, locating the correct departure platform to board trains and buses, all these stressful activities, caused tension and made me feel more alive. Plus, I get to travel and interact with locals while shooting photographs.

After our overnight flight into Madrid, we boarded a train heading south. The jet-lagged train journey was relaxing and quiet. Staring out my window, I watched the vast open spaces of the Spanish countryside flash by. The landscape was either dry parched land, covered with dried golden stems of grass, or olive groves. I observed more olive trees than I thought existed on the whole of planet earth, plus any olive trees growing on other planets in our solar system or other solar systems, on that four-and-a-half-hour train ride.

Most of the olives produced in Spain are pressed into olive oil, and some of that oil is turned into bars of soap. In a small, jam-packed gift shop, we found, no smelled, bars of olive oil soap scented with the essence of orange. It was such a pleasant aroma that we bought a bar and used it to shower for the balance of our trip. Occasionally, I noticed people sniffing the air after I passed. I brought new meaning to the phrase, "to bring a breath of fresh air." In sections of Valencia, orange trees full of bitter oranges lined some streets. Those bitter oranges are used to make marmalade. Nobody eats that stuff except the British, Sandy, and Denise Unland (my editor).

The first city we visited was Granada, the home of one of the most iconic tourist destinations in Spain, the Alhambra. This Moorish Islamic palace and fortress complex was constructed on a large hilltop, overlooking the surrounding landscape, for defensive purposes. Getting there required us, and any invading forces, to trudge up a long steep incline.

It was well worth the ascent. The Islamic detailed architectural features on the ceilings and walls inside the palace, caused me to pause and marvel at the craftsmanship required to execute the intricate designs. Outside were beautifully planted floral gardens. Water, which was routed around gardens and through reflective pools, provided both magical visual images and musical notes as it trickled throughout the complex. After spending the whole morning touring and photographing the buildings and grounds, we followed meandering roadways back toward our hotel. We were hungry and stopped to purchase take-away baguette sandwiches for lunch. As we walked out of the shop and toward our hotel, where we planned to eat on the rooftop patio, I suggested a glass of wine with lunch so we stopped in a wine shop and purchased a bottle of Spanish Tempranillo red wine.

We picked up two glasses from our room and headed to the roof top patio. There we sat and enjoyed our jamon and manchego cheese sandwiches, sipped the full-bodied wine, and relaxed in the warm sun. Soon, another couple joined us on the patio. We began to talk and discovered they lived in northern Germany. Being Americans, we shared our life stories in the next twenty-seven minutes and learned a few things about them. They lived east of Hamburg, on the water, and he was a psychologist. Before leaving, they accepted my offer to dine together that evening. As the sun began to set, we met in the lobby and walked to a nearby restaurant that they had suggested. It specialized in marisco frito mezclado, or mixed fried seafood.

The restaurant's interior, a large open space, was bright and filled with a special buzz that resulted from people eating and having a fun time. It appeared everyone was eating the specialty, so we followed suit and orders two platters of fried seafood, bright green salads, and a bottle of Verdejoa wine. The small bites of squid, octopus, shrimp, and fish, that had been lightly battered and flash fried were delicious, and the dry and somewhat acidic white wine paired perfectly with the fried seafood. We finished with the refreshing vinaigrette dressed salads. It was a lovely dining experience with new friends that we had met just hours before. After dinner, the four of us took a long walk and stopped for another glass of wine. We chatted, laughed, and enjoyed each other's company. The courage to say, "Hello," had led to another fun evening.

It is no secret that I love sweets. One evening while out walking, we passed a bakery. Well, we did not really pass it; we stalled, and then went inside. Always on the hunt for a sweet I have never eaten, I selected what looked like a piece of flan. The typical flan I have eaten is a light yellow custardy jiggly sweet eaten on a plate. This out-of-hand treat was a golden dense eggy rich sweet that had a deeper caramel flavor. As we walked, I became so engrossed in savoring each bite I walked into three people in front of me. I quickly shouted, "Perdoname." My high school Spanish classes were really paying dividends.

A few nights later, while again meandering around the city, I suggested a return trip to the bakery for another square of that eggy caramely goodness. An internet search had revealed it to be tocino de cielo, or egg caramel custard. We walked and walked and walked but could not find it. That made the first piece even more unforgettable and caused a tiny tear to run down my cheek. Another chance to possibly shed tears occurred when Sandy and I rationalized attending a bull fight.

Valencia is one of two cities we visited that had a bullring. Since bullfighting is a cultural phenomenon in Spain, of course I wanted the experience. The pros and cons of the sport are often debated in and outside of Spain. I decided to reserve my judgement until after I had a chance to see local Spaniards watching and reacting to the sport. Sandy was not sure she wanted to see death on display but finally agreed to accompany me. I purchased tickets and then did some reading about the sport that has a 1200-year-old history in Spain.

The fans, or aficionados, consider bullfighting a form of art important to their culture. I knew I had to experience the art show to determine if I would become an aficionado.

The weather forecast for the next day was cloudy with a chance of rain. By afternoon it did rain, and the organizers cancelled the bullfight. Apparently slippery surfaces and charging bulls could be a lethal combination, and not necessarily just for the bulls. Many disappointed faces were observed as I waited in line at the bullring ticket window to claim my refund. At least the bulls remained happy for another day.

Now, with a free evening, we decided to spend the ticket refund money on a nice dinner. That evening, with no destination in mind, we walked toward a new section of town. As we strolled along a busy commercial street, we watched for a restaurant that appealed to us. Next to a small square, filled with local people enjoying the summer evening, we found an inviting old established restaurant. We entered and were seated without a reservation. The wood dominated décor, and the advanced age of the male wait staff, led us to believe this was a place that would serve classic Spanish fare.

We ordered a Spanish rioja wine, to toast our good fortune, and looked over the menu. One item on the menu really intrigued me. It was roasted leg of baby lamb. I have eaten leg of spring lamb, which implies it is a young lamb, but I had never heard of leg of baby lamb. My wife asked if we could order the paella, and since an order had to be for two people, I agreed to her choice. Then as we sat sipping our wine, our waiter walked past with entrees for the table adjacent to ours. There it was. On a large oval serving plate was the entire tiny roasted leg of a baby lamb. I imagined myself picking it up, like a turkey drumstick, and biting into the luscious soft lamb meat with a crispy golden-brown exterior. Just then our paella arrived. It looked amazing and was delicious. It may have been the best paella in Spain, and yet I was a little disappointed. I promised myself I would return to Spain for the uniquely Spanish food experience I had passed up. Ordering and eating the leg of a baby lamb. That is a strange objective, unless you have read the back story.

We spent our last two days in Madrid. When we arrived, we checked into our hotel, and then walked for about twenty minutes along a wide boulevard, to get to the Spanish National Museum of Art, the Prado. After about three hours of dancing the museum shuffle while viewing the works of Goya, El Greco and Velazquez, we visited the museum café to rest and recharge with cups of coffee.

When we departed toward our hotel, we walked on the opposite side of the boulevard through a narrow floral garden that paralleled the street. Tired from many days of travel and the museum visit, when we entered our room I sat down and used my cell phone to check the soccer scores for the two Madrid teams. Before leaving home, I had checked their schedules to see if I might catch a match. Therefore, I knew Real Madrid was playing out of town, and I thought Atletico Madrid had played an early afternoon game. Turns out I was wrong. I discovered Atletico would play in about 90 minutes.

I raced down to the hotel desk and asked a clerk if it would be possible to secure tickets for the match. The clerk made a few phone calls that went unanswered. Finally, he advised me that if I went to the stadium, I might be able to get tickets. He noted that the team playing Atletico was near the bottom of the table, so the game might not sell out.

I rushed upstairs. After pleading with my tired wife, Sandy agreed to go if we hired a taxi rather than walk the two miles to the Vincente Calderon Stadium. From the back of the taxi we observed, at first a few, and then a flood of people wearing red and white stripped Atletico soccer gear. The taxi driver politely asked us to get out a few blocks from the stadium due to the crush of people. Exiting, we joined the river of stripped shirts and as we neared the stadium, we observed most of the 55,000 attendees milling around and drinking beer. They were tailgating without vehicles. Since drinking alcohol in the stadium seats is not allowed, and the cost of beer is lower outside than in the stadium, the local practice is to get a buzz on before entering. I approached and asked someone where I could purchase tickets, and they directed me to the opposite side of the stadium and the ticket windows. Once there, I waited in line until it was my turn and then requested two tickets. The ticket agent responded, "I do not have two seats together in the whole stadium."

I crossed my eyes, so I could keep one on him and the other on Sandy, and responded, "Give me two as close together as possible."

Yes, I am still married. Turns out Sandy's seat was a row in front of me and five seats to my left. Before the match started, I asked people if they would shift down so my wife could sit in front of me, and they kindly did.

The atmosphere at this sporting event surpassed that of any other sporting event I have ever attended. Watching the fans entertained us as much as the game on the soccer pitch. They sang and chanted tirelessly, when not smoking cigarettes or eating sunflower seeds. I observed multiple people who could shame a squirrel with their ability to quickly shell and eat one sunflower seeds after another. Sandy and I repeatedly looked at each other and just smiled. As we left, we agreed it had been an utterly unique experience to sit amongst fans so passionate about their soccer team. Impressed by the event, Sandy fell in love with soccer that day and will never have to be asked twice to attend another match.

I really enjoyed southern Spain, and the north of Spain still beckons me. Walking the Camino de Santiago, an ancient pilgrimage trail, has always appealed to me. Taking two to three months to walk 780 kilometers would be fun, right? Then I remember, while on the trail most hikers sleep in refugios (communal boarding houses) where hikers are jammed together like cattle going to slaughter, and I reconsider. Because of my ability to snore loudly, I know I would be dragged from my bunk nightly by gangs of angry-eyed hikers and thrown out into the cold dark night. So instead, I plan to continue my pilgrimage walk to Spanish restaurants, and the north of Spain has some great ones.

TOCINO DE CIELO (EGG CARAMEL CUSTARD)

Ingredients

Custard:
13 egg yolks
1 egg
I cup sugar
Zest of one lime
1 cup water

Caramel:
½ cup sugar
3 T water
1 T lime juice

Preparation

Heat oven to 350 degrees. In a medium bowl whisk the egg yolks, egg, and lime zest until well combined.

Create a water bath. Put a high-sided baking dish in the oven and pour boiling water into it until the water comes a third of the way up the sides.

To make the caramel, combine the sugar, water and lime juice in a saucepan and cook, without stirring, until the sugar has melted, and it is a dark caramel color. Watch carefully and pull from the heat near the end, while continuing to swirl the caramel in the hot pan, to prevent burning the sugar. Pour the caramel into a dry glass loaf pan or small square glass casserole dish. Rotate and tip the glass dish so the caramel coats the entire bottom. Let sit.

Next, to make the custard, add the sugar and water to a saucepan and cook over medium-high heat until it begins to boil. Continue cooking the syrup on medium for 8 minutes.

Then very slowly, pour and rapidly whisk the hot syrup into the bowl containing the egg and egg yolks. Pour this mixture into the glass baking dish containing the caramel.

Cover the dish loosely with foil, place it into the hot water bath, and bake for 30-40 minutes, or until a skewer inserted into the flan comes out clean.

Completely cool the flan and then release the custard from the sides of the baking dish using a small sharp knife. Set a serving plate on top of the baking dish and invert them both at once so the flan will release onto the serving plate.

Cut into serving pieces, (squares, rectangles, or triangles) and serve at room temp or chilled. To serve, squeeze some lime juice over each piece and garnish with fresh fruit. Or, cut yourself a nice piece and eat if off of a paper napkin while walking down a busy street, just as I did in Spain.

4

IRELAND

JAYSUS!

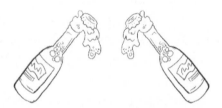

S andy and I planned our first trip to Europe in the early 90's with guidance and encouragement from our friends, Dusty and Ulla, who live in Germany. Our itinerary had us flying into London, where we would spend a few days, before flying to Shannon Airport in Ireland. It is there where our friends, who had ferried their car from Germany to Ireland, would be waiting for us. Our travel plans, for the next ten days, reversed that route so we would end up at their home in Bonn, Germany.

As we waited for our Chicago to London flight to depart, an airline employee called us to the counter to inform us we would be upgraded to business class. Apparently, we had been randomly selected to be the recipients of an expression of "kindness" from an airline. I know this is shocking to hear, but it did happen. What a fairytale beginning to our trip. Then we took off and once the plane leveled off, someone across the aisle lit a cigarette and the fairytale bubble burst. Yes, people could still smoke on airplanes.

When we arrived, we walked around London in a tourist stupor. At every turn we observed the familiar. Black, funny looking cabs, red phone booths, London bridge, the Parliament building, Big Ben,

Piccadilly Circus, Trafalgar Square, the Tower of London, and people who talked like the characters who appeared in Monty Pythons Flying Circus. These sites, and the people with an enchanting British accent, that had been burned into our collective memories via photos and film, appeared in real time right before us. It was exciting. I soon had Sandy posing with Bobbies and peeking out of a red phone booth so I could shoot the cliché photographs. We visited the Victoria and Albert Museum, the National Museum, took a black cab to the West End theatre district to see a performance of "Oklahoma," strolled through Harrod's food courts while drooling, and listened to an orchestral performance in Albert Hall. We were, as the British might say, "proper tourists."

Our central London lodging was in a dormitory managed and operated by nuns. It was in an old stone building located close to the Victoria and Albert Museum. During the school year, students filled the rooms. During the summer months, the nuns provided travelers cheap, less than $100 per night, London lodging.

Our Spartan dorm room contained two single beds. At this point the reader might expect me to describe the additional room furnishings, but I am sorry, the room only contained two beds. A common bathroom, located down the hall, gave us the chance to meet some fellow cheapskates, I am sorry, budget conscience travelers, during our two-day stay. Other highlights of our stay at the dormitory included new and unusual culinary delights, like canned beans and blood pudding on the breakfast buffet. We wrinkled our noses and stuck with the eggs and toast.

The two days in London flew by. On our last morning we packed and prepared to fly to Ireland. As we rolled our suitcases down a London Street, toward a tube stop that would transport us to the airport, an iconic black taxi rolled up.

"Going to the airport?" The driver asked.

"Yes!" I shouted back.

"I'll take you for the same cost as the two tube tickets," he responded.

We happily jumped in and chatted him up all the way to the airport. He had a lovely flowing English accent that required us to listen hard to understand what he said. Luckily, I had listened attentively to English accents while religiously watching every episode of Monty Python's Flying Circus.

As I sat there watching the row houses flash past the cab window, my mind flashed back to one of my favorite episodes.

"The parrots not dead, it's resting." "Hello Polly, RISE AND SHINE."

After clearing passport control in Ireland, we walked to the commercial area of the airport and as expected, our two friends, Dusty and Ulla, stood waiting for us. All the uncertainty and tension caused by travel to new places vanished when we sighted them. After hellos and hugs, we jammed our luggage into the back of their small European car, which they had ferried from Germany to Ireland. We then piled into the back seat and drove off for our "Bumping and Snacking" adventure.

When our arrival flight circled Shannon Airport before landing, the brilliant greens of Ireland had been on full display. Now we traveled across that green terrain on small two-lane roads that passed through rolling pastureland and small villages containing old stone buildings with brightly colored doors and window shutters. Each town was dressed up with window boxes and hanging planters that contained brightly colored flowers. Words like "rural," "quaint," and "cute" all came to mind as we bumped along the roadways. In between two small towns, my friend Dusty saw an elderly man sitting on a low stone wall up ahead. I could see the gray-haired man, who appeared to be in his sixties, was dressed in a wool Irish sweater and a wool flat cap. He looked like an Irish caricature. Was that a pipe in his hand? Was he paid to sit there? Dusty stopped the car and encouraged me to engage with a local by getting out and asking for directions to Doolin. I initially balked, but finally did after being harassed by everyone in the car.

"Excuse me, is this the way to Doolin?" I shyly asked.

He replied in a language I had never heard. I thought English was the first language in Ireland. Could I have been wrong? Turns out it was just his Irish brogue. Over the next week I had to listen awfully hard and watch the speaker's lips to catch half of what was being said.

Our first night was spent at a B&B just outside of the small village of Doolin. The fact that it was a quaint white cottage, with a red door and shutters, and a proprietress who spoke with a lovely Irish accent, all added to the magic. After being shown to our small rooms, we unpacked and then the four of us met to discuss our dinner plans. Doolin, a small remote city on the west coast of Ireland, contains a few small pubs that are notorious for music provided by whichever musicians walked in the door that night. We decided to make one of them our dining destination.

There are Irish pubs all over the world but walking into an Irish pub in Ireland for the first time made me feel excited. I ordered a Guinness and watched as the bar keeper slowly pumped the lever that filled the glass full of a dark, almost black, caramel colored liquid. The tiny effervescent bubbles rising to the surface created a creamy tan crown on the pint glass. After the foam had subsided a bit, the pint was topped off with a wee bit more beer and then set in front of me. Truth be told, at this point in my life, I did not drink very much beer. But drinking that beer, in that place, on that occasion, made it uniquely special. The mild malty flavored beer was cold, creamy, and refreshing. I enjoyed each sip while looking over the menu. Since we were sitting a stone's throw from the North Atlantic Ocean, I chose local mussels and salmon for my dinner.

While we tucked into the delicious freshly made food, musicians began to set-up in a corner of the pub. The mussels, which had been steamed in a broth of white wine and cream, and flavored with fresh parsley and thyme, were tender and delicious. My slow roasted salmon, accompanied by boiled potatoes and steamed asparagus, was moist and tasted of the sea. Then the pick-up band began to play their jigs and ballads to top off a special night, my first, in Ireland. It is always so thrilling and joyful the first time I have new experiences. I could return to that same Doolin pub, drink the same beer, eat the same meal, and listen to the same musicians, but the second visit could never match my first.

After dinner, we hung around for a while to listen to the music before stepping outside. It was a warm summer night, and the air was fresh. We walked about a block to the town's harbor. Even though it was about 10:45 p.m., and the setting sun was already below the horizon, it still illuminated the western sky enough for me to see the tiny fishing boats anchored in the harbor. I silently peered out into the North Atlantic, while muffled Irish music played in the background, and thought, "How lucky am I?"

The following day we drove North to the city of Galway. As we entered town, we pulled into a gas station and asked a man for directions to our B&B. Then as traffic cleared, we pulled out and drove a block before stopping at an intersection. Suddenly, the man from the gas station appeared at the driver's window. He clarified the directions he had given us and then turned to run a block back to the station. That single incident helped me begin to understand that the charm of Ireland was not the places we would visit, or the sights we would see. The main reason to visit Ireland should be to meet the Irish people and experience their friendliness, attitude about life, and unique humor by chatting them up. Oh, and eat fresh locally sourced food and drink plenty of Guinness.

While urban hiking the old section of Galway, we decided to eat lunch at a fish and chips shop. As I stepped inside, the alluring smell of deep-fried food caused my stomach to rumble. The menu contained only locally caught fish, served with chips made from locally grown potatoes. I ordered the haddock. Two breaded, and then deep fried perfectly crispy large hunks of fish, that were too hot to handle, arrived in a newspaper lined basket. The fish was so fresh and moist that it has made it impossible for me to order fish and chips again, anywhere, and expect them to be as good.

A few days later, we drove to the small farming community of

Cappawhite, in County Tipperary. My wife and I checked into a B&B just outside of town and our friends went to stay with a good friend who lived nearby. The B&B accommodations were in a small modest Irish home. We entered through the front door and into the knickknack filled living room with lace curtains. A doorway in the living room led to the small bedroom where we would sleep. We felt like we were visiting friends or relatives who had invited us to spend the night, but these were strangers. Thinking we had disrupted the family life of the home's occupants; we took a walk into town to stretch our legs and get out of their way.

Cappawhite was as spartan as our accommodations. In addition to few quaint homes it contained a postage stamp sized Post office, a Catholic church and two pubs. I suggested a drink at one of the local pubs to kill some time. As we walked inside, some older men sitting at the bar gave us a look over and continued their conversation. Listening to them talk, while trying to understand what they were saying, entertained us. One of them loudly shouted, "Jaysus!", to begin his response to something someone else had said. For the rest of the trip and the balance of my life, I have looked for opportunities to speak in my Irish brogue and shout, "Jaysus!" But only when it seems appropriate, which is too often according to some friends.

The next morning, Sandy and I attended Sunday morning Mass at the Catholic church in Cappawhite along with our traveling companion's local friend and his mother. Most of the Irish men attending the Mass stood outside the church. Some smoking, while others occasionally looking through the propped open church entrance doors. All the women, wearing their Sunday church dresses, paraded into the small but comfortable church. The structure of the Catholic Mass is the same all over the world but having a priest with an Irish accent made this experience different.

After Mass, the four of us walked together to the community center for a church-sponsored bake sale. The large open room was lively with conversation and filled with the aroma of sweet baked goods. All the lovely and lively Irish ladies, dressed in their Sunday's finest, who had baked the pastries, cakes, and cookies, greeted us like family and wanted to know where we lived in the States. When we said, "The Chicago area," they continued the conversation as they mentioned relatives who had emigrated to the Chicago area in years past. Then, before departing, we purchased a lovely Irish cream cake from one of them. We drove back to our new friend's home and enjoyed the delicious vanilla scented soft and airy sponge cake, frosted with sweetened fresh whipped cream, and cups of steaming hot PG Tips tea. The experience of talking with locals and eating food they had lovingly prepared made me feel like I was part of the local community.

After our week in Ireland, we departed via a car ferry for Wales. We then spent a few days bumping and snacking our way across Wales and England, before boarding another ferry for the Netherlands. From there we would drive to our friend's home in Bonn, Germany before flying home.

Our first night in the UK was spent at a B&B in Wales. Built in 1740, the stone structure was the oldest building I had ever slept in. The weathered and worn exterior was balanced by old rose bushes covered in pink flowers. Another stop was to visit Hay-on-Wye, the town of books, that contained no less than twenty bookstores. The quant village had a meandering main street that followed the contour of the Wye River. Eventually we arrived in the port city of Harwich, where we waited to board the second ferry boat.

The ocean-going ferry was a large ship that could accommodate over 200 cars and 300 freight trucks. As we waited in our car, I watched as a large gate, hinged at the bottom of the bow of the ship, was lowered and became a bridge from the dock to the ferry boat. We, along with the other cars and trucks, were directed by the crew onto the ferry and to our parking spot in a log row of cars. After parking we climbed a stairway to the top deck. Below deck, the ferry had a restaurant, lounge areas with rows of chairs, and even a movie theatre. My three traveling companions all went below deck to watch a movie while I decided to stay on the upper deck. It was a sunny warm day and I enjoyed watching the other boat traffic crisscrossing the channel. Then my sense of place suddenly transported me mentally back several decades. As I watched our ship's progress from England to the Hook of Holland, I remembered the tens of thousands of soldiers who crossed that same body of water, the English Channel, on D-Day. Their rough crossing, hostile landing, and subsequent sacrifices in June of 1944, changed the world for the better. Thinking of them, rather than watch a movie, seemed to be a more meaningful activity.

Looking back on that first trip to Europe, I realize what an important role our friends had played. They guided and pushed us to be and become independent travelers by their example. Seeing and experiencing how they traveled on this trip gave us the courage to continue to travel on our own. Anyone who is unsure or uncertain about planning and then traveling independently should partner with friends and just do it.

A few years later, in the mid-90s, we returned to Ireland with two teenaged daughters. We again flew into Shannon airport, cleared customs, retrieved our luggage, and then proceeded to the car rental desk. After completing the rental agreement paperwork, we walked to the parking lot with the clerk to find our car. I will admit I was a little apprehensive about driving in Ireland. Driving while seated on the right side of the car and traveling on the left side of the road was an unnatural act. I think the nuns in grade school talked and warned us about unnatural acts, but I do not remember the details. Friends had told me, "It will take you three days to figure out you have a rearview mirror." Or "Wait until you get into your first roundabout with a lot of traffic, you will be going in circles until you run out of gas." Fear mongers, I thought.

Then as I looked over the rental vehicles, while in a zombie day stupor, I noticed all the left side rearview mirrors were dangling or missing. I soberly got into our rental, asked my family to remind me to "stay left" whenever I drove onto a roadway, and off we went.

It did not take long to understand what happened to the left side mirrors. Almost every rural road in Ireland, oh, and most of Ireland is rural, are at best a lane and a half wide. Both sides of the road have either ancient stacked stone fences or six-foot-tall hedgerows. Combine those obstructions to your view with curvy roads and driving becomes a tense white-knuckle activity. Every time I approached a curve, a car, tour bus or truck, could be driving toward me. When at the last moment I would see a vehicle, which was taking up most of the lane and a half of road, I would swerve to the left to avoid a head-on collision. While Sandy was screaming, "You are going to hit the hedge," I felt good about the fact that my rental car did not have a left side mirror. If it had, I would have scrapped it off. The sound of hedge branches brushing the side of the car soon became music to my ears and provided real comfort. Those hedges acted as an early version of lane guidance sensors.

Since that initial left side of the road driving experience, I have driven in England and Australia to hone my skills. What I have found is that, after a few days behind the wheel, I become accustomed to the new driving routine. The real problem occurs after I return home. Within a few days of my return, I will be driving somewhere and suddenly be panic stricken. My brain short circuits because, for just a fraction of a second, I will not know which side I am supposed to be on. Left, right, left, right?

Our three days in London, followed by travel with friends in Ireland and England, introduced Sandy and I to European travel. Because both countries are English speaking, discounting the accents, they were safe havens for new travelers like ourselves. Exploring London on our own gave us confidence in our ability to plan and travel independently. Then as we bumped and snacked across Ireland and England with our friends Dusty and Ulla, we learned how to travel. Although we were literally along for the ride, for they had planned our route and reserved our accommodations, we experienced the joy of "Bumping & Snacking" travel.

SLOW ROASTED SALMON

Ingredients

2 T olive oil
4 pieces of salmon fillet (about 6 oz each)
Zest of one lemon
1 T chopped fresh thyme
Salt
Pepper
Lemon wedges
Irish butter

Preparation

Heat oven to 275 degrees. Line a baking sheet with parchment paper or foil and brush with some of the olive oil. Mix remaining oil with the thyme and lemon zest. Lay the salmon fillets, skin side down, on the baking sheet. Divide and spread the thyme mixture over the top of each fillet. Season the fillets with salt and black pepper.

Bake for 14-18 minutes or until the salmon is opaque. Garnish with lemon wedge and serve with a side dish of your choice. To make your dining experience a wee bit more Irish, add a pat of room temperature Irish butter on each fillet as you set them on the serving plates. And do not forget the Guinness. It pairs well with everything!

5

CHINA

AN ASIAN CULTURAL EXPERIENCE

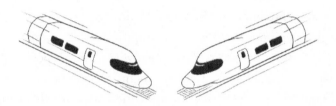

Traveling for work is a way to see the world on someone else's dollar, euro, or in this case renminbi. I have been to Shanghai twice to lead two-day training workshops. A local Chinese firm did all the marketing and selling for the workshop, or as we consultants say, "They put the butts in the seats." Flying to the site, in this case Shanghai, and delivering the workshop content became my responsibility.

Since this was a chance to visit a culturally unique part of the world, and the client would cover all of my travel expenses, Sandy decided to accompany me. I was quite surprised at her decision. For years I had shopped at a local Asian grocery store, and she occasionally would come along. The smells emanating from open plastic tubs of fish and crab, combined with other unusual aromas in the store, appealed to me but not to her more acute sense of smell. More than once she stated, "I would never want to go to China." One should never, say "never."

To prepare for the trip we had to visit the Chinese embassy in Chicago to obtain travel visas. We also scheduled a visit with our family doctor to be inoculated for some unusual diseases. The list of possible inoculations included hepatitis A, hepatitis B, typhoid, yellow fever, Japanese encephalitis, rabies, meningitis, polio, measles, mumps and rubella (MMR), Tdap (tetanus, diphtheria and pertussis), chickenpox, shingles, pneumonia and influenza. Luckily, our family doctor pared down that list to just a few. While waiting on our travel visas, we researched and planned a two-week stay in China. We decided to visit two cities, Shanghai where I would work, and Beijing because of its historical sites like the Forbidden City and Tiananmen Square, and its proximity to the Great Wall.

Our thirteen-hour flight was non-stop from Chicago to Shanghai. The unusual flight path took the plane over the north pole and then across Mongolia. As I looked out the plane window at the vast ice-covered land below, I reflected on my anticipation for this trip. The fact that the destination was so different from the western world in which I lived, made me excited to get there and experience the differences.

My Chinese host had promised to be waiting for us at the airport when the plane arrived. Then our flight landed early. After failing to find my name on one of the placards held by about 100 people waiting to pick up passengers, we decided to find our own way to the hotel where the workshop would take place. We located an ATM, withdrew some renmimbi, and then proceeded to a high-speed rail line. I asked a German national, who was standing nearby, if this train would take us to the Pudong area of Shanghai, the location of our hotel. After he confirmed the route, we purchased tickets for the Maglev German engineered train. I had read that it used magnets to both lift the train from the surface of the rails and propel it forward. It proved to be the fastest and smoothest train ride ever while it transported us at 300km an hour to our destination.

We departed the train and walked down a stairway that took us from the elevated platform to a ground level taxi stand. Before leaving home, I printed a document containing the name of our hotel in English and Chinese. As we entered a taxi, I handed it to a driver who then drove us to the front door of a large western style hotel. The hotel, with its sweeping driveway and oversized façade, would have fit nicely in any large city in the US. But when we entered the front door and encountered the Chinese staff it became clear that we had traveled to the other side of the world.

While I worked the next two days, my wife went on mini tours of Shanghai arranged through our hotel. Once I was free, we spent the next two days exploring Shanghai, a city of twenty-three million people.

On the first day we took a cab to the center of old Shanghai to stroll along the Bund, a riverfront park that is in between the Huangpu River and an exclusive shopping district. Shanghai's new financial district, located across the river and built in just twenty years, contained numerous tall and architecturally interesting skyscrapers. Shapes that included large globes, spires, ovals, and rectangles were covered in reflective glass. One building had a large rectangular opening near the top that made me think of a beer bottle opener. After being awed by that view, I stopped to take a photograph of three Chinese men using hand hammers and chisels to break up a section of the walkway that needed to be replaced. Most anywhere else in the world a construction crew would be using a pneumatic jackhammer to quickly break up and remove the concrete. In China, where labor is cheap and people need employment, hand tools still do the job. Made me wonder how the skyscrapers had been built.

It was a beautiful sunny day and thousands of Chinese joined us on the walk along the Bund. Being from the west, we drew attention because we stood out.

Occasionally a Chinese family would hesitantly approach Sandy, and then use sign language to ask if they could have their picture taken with her. At first Sandy felt honored and would agree. The parents and children would all line up alongside her, raise one hand to give the peace sign, and smile for the photograph. Using their cameras, I snapped their picture while wondering what they would say while showing the photograph to their friends and family.

Initially, Sandy thought they had mistaken her for someone famous. I had a different theory. I explained that they, based on their dress and demeanor, might be from country villages and were only visiting Shanghai. I continued by saying, "They probably never see westerners, especially one as beautiful as you." She quickly agreed. If she had not tired of the activity, we could have charged a small fee for each staged photograph and covered our travel expenses.

While traveling, I attempt to take photos that contain local people. Including people increases the interest level of the photograph for the viewer. Because people often do not like their picture taken, especially by a stranger, I must be a bit sneaky in my approach. I will often take multiple photos of a subject without raising the camera to my eye, in hopes that one of the hipshots will capture the moment I am after. While resting on a bench, during our walk along the Bund, I shot multiple photos of two gray haired Chinese ladies who walked by. They are both wearing dresses with blue in the fabric and one of them is holding a royal blue umbrella. Because I am shooting up from my seated position, it turned out to be an interesting photograph because the umbrella frames their faces.

Unlike me, the Chinese were very bold and direct when taking photographs of people. Over and over, I observed people unashamedly taking pictures of us. Then, when I observed two Chinese men, with their cameras pointed directly at us, I raised my camera and took a photograph of them photographing us. We all looked at each other and smiled, knowing we had something in common, an interest in each other.

The next morning, we departed from the hotel in a taxi to visit the Shanghai Museum. It had made our list of "things to see" in Shanghai because it contained many old and rare Chinese cultural artifacts from a civilization that goes back three thousand years. As we entered the glass fronted circular shaped building, we could see an airport type scanner ahead. All visitors were being asked to put their purses, backpacks, and bags through it. We immediately became nervous. Fearful of drinking tap water in China, both of us had put a bottle of water in our small backpack before leaving the hotel. Conditioned by U.S. airport security, we pulled out the water bottles and expected to be asked to trash them. Instead, the guards instructed us to take a drink from our bottles. We did not balk at the request nor did we drop dead after taking the drink, so the guard waved us through. As we put the bottles back into our backpacks I commented, "That was a commonsense clever approach."

The museum was filled with national treasures. This Chinese cultural collection featured ceramics, pottery, glass, metal castings and costumes displayed beautifully in well-lit cases. Photographs were allowed, so I pulled my Nikon DSLR from my backpack and had some fun. The artificial lighting illuminated the collection and cast shadows to provide contrast. The calming effect of multiple figures of Buddha and the sculptural richness of horses, with and without riders, drew me in. The glaze on the surface of ancient ceramics was cracked into an infinite and indistinguishable pattern. The brilliant bright colors woven into a pair of shoes, with curled up pointed tips, made me stop and stare. The information placard next to a dull colored ceramic figure, in a lying down position, noted it was a pillow. Intricately carved jade pieces, like a hair pin containing a crane and a turtle, caused me to wonder how the craftsman had made the piece. All the artifacts, which had been made hundreds, or in some cases thousands of years ago, showed amazing craftsmanship. After a few hours we visited the museum café for a pot of tea. As we sipped our oolong tea, we agreed it had been a museum well worth visiting because it helped us better understand the long cultural history of China.

We really enjoyed our introduction to the Chinese culture while exploring Shanghai, the largest city we had ever visited, but it was time to move on to Beijing. When we first arrived at our Shanghai hotel, we asked the concierge to help us obtain tickets for a newly operational high-speed train that traveled between Shanghai and Beijing. At the time of our arrival it had only been operational, and available to the public, for a few weeks. Fortunately, he was able to get the tickets. With them in hand, we caught a taxi to a large railway station, where we boarded a high-speed train that was really a 200-mph rocket ship that traveled on rails.

The modern new station provided a contrast to the old rail stations of Europe. Rather than vaulted ceilings and massive architectural features the design of this station focused on functionality. The plain rectangular main hall contained large seating areas that were filled with Chinese travelers. Unlike modern airports, which serve as shopping centers as much as transportation hubs, this rail center was free of commercialism. We sat and waited for an appointed time when we could move to a boarding location. About ten minutes later, gates opened, and we walked toward our train. Before boarding, we took photos at the front of the train. The gleaming new lead car had a bullet shaped nose that gave it a futuristic look. We were excited to climb aboard for the ride.

Our five-hundred-mile journey north followed the Eastern seaboard of China. For the entire trip, the haze and smog that plagues China was visible from our rail car window. It reminded me of foggy fall mornings in the Midwest. This new rail line was elevated, which eliminated all railroad crossings, and the rails had been laid on a concrete bed. This resulted in a ride so stable, it reminded me of sitting in my favorite living room comfy chair.

The other passengers, many who appeared to be businesspeople, sat quietly during the trip. The exception was a man who yawned so loudly that it reminded me of the roaring lion in the movie, "The Wizard of Oz." Then, when he did it again, I figured it must be culturally acceptable, so later I imitated him. My ribs were sore for two days. Not from the yawn, from my wife's elbow.

Upon our arrival in Beijing, we sought out, and found, the taxi stand. The line of waiting passengers far exceeded the available taxis. After a fifteen-minute wait, we loaded our luggage into a cab and left for our boutique Chinese hotel located in an old section of Beijing. I had read that most of Beijing's older housing, single story small structures that were jumbled together like rabbit warrens, had been torn down in preparation for the 2008 Olympics.

When our taxi pulled into what looked like an alley to drop us off, we discovered our hotel had been converted from some of that old-style housing. It consisted of many small structures rather than a large hotel building. Young Chinese ladies, in their early twenties, dressed in traditional silk dresses embroidered with floral decorations, checked us in and showed us to our room. The room was decorated with Chinese motifs and fabrics. As we unpacked, we agreed that this single-story hotel would offer us a more authentic stay in Beijing than any western type hotel could have provided.

As we walked down the alleyway, to and from our hotel, we observed residents entering or leaving their neighborhood public restroom/shower facilities or just sitting in groups along the alleyway watching us pass. The alley, like the plazas in small European towns, seemed to be their public space. Older men sat on plastic crates while chatting and smoking, while women gossiped as they watched children at play. As we passed them daily, they helped us become experts at saying "Ni hao", or hello.

The hotel staff spoke "hotel English" which helped make our stay a pleasant one. When I asked them common guest questions like, "What time is breakfast served," I was answered promptly. But if I asked about the location of the closest grocery store, or where I might buy an SD card for my camera, they looked at me with a puzzled expression and no response. We did rely on them to write our destination, in Chinese characters, on the back of the hotel business card before we headed out to explore for the day. With business card in hand, we would walk down the alley to a busy street, flag down a taxi, show him the back of the card, and off we went on a new adventure. For our return trip we would use the front of the card to display the hotel's address. Simple but effective.

Our first escapade was a visit to what had been historically called, The Forbidden City. In today's China it is referred to as the Palace Museum. As I walked under the massive portrait of Mao and through the gates, I felt exhilarated. I had seen that image of Mao hundreds of times on film and photographs, and now I was about to walk under it and into the Palace Museum. In the crowd of people, we noticed a few other westerners, but most were Chinese, the people who in the past had been forbidden to enter this palace. As we walked down a set of stairs, and for the first time viewed the vastness of the royal compound that lay before us, I wondered what was going through the minds of all the Chinese visitors. Thousands of people, many of them Chinese tour groups wearing the same colored hats or T-shirts, walked ahead of us. In the U.S., we view history as the rise and fall of other countries. Their view of history is tied to the rise and fall of their own country, which for thousands of years endured a cycle of rulers and invaders. This temple compound, first occupied in 1420 during the Ming Dynasty, represented just a fraction of their long history.

Once inside I admired the architecture of the red wooden struc-tures with sloping ceramic tile roofs. I was also intrigued by the inten-tionally planned layout of the complex. Large open spaces had been left between the buildings, which made it impossible for an enemy to plan a sneak attack. The Chinese visitors walking through the Palace Temple with me had to view the place differently. Clearly their views, and thoughts, more insightful than mine, had to also encom-pass the historical events that occurred here.

Seeing the Great Wall required us to book a tour since foreign visitors are not allowed to drive in China. So, to make the ninety-mile trip, the hotel staff booked us seats on a mini-tour bus. Six other trav-elers, including a family of three from California, joined us on the day-long trip. The California man had married a Chinese woman, and they, along with her daughter, had traveled to China to both visit family and vacation. It felt liberating to talk with them during our day together, because it is easy to feel isolated when you do not speak the local language.

I was now a tourist and tourists are a captive audience, which caused me to feel trapped for much of the day. The tour schedule, that included two pre-defined shopping stops and lunch, had been arranged by the tour company. On the way to the Great Wall, we stopped at a jade factory. With a jaded attitude, I walked through the vast showroom scanning the carved jade that filled the display cases. The bright lights within the display cases caused the jade jewelry, colored either a pearly white or somewhere on an endless spectrum of light greens, to glow. Through some windows on the back wall, I saw artisans bent over grinding and cutting wheels, transforming raw jade into jewelry. That is where I wanted to go, but of course that was not allowed. I instead followed Sandy around while doing the shopping mall shuffle. She looked over the jade offerings while I checked my watch. When the forty-five minutes of required shopping time ended, we climbed back onto the bus and departed.

Before completing the drive to the Great Wall, we stopped for lunch. The wait staff seated us at a large round table before taking our drink order. I ordered a Tsing Tao lager beer that came in a bottle twice the size of a beer back home. It was ice cold, light and refreshing. Soon we were tucking into plates of fried rice and a variety of stir-fried dishes, some vegetarian and others with chicken or pork, that the staff delivered and set on a large lazy Susan in the center of our table. As the serving device rotated, we all helped ourselves to the still steaming dishes. As I fumbled with my chopsticks, I watched the Chinese at our table skillfully use theirs and felt inadequate.

After lunch, we completed the drive to the Great Wall. As I disembarked from the vehicle, I followed our small tour group through an area of vendors selling souvenirs and snacks, making the site seem touristy.

To my surprise, our driver informed us we would ride a cable car to get up onto the Great Wall. Apparently, my understanding of the Great Wall's structure, based on aerial photographs of it snaking across a hilly terrain, might be different from reality. Sandy and I boarded a car and up we went, way up, at least 80 feet. As I stepped onto the Great Wall, I immediately felt that special euphoric buzz that comes with visiting something or somewhere I have heard about for a lifetime. Sandy was giddy with excitement. Her eyes were lit up and she was smiling like a child on Christmas morning. Standing upon the Great Wall while trying to get our heads around the scope and actual size of the structure, was a thrill we will not forget. The walkway atop the wall had to be at least fifteen feet wide. We peered through the openings in a six-foot defensive tall wall built on one side of the walkway, intended to protect the soldiers from the invader's arrows. Next, we followed the walkway in both directs while recording our memories in digital images. This required us to climb up and down large stairs that followed the elevation changes in the wall. As I stood there observing the wall zigging and zagging while it rose and fell to follow the mountainous terrain, I thought about the effort and cost required to construct this temporary impediment. I wondered how many lives had been lost or disrupted in the futile attempt to stop the inevitable movement of people? For people are just like flowing water. They will eventually find a way around, under, over or through structures intended to block their movement, just like Genghis Khan and the Mongols did. I found it funny that an ancient Chinese place caused me to think philosophically about the folly of some men's thinking and actions. Confucius, the Chinese philosopher, and politician, who emphasized personal and govern-mental morality, correctness of social relationships, justice, kindness, and sincerity, might be a good role model for some modern-day wall builders.

When not visiting the major sites, like Tiananmen Square, the Palace Museum, and the Great Wall, we urban hiked the area near our hotel. Sandy and I love to visit food stores when traveling since they are cultural research centers. Near our hotel was a large four-story grocery store with escalators that moved shoppers and their grocery carts between levels. The store, not unlike grocery stores at home, had aisles with packaged goods on shelving. Then when I walked through the meat department, I noticed something unusual. An eight-foot square table, piled high with cut up chicken parts, caused me to stop. Instead of what I would see at home, processed chicken in plastic wrapped foam trays, the local shoppers could pick and choose from a mountainous pile of seemingly un-refrigerated chicken pieces. I became concerned about contracting a salmonella infection from walking too close to the display, so I quickly moved on.

Another stop while out urban hiking was to a large building filled with small vendor stalls. I would compare it to an indoor flea market. Most of the clothing stalls were staffed by women who would shout out, "Hey lady," as Sandy walked by. It became a never-ending soundtrack that played as we strolled through the labyrinth of aisles and stalls. For the rest of our trip, if I wanted to get Sandy's attention, I would say, "Hey lady." She would respond by giving me the evil eye and then laugh.

One day as we walked back toward our hotel, we stopped at a local restaurant for lunch. With no English menu available, we relied on a Chinese language menu that contained pictures. To place our order, we pointed at the photos of a steamer basket of dumplings and a platter of green beans. The dishes, when served, looked like the photos, and tasted delicious. The plump dumplings, with a fragrant ground pork and chives filling, were steaming hot. The green beans had been flash fried in a wok and then garnished with fine crispy bits of pork. After finishing our meal, I paid the bill and left the coins I had received as change, on the table for a tip. Their value could not have been more than a few cents. We left the restaurant and walked back toward our hotel. Suddenly, the waiter from the restaurant ran up to me and returned the coins. He had no concept of tipping, and I did not have the language skills to explain it, so I graciously accepted my coins.

During another urban hike, we rambled through a park that went around the circumference of a lake. It was an open area in which the city dwellers could relax and enjoy nature. Passing through the park we sighted a permanent concrete ping pong table. I stopped and watched the two people engrossed in a game. After a few minutes one of them walked up to me, offered me their paddle, and motioned for me to take their place at the table. I accepted the offer and for the next five minutes felt engaged, energized, and outclassed. As we walked away, Sandy asked, "How did it feel to get your ass whipped by a woman?"

Since breakfast was included in the cost of our room, we started our days eating with the other hotel guests. Breakfast was a mixed offering with items for Chinese and western guests. After a couple of fried eggs with toast, I would have a bowl of congee, or rice porridge, topped crispy onions, dried shrimp, and some hot sauce.

Sitting near us one morning was a pair of westerners. As we began to chat, their accents indicated, and then they confirmed, they were both British. She had inherited some money and decided to see some of the world, and he had agreed to accompany her for the first leg of her journey. They had traveled by train across Russia on the Trans-Siberian Express before making their way down to Beijing. I will always remember their referring to Russia as "the land of the un-smiling." Funny how someone else's negative experience can influence another traveler. Russia had never made my list of places to see, so I added it to the list and immediately crossed it off.

As we talked with them, we discovered a common objective while in Beijing, to eat a local specialty, Peking duck. So we checked with the hotel staff for restaurant recommendations, and they made reservations for us the following night. I was familiar with this iconic Chinese dish for I had attempted to make it some years back. The recipe was involved. The first step required the use of a bicycle pump to inflate the skin of a whole duck before pricking the skin and then dousing the carcass with boiling water. The next two steps, hanging the duck in front of a fan for twelve hours before placing it, uncovered, in the refrigerator for another day, dried out the skin. All these steps were intended to ensure a dry crispy skin on the finished roasted duck, for savoring the skin is the ultimate pleasure when eating Peking duck.

When it was delivered to our table, we all moaned, "Mmmmm," in unison. As a waiter skillfully sliced the whole duck into thin slices, another waiter set down the condiments. Small flour crepes, sticky sweet hoisin sauce, julienned cucumber, and scallions. Slices of duck were set on a crepe followed by the other condiments. It was then rolled up and eaten. The contrasting textures of a warm soft flour pancake filled with warm fatty duck, crispy duck skin, crunchy cucumber, and scallions, topped with the sweet sauce made it a very memorable shared experience with fellow travelers.

A westerner from the Netherlands, who had attended my workshop in Shanghai, recommended we attend a cooking school while visiting Beijing. He noted a Chinese cook and cookbook author had started the cooking school. Since I love to cook, we contacted the school and signed up for a noodle making class.

Getting to the cooking school, located in a home, required a taxi ride and then a walk through a maze-like area of small homes in an old Beijing neighborhood. We felt like we were on the Candyland board game as we twisted and turned on our way into the housing area to locate the cooking school. When we arrived at the school an English-speaking host, who worked for the school's owner, greeted us warmly. Although born in China, she had been adopted by American parents and raised in the U.S. Our instructors, Chinese chefs, taught us and some travelers from the Netherlands. We were each given an apron and started the lesson by making a wad of dough using only flour, water, and salt. We then converted the dough into four different noodle shapes. Hand-pulled, hand-rolled, cat's ears and knife grated. The first two are self-explanatory, while the cat's ear noodles resembled the Italian orecchiette, and were formed using a small piece of dough and a push of your thumb. Making the knife grated noodles requires one to hold a large block of noodle dough in one hand, while quickly moving a horizontally positioned sharp knife or cleaver held in your other hand, across the surface of the block of dough to shave off small pieces. We all sat transfixed as a Chinese instructor repeated this motion over and over while the cut noodles flew into a pot of boiling water in front of him.

The instructors then used the noodles that they and their students had made, along with other ingredients, to make two traditional dishes that we shared during a communal lunch. One, a simple dish of eggs and tomatoes with hand pulled and rolled noodles, was followed by a caramelized pork belly and cat's ear noodle dish. I had never eaten a savory dish that started with making caramel first. The caramelized sugar, which added a real depth of flavor, and black vinegar balanced the sweet and sourness of the pork dish. When finished, the chefs plated the dishes, and we all ate our meal together. After some remembrance photos were taken, we meandered out of the maze, caught a cab, and went back to the hotel to begin packing for our morning departure.

The next morning, we caught a taxi to the train station to catch the high-speed train back to Shanghai. Two days later, we boarded our flight for the thirteen-hour non-stop flight home.

The following year, in 2012, I was invited back to Shanghai to lead two more workshops. This time I traveled alone. My hotel, and the location for the workshops, was just down the street from the prior year's location. It was another large western-style hotel. The hotel's location brought some comfort for I was familiar with the surrounding area and the local businesses. Soon after checking into the hotel, I decided to take a walk to find some lunch.

Except for breakfast, which is most often included in the room price, I always try and avoid eating at the hotel in which I am staying. My reasoning is that hotel food is most often predictably safe, uncreative, and overpriced. I prefer to go out and find something different and unpredictable, especially when visiting new places.

Within two blocks of my hotel was a vegetable and fruit store that looked, based on the building's age and architectural style, like it had been at the same location for decades. The age of the structure made it look out of place in a neighborhood dominated by newly built high-rise apartment buildings. It had an open front with the brightly colored fresh produce spilling out of the storefront to lure in shoppers who resided in the nearby apartments. As I walked by, what caught my eye was not the produce, but a small food stall located at the front of the store.

Two ladies working inside the cramped stall space made and sold two versions of Chinese fast food, steamed buns, and fried scallion bread.

To make the buns one of them filled pieces of soft leavened white dough with either a meat or a chopped greens filling. Then, using just her fingers, she deftly and decoratively sealed the tops into a uniform pleated round shape before setting them into woven bamboo steamer baskets whose dull, almost gray color, indicated their age. After filling a stack of four baskets, she set them over a large wok of boiling water to steam. Fifteen minutes later, when the lid was taken from the top steamer basket large snow-white steamed buns were visible.

For less than a dollar the women handed me a plastic bag containing one of each. The beef and onion filling in the first bun tasted like my mother's Sunday pot-roast and the second, filled with chopped greens, onion and garlic was a vegetarian delight. More than once, after that first experience, I would pull some green leaves off a bush before approaching the food stall. I would point to the leaves in my hand and then to the steamed buns to ensure I was ordering the ones filled with healthy greens. My communication technique caused them to smile at me with twinkling eyes, and I would smile back.

The second lady, who was making fried scallion bread, skillfully rolling out small balls of dough into flattened disks. She next brushed the flattened disk with oil before sprinkling the entire surface with finely sliced green scallions. She would then roll up the round disk up into a snake shape. Next, she would coil the dough into a spiral before again rolling it into a flat round disk. The onion filled raw dough was then fried in a puddle of oil on a flattop griddle. Hot from the griddle it tasted so good I cannot describe it. The only way to understand how good this crispy and flaky exterior, soft interior, onion flavored round of fried dough tasted is to find a place to order one for yourself. Or make them at home.

I used sign language and pointing to order street food but spoke English when presenting my workshops. I could do that because the Chinese who attended the workshops had studied English in school.

This allowed me to talk with them while eating lunch. On one occasion our lunch was a traditional Chinese meal, so we sat together around a large round table. Positioned in the center of the table, a lazy Susan held at least fifteen different dishes. Though impressed with the Chinese stir-fried food, the best part of the meal for me was listening to some of them describe life in China. I listened intently to one of them who talked about having to pay a heavy fine because he and his wife decided to have a second child. Another student, when I asked where he lived, said that almost everyone lives in apartments in China for the government owns all land. His comments rang true for all over Shanghai I had seen blocks of apartment buildings, maybe ten to fifteen identical structures in each block, which stood about fifteen stories high. In some spots these large apartment blocks, or blocks under construction, filled the skyline as far as I could see. Also present in great numbers, stood the large cranes used to erect these building. I remember hearing someone refer to them as the national birds of China. During lunch I also learned that because of their English language skills, most of them worked for western headquartered companies, and they had no qualms about changing jobs frequently to get ahead financially. They were intelligent and ambitious. That lunch helped me better understand China and the people who represented the future of the country.

I finished my consulting work on a Friday and had booked a Sunday flight back to Chicago. This meant I had Saturday free to do something in Shanghai. Along some of the major roadways, earlier in the week, I had noticed advertising banners for a European Professional Golf Tournament which would taking place in Shanghai. An internet search revealed tournament play started Thursday and finished on Sunday. Because I golf and have an interest in professional golf, I asked the concierge to inquire about the availability of tickets. He made some calls and informed me entrance to the tournament was free. I decided to attend.

The golf venue was about twenty miles outside of Shanghai, so it required me to hire a car and driver to transport me to and from the event. As the car approached the golf course, a new view of China emerged. Large single-family dwellings had been built on the land surrounding the course. In all of China, individuals cannot own land. They can own the structure but must lease the land.

Seeing these mansions, surrounding the beautiful new golf course and the site of the professional golf tournament, caused me to wonder who built and owned them. As we drove past, they appeared mostly unoccupied. Obviously, they had been built to attract wealthy individuals. Maybe hosting this world class golf tournament was part of the marketing strategy to sell or rent the homes.

I have attended PGA tournaments in the U.S. and this European Tour event had just as many world class players on the course competing. The reason for the no entrance fee policy became clear quickly. Very few spectators lined the fairways and many of them, like me, worked in China but lived in the west.

I struck up a conversation with an Indian National, a man in his fifties, as we waited and then watched a foursome tee off. We hit it off quickly and decided to share lunch. We walked to the concession tent area, ordered, and then sat eating baguette ham and cheese sandwiches while we talked. We also got a bit of a buzz on when we sampled some Scotch whiskey given away as part of a promotion. After lunch, we headed back onto the course to watch the action. When it was time for me to depart, to meet my driver at our pre-arranged time and location, I offered my new friend a ride back into city-center. He accepted, and during the ride, he continued to share his experiences related to working in China. He stated he changed work locations by alternating between manufacturing facilities in India and China every two weeks. He noted that the cheaper wages in China caused his business to make the decision to manufacture there, but the Chinese facility required constant oversight which is why he traveled back and forth so frequently. Since my work career before consulting had been in manufacturing, we had much in common.

Business travel is often a lonesome activity. Simply saying "hello" to a stranger had led to a very enjoyable afternoon for both of us. I have found that no matter where I travel, if I have the courage to take that first step, I meet some wonderful people.

Both of my trips to China were eye opening cultural experiences. The rate of change in China, driven by the influx of Western money and a single party government that makes rapid decisions without the need for broad consensus, is breathtaking. As an example, in the U.S. high speed rail lines have been discussed and debated for decades yet not one has been built. In China, they just made the decision and quickly built them all over China.

China went from being an agrarian society to one of the dominant world powers in around thirty years. I am glad I had the chance to see and experience a culture that is still in flux and trying to understand itself.

CONG YOU BING (FRIED SCALLION BREAD)

Ingredients

3 cups all-purpose flour
2 t baking powder
1 t salt
1/3 cup canola oil
1-1/2 T toasted sesame oil
1 cup thinly sliced scallions (green onions)

Preparation

Place 1-1/2 cups of the flour and the baking powder in a food processor. With motor running, add 1/2 cup of cold water and process for
about 30 seconds or until dough comes together. Remove dough and
then add remaining 1-1/2 cups of flour and salt. With motor running,
add 1/3 cup plus 3 tablespoons of boiling water and process until
dough comes together. Return reserved dough to the processor and
process both doughs together for about 30 seconds.

On a floured surface knead the dough until smooth (3-5 minutes).

Set dough in an oiled bowl and cover with plastic wrap. Set bowl aside for 2 hours.

Combine the canola and sesame oils together. Divide dough into quarters. Form each piece into a ball. On a floured surface roll balls, one at a time with a rolling pin, into 10-12-inch rounds. Liberally brush the top surface with the oil and then sprinkle with ¼ cup of the onions. Roll up the dough into a log shape. Then coil the log into a round and pinch the outer edge under the coiled dough. Using the rolling pin, roll the dough into an 8-inch round. Repeat the process with the other three pieces of dough.

Add 2 tablespoons of oil to a non-stick skillet and heat. When hot, add a flatbread and cook, while swirling the pan occasionally, until it has browned. Flip it once and cook until lightly browned. Repeat the above process, adding more oil when needed, for the three remaining flatbreads. Cut into wedges, eat while warm, dipped into soy sauce.

*Warning: If you have a vented exhaust hood above your stove, which will disperse the smell of the frying scallion bread into your neighborhood, expect neighbors you have never met to show up and knock on your front door.

6

SWITZERLAND

FOUR COUNTRIES WITHIN ONE

U sing a Swiss Pass, that covered transportation on trains, boats, and some cable lifts, is how we traveled around Switzerland during our stay. It has been said that Swiss trains run like Swiss watches, smoothly and on time, and that proved to be correct.

At the beginning of our trip, we boarded a train in Zurich that would transport us to a small farming community. Once there, we planned to meet up with our traveling companions, Mark and Kitty, the ones we had met at the agritourismo in Tuscany, at a guest house where we planned to spend the first two nights of our two weeks of travel.

We paid attention to each stop the train made as it rolled through the lush green valley pasturelands with mountain backdrops, for we knew we had to switch trains to get to our last destination. When our stop was announced, we gathered our luggage and waited by the exit door. As we exited, we searched for and found the schedule board to find out which platform our next train would depart from. Noting it was a platform on the other side of the tracks, we headed down a set of stairs, walked under the tracks, and then walked up a set of stairs to reach the platform. Just as we reached the top step, the train pulled into the station and we stepped on. It was Swiss precision. If one of us had stumbled or sneezed, we would have missed our connection.

Two stops later, the second train slowed and stopped at our destination. While departing the railcar, I looked right and to my surprise observed Mark and Kitty doing the same from the car behind ours. We had each traveled from different parts of the U.S. and ended up on the same regional train. Happenstance, not the Swiss railway efficiency, was responsible for this special surprise.

The four of us then took off walking, down a narrow asphalt roadway, toward the guesthouse. As we walked and talked, a station wagon pulled up. It was the owner of the guesthouse. She invited us to stow our luggage in the back and get in. As the car pulled up, I could see the dark brown, wooden two-story guesthouse, with green shutters framing the windows, was outside of town and in the middle of pastureland. The exposed wood lobby, decorated with lace curtains and large cow bells hanging on the wall above a massive fireplace, seemed appropriate. After checking in, we all met for lunch in the dining room.

I ordered an ice-cold Swiss beer, Feldschlosschen (not as easy to say as, "Give me a Bud."), and wiener schnitzel with spaetzle and red cabbage. The veal had a crispy exterior and was still moist. The spaetzle, finished with some Swiss butter, was luscious and the sweet-sour flavor of the red cabbage balanced the fat of the meat and buttered noodles. The delicious food made me think I was in Germany, and this area of Switzerland was close to Germany. One of the unique features about the small country of Switzerland is that it is positioned between Italy, Germany and France, and the culture of each of those countries bleeds across their common physical borders. So sometimes, based on the language being spoken or the food I was served, I was not sure in which country I currently stood.

The next morning, we went back to the dining room for breakfast. One item, Swiss muesli, really impressed me. Oats had been soaked in milk overnight to soften them. In the morning fresh and dried fruit, nuts and yogurt were mixed in before serving. They may have also added a bit of honey to balance the tartness of the yogurt. The cold sweetened concoction provided a healthy start to our day and was delicious. After I returned home, I made and ate my version of Swiss muesli until I became sick of it. Too much of a good thing.

While in Southern Switzerland, where people spoke Italian, we caught a ferry boat that would transport us to a point from which we would hike back toward our departure point. As the ferry slowly made its way up a long narrow alpine lake, I walked around the top deck taking photographs of the beauty all around me. Watery reflections of small villages and anchored boats, passing boats, and the alpine mountains, all drew my attention as we passed their location. We disembarked at the furthest stop and walked through the hilly, winding streets of a quiet old village built on the shore of the lake. It was composed of a jumble of old stone two-story structures. Our walking route was more of a path than a road for cars would not have fit through the tight spaces between the buildings. Before starting the hike back, we selected a restaurant overlooking the lake for lunch. The outside was old and worn, like most everything in the town. It was the name of the "daily special," written on a chalkboard that made our lunch location decision an easy one. Just reading the words, "fresh porcini risotto", provided me joy, for I love risotto and the opportunity to eat fresh porcini mushrooms only happens in Europe. We entered the tiny, eight-table restaurant and were seated near the windows. The interior was anything but glamorous, but the view of the sun reflecting off the water with the mountains as a backdrop caused us all to stop talking and just stare. We all ordered the risotto, and it took thirty minutes to arrive tableside, meaning it had been made to order. Each creamy spoonful of that risotto warmed my soul while the sunlight streaming in from the lake brightened my day. Often, when I am served a really good meal, I like to thank the chef who prepared it. So, on our way out, I pulled back a cloth curtain that hid the tiny kitchen from the patrons, to reveal the chef who had made my plate of risotto. Just as the curtain opened, she turned to look at me while she stood at the stove stirring another order of risotto. The stove faced the lake and an open window above the stove flooded her in beautiful daylight. She smiled broadly while I snapped her picture. Her love of cooking was evident not only in her smile, but also in the dish of risotto I had eaten. I have learned through experience that it takes skill to cook risotto to perfection. I would have loved to be her apprentice for an afternoon so I could compare her techniques to mine.

On a train headed to Lausanne, on the western side of Switzerland, I learned about the importance of acknowledging someone who is talking to you. Improving my listening skills has been a lifelong objective for my wife. Whenever I respond, without fully listening to what she has to say by acknowledging her dialogue, Sandy quickly points out my inability to listen to understand. Well, on this train ride, it became clear that I needed an immersion learning experience, and I got one. Two ladies, sitting directly across from us became my instructors. One of the two ladies talked incessantly while the other looked at her, nodded, and said, "YA" loudly with enthusiasm and understanding every twenty seconds for over an hour. That was a lot of "YAs" but hearing them taught me a life lesson.

We arrived in Lausanne mid-day. While rolling our suitcases toward our hotel we noticed a sandwich shop with a line of patrons patiently waiting their turn. Inside the open-fronted shop I saw vertical rotisseries, loaded with different meats, spinning in front of heating elements. Immediately I thought gyros sandwiches, but I was wrong, these were doner kabobs, a Turkish sandwich.

After placing my order, I watched the assembly of my sandwich. Thin slices of lamb, cut from the rotisserie, fell directly onto a fresh pita bread. A salad of lettuce, tomato, cucumber, and raw onion went on top of the lamb. Before folding and packaging my sandwich the cook asked, "Would you like harissa sauce?"

Still thinking gyros sandwiches topped with garlicky, cucumber and yogurt tzatziki sauce, I was puzzled, but said, "Yes."

One bite confirmed I had made the right choice. Soft tender

bread, crispy bits of spiced lamb, fresh crisp salad and that spicy red chili sauce all combined to make a memorable sandwich.

Another train journey took us to the village of Murren, in the high Alps, where we spent three days. This small alpine community, accessible only by train, sits about 5,500 feet above sea level. To make the ascent up to Murren, from the valley below, we boarded a small, dedicated cog (gear-driven) train that transports visitors in and out of the village. Sitting on a wooden bench seat I stared out the window as the small train slowly climbed up the mountain. Occasionally there were breaks in the surrounding forest and I caught glimpses of the valley far below and the three imposing snow topped mountains, the Eiger, Monch and Jungfrau, that flanked the opposite side of the valley. Walking from the train station, with our luggage in tow, we stopped at multiple viewing points along the route to our guest house accommodations. With my mouth agape, I viewed and photographed the rocky mountain tops and sheer cliffs that dropped straight down to the green valley far below. The beauty all around me made me giddy with excitement.

Over the next few days, as we hiked the many alpine trails in the area, we encountered small herds of dairy cattle grazing on the summer plants. The sound from the large bells strung around their necks announced their presence. The simple movements associated with grazing caused the cows to create unique, ever changing, magical cowbell compositions as clear as the air in the Alps. This unique sound of Switzerland made me stop and smile, so I recorded a thirty second soundbite. Playing it today transports me back to the Alps, as does eating rosti, or fried potatoes.

On our second day we rode the same cog train down to the valley where a local train transported us to a mountainside lunch destination. After exiting the train, we crossed the road and stood in line waiting for a cable car that would transport us up to the restaurant. We stepped from the cable car into a mountain top mist that obscured the valley below. Bleating sheep, feeding on the sparse green foliage, appeared, and disappeared in foggy mist. We followed a narrow trail that ran along a shear vertical face of rock. Then we sighted the restaurant. It appeared in the distance like a dwarf mirage clinging to the base of the immense rock face. After a ten-minute wait, we were seated and looked over the limited menu. I ordered a dark brown Swiss beer, a bratwurst and rosti. Swiss rosti can be a simple dish made of grated fried potatoes. Or it can be elevated to gourmet fare if the chef has the courage and patience to leave the grated potatoes untouched until the hot butter in the small frying pan creates the perfect crispy brown exterior on the potato pancake. My rosti was perfect. It was simple food cooked well.

Food or dishes endemic to an area always seems to taste better when eaten there because the location adds some level of authenticity. Makes me wonder if Rocky Mountain oysters would be tastier in the Rockies? Following this line of thinking we decided to eat a local dish at a nearby restaurant that night. The three-story chalet style building had a typical unfinished wooden exterior that had weathered into an almost burnt toast brown color. A yellow and white stripped awning, and the Swiss flag, hung out front to greet us as we entered.

Our guesthouse host, a friendly middle-aged housewife and mother, recommended this place to enjoy a local specialty that utilized the cheese those bell-ringing cows helped to produce. So before entering we had decided to order cheese fondue for four. When it was set in the center of the table, the buttery, nutty aroma wafting from the bubbling pan of cheese became a smell I will forever associate with Switzerland. We gleefully speared, dipped and consumed countless cheese covered chunks of crusty bread until we all felt as if we had a wheel of cheese in our bellies. Later, I was surprised to find that there is a direct relationship between constipation and the amount of cheese consumed.

But that small self-inflicted problem did nothing to take away from all the wonderful experiences we had in Switzerland.

ROSTI (POTATO PANCAKE)

Ingredients

3 medium size red (waxy) potatoes
2 T butter
2 T canola oil
Salt and pepper

Preparation

Three hours before you plan to eat, parboil the potatoes. Boil until just tender but not soft. Test for doneness with the tip of a sharp paring knife. Run under cold water and then refrigerate the potatoes for 2 hours.

Grate the potatoes using the large openings on a box grater. Heat 1 tablespoon of both butter and oil in a small heavy bottom non-stick skillet until very hot. Add the potatoes and press them, using a spatula, into a round flat cake. Salt and pepper to taste. Tent the potatoes with foil and cook undisturbed for 10 minutes. Pancake should be well browned.

Remove the skillet from the heat and place a large serving plate on top of the pan. Flip over, return skillet to the heat, and add a tablespoon each of butter and oil. When hot, slide the potato pancake, uncooked side down, into the skillet and cook for 10 more minutes.

Slide potato pancake onto a plate. Cut into wedges and serve with sides of your choice. Ham, cheese, eggs, smoked salmon, an ice cold Feldschlösschen beer, or a simple side salad are some choices.

7

BELGIUM

THE BEST STRAWBERRIES IN THE WORLD

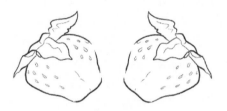

At this stage of life, semi-retired and slowing down, I love travel trips where we have a home base for multiple days. It allows me to develop a sense of place, so I feel like I am part of the neighborhood. Heck, by the end of our six-day stay in Brussels, both me and the Middle Eastern guy, who owned the convenience store located across the street from our rental flat, became comfortable with nodding at each other.

Because I had just finished consulting in England for three days, when our short ninety-minute flight from London arrived in Brussels, we were ready to urban hike the city. Our rental unit, or flat, as they would say in Europe, was a furnished one-bedroom apartment. The cost, under one hundred euros a night, was more reasonable than any city-center hotel. Soon after the owner let us in and showed us the unit, we left to wander the city without a destination in mind. At some point we heard singing in the distance and used it as our true-north compass reading to guide us toward the joyful noise. Following the sound, we traversed city streets filled with small shops, restaurants with outdoor seating, and multi-story buildings decorated with colorful cartoon book murals. After fifteen minutes of walking, we stood overlooking a large public space filled with walkways, trees, and floral gardens. At the far end stood a stage with seating fronting it. As we approached, thirty dancers in colorful folk costumes and a choir of around fifty singers performed on stage. The women wore long dresses, white blouses, colorful sashes around their waists and shawls covering their shoulders. The men had on long coats, held closed with sashes, and felt hats. I asked someone about the event and was told it was a Latvian summer solstice celebration. We sat down on two of the uncomfortable folding metal chairs and spent the next hour being entertained. As we departed, I rubbed my sore ass and commented, "This is another good story. We had to travel to Brussels to find out the Latvians love to sing and dance."

On most days, we walked about a half-mile to the modern railway station to catch a train headed to a different Belgium city. A chance meeting in Utah earlier in the year helped to define some of our destinations, along with the experiences we pursued while there.

After some business in Denver, my wife and I headed to southern Utah to explore and hike some of the National Parks. While walking along the canyon rim at Canyon-lands National Park, I noticed a young couple standing nearby. After he photographed her, I offered to take their photo. When done, we chatted for a few minutes about the natural beauty of Utah and then went our separate ways. Two days later, while hiking in Arches National Park, our paths crossed again. As we talked with Nick and Elisa, we learned they lived in Belgium. When we informed them that we would be in Belgium two months later, the young man asked for our contact information. A few weeks after we returned home, I received an email from him that contained a personalized Belgium travel guide. It included recommendations for cities to visit, restaurants, specialty foods and notable beers.

One recommendation was to visit the North Sea coastal town of Blankenberge and eat Liege waffles at their favorite beachside restaurant. Walking from the train station we viewed a city of buildings with worn exteriors and tourist gift shops. Think salt-water taffy and funny beach hats. It seemed locked in a different time, like many tourist cities who try and preserve an image of the past. Missing from town were visitors like us, but to be fair it was a beach town, and this was early spring on the North Sea. Too early for the summer crowds that must fill the town and the beaches come July and August.

Waffles are a national obsession in Belgium, and we found ourselves talking obsessively about waffles as we approached the restaurant.

"I do not understand how the waffles here could be much different from the ones we make at home," I said.

"Well, we will soon find out," Sandy responded.

It turned out the restaurant, with a large outdoor seating area, was closed for the day. Feeling like we had an obligation to eat a waffle we selected a nearby beachfront place and ordered one to split. Served with a few strawberries, blueberries, and a dollop of whipped cream, it looked inviting. Disappointment filled our faces as we ate it, for it tasted exactly like one from home and could never live up to the waffle we had conjured up in our imaginations.

We departed and strolled along the beachfront looking at the now deserted beach. I pulled out my camera to photograph two rows of twenty tiny wooden beach houses. These small buildings, like back-yard storage sheds, were lined up, side by side, on the beach. Most were all white, but the few that stood out had roofs painted bright red, yellow and blue. At the far end of the beach was a pier that jutted out into the sea. We walked out onto the pier, watched, and photographed a passing sailboat. One of the men on board was working to raise the sails while the other manned the wheel to guide the boat from the port and into the North Sea.

Leaving the beach area, we turned inland to find a restaurant for lunch. An open table in the outdoor seating area of a non-descript little eatery called to us. Eating outside while traveling is a priority for us for it allows us to people watch. While being seated, a waiter set a beer in front of a man at the next table. Sunlight hit the glass and caused the beer to glow like a bright red beacon.

I asked, "What are you drinking?"

He explained, "It is a framboise Lambic ale, ever have one?"

"No, I have never seen or tasted a red beer," I responded.

"You should," he said, while smiling knowingly.

So, I ordered one. When it was set in front of me, I raised the glass to my nose. The aroma of raspberries was pronounced and intense. This caused me to think it might be a sweet sissy beer, so I took a taste. It was anything but that. This ale had a tart fruity flavor and a clean aftertaste. It was delicious. Later when I checked the list of recommended beers given to me by my guide Nick, it of course was on the list. Lambic ales, like the one I was drinking, use natural airborne yeast for their fermentation and are a specialty in Belgium.

A few weeks prior to our departure for this trip to Belgium, Sandy had read about another Belgium specialty. The New York Times newspaper had featured a story about the strawberries grown near the town of Wepion, Belgium. If I remember correctly, the author of the story claimed they were the "best strawberries in the world." So, when our friends from Germany, Dusty and Ulla, joined us in Brussels for a few days, we suggested a jaunt into the country-side for a strawberry tasting.

The next morning, we shared the back seat of the car with their dog, a deaf Parson Russell terrier named Indie, who had the ability to snore like me. Even if he had a wife, like me, he could not be informed, as I often am, that he was snoring. He was a lucky dog indeed. We entered Wepion into the GPS unit and drove off to sample the best strawberries in the world.

Arriving in the sleepy riverside town with little traffic, motorized or human, we stopped at a bakery for a coffee and a snack. A whipped cream topped white cake that had been decorated with strawberries drew our attention. Biting into the slice of moist cake, covered in sweetened whipped cream, provided a cool and refreshing food experience. As far as I am concerned, whipped cream, rather that sugar laden fat-based frostings, are the perfect cake topping. I reserved the two strawberries that topped my cake until the cake was gone, so I could savor them. Ordinary, and certainly not world-class, best described them.

In the New York Times article, the name of a strawberry distributor was mentioned. We searched the internet for the distributor's address and then entered that location into the GPS unit and continued our search. Keeping an eye out for fields of ripening strawberries, we followed narrow winding roads out of the river valley and eventually sighted the small concrete and corrugated metal sided warehouse ahead. As we turned onto an access road to get to the building, I was provided an unexpected history lesson. The road sign read, the "Rue de la 1 Armee Americaine." The 1st US Army division had helped to liberate Belgium in 1944 and I secretly hoped it had been spring when the American soldiers passed through, and the locals offered them strawberries.

We pulled into the parking lot, got out and walked toward the warehouse. A man who observed us approaching walked to meet us near the shipping dock. He quickly made it clear this was a wholesale warehouse and we could not buy what we coveted. He directed us down a nearby two-lane highway where he said we would find a fruit stand at which we could score some strawberries.

We pulled up to the fruit stand and excitement filled the car. Even Indie, the deaf dog woke up. He must have sensed the energy change within the car for he leapt up and looked at each of us. After purchasing three pint-sized baskets of the most perfect looking strawberries, we returned to the car. Each big, uniform, deep red berry had a glossy shine. They looked so alike I asked, "Do you think they were cloned?"

By now the car was perfumed with the smell of ripe strawberries. We all selected a berry and bit into the best strawberries in the world.

"What do you think, best strawberry ever?" I asked everyone.

"Amazing, sweetest berries ever," replied Dusty.

"No un-ripe white top or core, meltingly soft and delicious," noted Sandy.

"Yummy, each one is the same – delicious," said Ulla!

They were the sweetest, most strawberry tasting strawberries any of us had ever eaten. Juice ran down our chins as we happily devoured two baskets.

As we drove away my friend Dusty commented, "I think I know the secret to the sweetness of those strawberries."

I responded, "Really?"

With a straight face he said, "An English pronunciation of the city name, Wepion, is "We-pee-on-em."

Laughter erupted in the car. I guess that is why fruit should always be washed before it is consumed.

On our last evening in Brussels, we joined my cousin Lee's son Steven, who lived and worked in Brussels, for dinner. We met at his flat and then walked to one of his favorite Brasseries. The restaurants interior included tables with white tablecloths, cushioned chairs, low-lighting, and a well-stocked bar which had the look and feel of an old French restaurant. Since French is the dominate language in Brussels, our host greeted the waiter in French. Once seated, the waiter, dressed in a black suit and tie, described in French, and translated by Steven, a few specials that were available. His eyes sparkled and his voice sped up with excitement as he mentioned it was herring season, and we could order the local ocean fish as an appetizer or entree. I have always loved the sweet tart taste of pickled herring, so I followed my host's lead, and ordered it for my appetizer.

Just as I was daydreaming about past lunches of Noon Hour brand pickled herring with saltine crackers the server set my appetizer down. My preconceived notion of what I would be served did not match what lay in front of me. It appeared that no pickling liquid or cooking method had altered the fillet of herring. The raw reddish gray slab of fish looked lonesome. It sat isolated on the plate with a pile of chopped green onions, a small mound of mustard and a slice of lemon. My first bite confirmed its rawness and fishy taste. The sharpness of the onions, lemon juice and mustard tempered that taste, which helped me finish a dish of which I was not that fond. When the waiter asked how I enjoyed the herring, I said, "I was glad to have tried this local specialty, once."

The length of our visit to the small country of Belgium was exactly right. During our weeklong stay we had visited and explored enough of the country to appreciate it and its people.

LIEGE WAFFLES

Ingredients

1 cup milk
1 pkg instant dry yeast
4 cups all-purpose flour
2 eggs (beaten)
6 T brown sugar
2 t vanilla extract
½ t cinnamon
¼ t salt
10 oz butter
1 cup Belgium pearl sugar (order online)

Preparation

In the bowl of a stand mixer add the yeast to the cup of warm milk. Stir and let sit for 5 minutes. Then, add the flour, eggs, brown sugar, vanilla extract, cinnamon, and salt. Mix on medium speed to form a sticky dough. Add the softened butter and mix until it has been incorporated into the dough. Cover bowl with plastic wrap and let it rest for 2-3 hours.

Gently stir the pearl sugar into the dough so it is evenly distributed. Divide the dough into 10 equal pieces and let them rest for 10-15 minutes.

Cook the waffles in a hot buttered waffle iron until browned. Be careful when removing and handling the waffles for the caramelized pearl sugar on the exterior of the waffles is extremely hot.

Eat out of hand or serve with fresh fruit and whipping cream. As you tuck into your second waffle, because one of them is never enough, think of Nick and Alisa, the Belgium couple who helped us plan the trip where we discovered these tasty waffles.

8

JAPAN

A CULTURE OF RESPECT

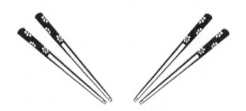

E veryone should visit Japan at least once, if for no other reason, just to use the toilets with electronic controls. Just imagine, if you can, a cold winter's morn with a warm toilet seat waiting for you, and jets of warm water cleaning you up when finished. If in the distant future, old civilizations are assessed by their toilet technology, Japan will be revered.

We flew directly to Japan from Hawai'i, where we had gone to escape a portion of a cold Midwest winter. For some reason, when we began planning the trip, we thought we might be halfway to Japan while in Hawai'i. We were wrong. Hawai'i is a nine-hour flight from Chicago, and Tokyo was a nine-hour flight from Hawai'i. Our return trip from Tokyo to Chicago took eleven hours. Truth be told, while in Hawai'i, we had been at one corner of a large obtuse triangle.

As we boarded the Tokyo bound flight in Honolulu, it became obvious that we, as westerners, were the minority. In total, there looked to be around six of us in a plane full of what appeared to be Japanese passengers. This situation provided insights into the Japanese culture long before we landed in Tokyo.

My first cultural indicator occurred during the plane boarding process. It was orderly and quiet and once people took their seats, they stayed seated. Once we were airborne, in my area of the cabin I observed just one individual with their seatback reclined during the nine-hour flight. Quite different when compared to flights to Europe, on which I have had people recline their seatback so far back they literally pinned me in my seat.

Because my seat was located on the aisle, I had a view of the aisle in front of and behind me. No elbows, shoulders, heads, knees, or feet were visible in the aisle space. Compare that with U.S. domestic flights, where you must do the tango, or some variation of this Latin American dance, on the way to the washroom to avoid all the body parts sticking into the aisle. The Japanese culture of respect, care, and concern for others, which I witnessed throughout the flight, would be reinforced repeatedly during our two weeks in Japan.

We landed after eleven o'clock in the evening, cleared passport control, and retrieved our luggage. At the taxi stand, we boarded a Toyota Camry taxi, scented with the smell of old cigarette smoke, for our hotel located near Tokyo Station. From the back seat, the night-time view of large buildings and streets devoid of people looked like every other large city in the world. Daylight, and a crush of people would confirm our location in Tokyo the next morning. Knowing it was late, and we were tired, the English-speaking hotel staff hastily checked us in so we could quickly prepare for bed. We planned to meet our traveling companions Mark and Kitty, from Colorado, in the hotel lobby at 8:00 am.

In the morning, as we exited the elevator, we sighted our friends. Broad smiles, heartfelt greetings, warm hugs, and our individual stories of travel to Japan, rekindled our long friendship. They arrived in Tokyo the prior afternoon, had mapped the walking route to the train station, and were prepared to guide us there. We collected our luggage from our rooms, checked out of the hotel and prepared to leave. As we exited the hotel, we passed the hotel smoking room. It was the size of a double phone booth. Years of smoke and nicotine had stained the walls an uneven grimy yellow and inside was a dutiful smoker, a follower of the rules. Following the rules, I would find in my two weeks in Japan, is important culturally.

Our first day of travel, a five-hundred-mile trip south, would involve a shinkansen bullet train, a regional train, and a ferry. Planning for our lunch on the train, we decided to purchase a Japanese single-serving boxed lunch, a bento box, at one of the many retail kiosks located within the railway station. I did not understand the language or the currency, so to calm my nerves I walked into the kiosk, tried to avoid all of the commuters who rushed in and out, and went directly to a refrigerated case containing bento boxes. I could not read the Japanese characters on the content labels, but the pricing labels scared me. Seventeen hundred yen for a modest lunch! Then I noticed a few bento boxes that had a cellophane window in their top cover allowing me to view the contents. Inside of one I could see a pile of rice, a few grilled spring onions, and chunks of something that appeared to be deep fried. I grabbed it along with a triangular block of rice wrapped in seaweed (nori). It looked like a musubi, a snack food item I had brought and eaten in Hawai'i. Off to my left was a line at the checkout register. I took my place and while waiting pulled two one-thousand-yen notes from my wallet. When it was my turn, I mumbled an attempt to say hello in Japanese and handed the clerk the currency. She bagged my purchases and handed me my change. We both said, "Arigato," and I stepped outside to wait for Sandy and our friends. We all had looks of relief on our faces after completing our first transactions using yen.

While waiting to purchase anything on this trip, invariably someone would get in line behind me, making me a bit nervous. To ensure both a speedy purchasing process, and to keep from appearing like a bumbling idiot as I fumbled with coins whose value I did not understand, I continually used paper currency as we traveled around Japan. This tactic may have preserved my ego but resulted in pockets full of coins. So full that I had to tighten my belt on a few occasions, fearing my pants would fall to my ankles in a public space. Then, when my traveling companions began to call me Mr. Bo Jangles, I started looking for panhandlers on the street so I could unload some coinage. In Chicago, there is a someone asking for a handout on every corner of North Michigan Avenue, but during my two weeks in Japan I did not observe any, and I am not sure why.

With our bento boxes in hand, we proceeded to our platform and when it arrived, boarded a southbound shinkansen bullet train. We could have flown south but decided to take the train to experience high speed rail travel. The 200 mph shinkansen trains, that crisscross all of Japan, are a convenient and efficient way to get around.

As we located our reserved seats, after stowing our suitcases in a rack near the railcar entrance, I found myself sitting across the aisle from Sandy and our friends. Next to me, in the window seat, sat a casually dressed middle-aged Japanese woman. Because of the language barrier we both ignored each other. I chatted with my companions across the aisle and she stared out the window at the passing landscape.

Not long after the train departed, a railroad employee walked through our railcar. After exiting the sliding glass doors at the far end of the car, he turned toward us and bowed. For the balance of this train trip, every other railroad employee did the same thing. I have ridden on trains in many different countries, but never had I seen anything like this overt sign of customer respect. Each time it occurred, we just looked at each other and smiled. Our smiles continued for the whole two weeks for in restaurants, hotels, and retail establishments this sign of respect for customer was ever present. We often found ourselves awkwardly attempting to return the bow.

Around noon, hunger drove us to open our bento boxes. I removed mine from the bag, opened the top lid and found my utensils inside. A pair of chopsticks. Great, I thought. Here I am sitting next to a lady who has eaten every meal of her life with chopsticks. "This should be interesting," I nervously said to my companions.

Mark commented, "Yeah, eating our meals on this two-week trip might consume most of our waking hours, due to our lack of chopstick skills."

Just as I started to dig into my meal, and confirmed that those chunks of fried something were chicken, or karagge in Japanese, my friend Mark leaned across the aisle and said, "Here is something to wash down your meal," as he handed me a small bottle of rice wine or sake.

"Where did you get that?" I asked.

"Kiosk at the station."

"Perfect, thanks Mark!"

When finished, as I cleaned up the meal rubbish and picked off the countless pieces of rice stuck to my shirtfront and lap, I again thought about the Japanese women sitting next to me. She must have been chuckling to herself watching me eat with chopsticks.

Suddenly, I stood up and said, "Hey, I forgot, I have dessert for us. I bought a bag of dark chocolate squares that contain bits of dried cherry before we left Hawai'i."

I retrieved the chocolates from my backpack and passed them across the aisle.

"Here you go, help yourselves."

Because I am gregarious and love to talk with people, it had been uncomfortable sitting next to someone for two hours and not chatting. A language barrier had prevented both of us from even trying to communicate. I have always believed that food is a universal language, so when the bag returned to me, I decided to offer her a chocolate. I leaned slightly forward and looked at her to make eye contact. Then, with my face lit up by a sake enhanced smile, I held the bag in my left hand, and with the open palm of my right hand, I offered the bag to her. She looked up, smiled, and said something in Japanese that included the word "arigato" (thank-you), before accepting the bag and removing a chocolate. A few minutes later I again passed the bag across the aisle, it was returned, and I offered her a second piece. At first, she used hand gestures to decline, but then graciously accepted my offer as she bowed and said, "arigato."

About fifteen minutes later, she retrieved her travel bag and pulled out a box. The exterior design of the box had the appearance of a gift-wrapping paper. She removed the box lid, exposing two rows of beautifully decorated heavy paper sleeves. She removed four little packages, and with an outstretched arm offered each of us one. We tried to decline, thinking it was too generous, but she persisted, while displaying a smile only gift givers can possess. We opened the end flaps of our gift and slide out a cellophane wrapped custard-filled cake. We ate the tender moist cakes, filled with a creamy vanilla custard, while emitting sounds of pleasure.

"Mmmm, delicious, wow, and whaah (read the chapter on Spain for the translation of this word)."

We looked at each other with smiles on our faces and in unison shouted, "Arigato, arigato!"

She returned to her seat and began to put the box of cakes away. I pulled out my cell phone, put it in selfie mode, and held it out in front of me. Seeing the camera, she sat down and leaned against me. While she held up one of the cakes, and we both smiled, I snapped a photo that I cherish. That photo, of our smiling faces, supports my long-standing belief that food can break down cultural barriers and bring people together.

Sitting there, I wondered how she would tell the story I just relayed, to her family and friends. To facilitate that conversation, I filled my empty cake sleeve with chocolates and handed it to her. Later, as I stood up to exit the train, we instinctively, like old friends, made eye contact and smiled. We had bridged the language barrier.

That touching moment set the stage for a two-week-long look at a unique culture. Everywhere we went in Japan, the streets and sidewalks were as clean as someone's house just before the invited company arrives. Clean, not because there are people paid to pick up discarded trash, but instead, clean because no one would ever consider littering. I wondered if there was a word in the Japanese language for litter, for in the cities we visited litter did not exist.

Supporting this culture of cleanliness was another cultural norm. It is unacceptable to eat while you are walking in Japan. Even in large markets, where many opportunities to sample the local food existed, English language signs stated, "Do not walk and eat." The vendors, to support both this cultural norm and the tourists, had small benches along one wall, where one could sit, eat, and enjoy the local street food.

Another cultural anomaly was the courtesy shown when waiting in any line. Orderly lines are formed to the side at all rail, bus, and subway boarding locations. Only after everyone exited, did the passengers waiting in line board in a methodical fashion. Also noteworthy was the fact that everyone stepping onto an escalator did so to the left. This meant the right side was always clear for someone who was in a hurry and wanted to walk up.

When spending money for anything, lodging, transportation, food and drink, garments, and gifts, you will never have a better customer experience. There is always someone, and often multiple people, at your service. At every hotel, we were greeted at the door each time we entered or departed. Individuals who are serving you do so with a sense of purpose. They move rapidly, and I witnessed a few clerks break into a trot if they had to move very far.

The packaging of everything we purchased was over the top. Clerks spend an inordinate amount of time wrapping everything like it was a special gift. When we purchased strawberries at a food store, the clerk gave them a final wrap in bubble wrap for protection. When my wife purchased a small box of chocolates, a frozen gel pack was included in the paper packaging to ensure they stayed cool. All pastries were individually wrapped and placed in delicate bags with handles. Boxes of specialty cookies and pastries all came in gift wrapped boxes.

Technology advances witnessed on our trip both reduced the cost of doing business and improved the customer's experience. One evening I walked four blocks to get from our Kyoto hotel to the large train station. I was on a mission to purchase some pastries for our breakfast meal. I located one of the French bakeries in the rail center and entered. Grabbing a tray and a pair of tongs at the entrance I headed toward the pastry display. I looked over the selection that, if I did not know I was in Japan, would have convinced me I was in Paris. They all looked that good. I selected two kouign-amann, hunks of butter-infused pastry covered in caramelized sugar, that were studded with macadamia nuts. That should have been enough. But then, I saw a tray of all butter croissants. I have zero will power in bakeries. I added two to my tray before partially closing my eyes so I would not see and buy anything else. I slowly shuffled to the back of the check-out line. I watched the people in front of me set their tray under some type of scanner at the checkout station. I thought to myself, there are no barcodes or QR codes on bakery, so the scanner must use image recognition software to identify and price each item instantaneously. When I stepped up, I set my tray under the scanner and then I inserted a credit card into an automated teller. At the same time, a clerk individually wrapped my pastries and placed them in a logo bag with handles. My change discharged from the automated machine and she handed me my bag of goodies as we both said, "Arigato." On my way back to the hotel I opened the bag, lowered my face to the opening and inhaled. Breakfast could not come quick enough.

In Tokyo, based on a recommendation from our cooking class instructor, we ventured into a one-season clothing store (clothing so cheap you wear it for only one season). It reminded me of an Old Navy store for adults. The reason for our visit was to observe the technology employed at the twenty check-out stations. Here the usual customer service, driven by human interactions, had been turned on its head. We stood and watched as customers put the garments they wanted to purchase into a box at one of the checkout stations, and then closed the door. A scanner read the smart tags on the items and displayed the total price. The customer then inserted a credit card or cash into an automated teller. When the transaction was complete the door opened and the customer bagged their purchased items and departed. No clerks required.

Another self-service option are vending machines that are everywhere you look in Japan. One morning the four of us took a cab to a shrine site outside of Kyoto. Even though the cab driver could not speak English, he communicated using art when he handed each of us a small origami crane that he had made. That was a special moment. The shrine we visited was noted for hundreds of cast concrete heads that were lined up in rows all over the site. Each face was different, and many of them were covered with lichens and moss. It was a surreal place. To get to our next destination, a popular bamboo forest, we planned to hike there from our current location. We followed a small winding paved road that passed through a mostly rural area with modest homes, along with a few gift shops and restaurants. Near a small industrial building, right on the side of the road, was a vending machine with an English language title. I sighted it first and asked Mark, "You thirsty?"

"No, why?" He responded.

"Well, because here is the Liquor Store," I said and laughed.

Inside the glass fronted vending machine, with an English language marquee that read "Liquor Store," were twenty-three different Japanese canned beers. Throughout our trip, the four of us continually referenced elements of the Japanese culture like this, for it intrigued us.

Our trip south on the high-speed shinkansen train took us to the first location we visited in Japan, Miyajima Island. Our stay there gave us a glimpse of Japanese life in the past, because we stayed in a Ryokan. This was a traditional inn, and they have a long history going back 1,200 years. They feature public baths (onsen), traditional kaiseki (multi-course) meals and an opportunity to sleep on mats laid on the floor.

As we walked into the Ryokan, three bowing staff members, two young men and a middle-aged woman, and rows of slippers greeted us. They asked, and we removed our shoes, which they placed into a cubbyhole shelving unit sitting against a wall. The four of us then scurried around trying to find a pair of slippers that fit. They all looked too small, and when I tried them on it became obvious that I had feet larger than most Japanese. When I slipped my feet into the largest pair I could find, my heels hung off the back, and my toes were scrunched into the front. As I gingerly walked toward the registration desk, I observed Mark, who is well over six feet tall, also hanging out of his slippers. It looked like he was gingerly walking over hot coals as he moved slowly forward. "Perfect fit, huh Mark?"

"It is all part of the experience," he said and chuckled.

After registering, a staff member guided us onto an elevator and up to our second-floor room. The entire floor in the sparsely decorated room was covered in tatami (woven straw) mats so we were instructed to leave our slippers at the room entrance. Two chairs, with a small table between them, sat by the window overlooking the bay. The only other piece of furniture was a low table, at which you could sit cross-legged and eat or drink tea, centered in the room. Before leaving, the staff member told us that while we were dining that evening, someone would set up our beds.

After exchanging my clothes for one of the two silk robes laying on the flat surface of a small alcove, I settled into one of the two chairs and peered out the window and across the bay. Boats, safely anchored in a small harbor, and rows of vertical posts with netting strung between them up and down the waterway, led me to believe aquaculture was a local industry. I wondered what type of seafood they produced. Our evening meal at the inn, one of the highlights of our stay, would reveal the answer.

After being seated for our multi-course kaiseki meal, we all declined the offer of western utensils and readied our chopsticks. The meal featured eleven different and varied dishes. Some, easy to identify, like a small grilled fish, while others, like a salted plum, left us guessing with puckered lips. The highlight of the meal, four immense locally farmed oysters, were served two ways. Steamed and deep fried. The naked steamed oysters had nothing to hide. They were plump, firm, and delicious. The fried oysters worn a thin coat of crispy tempura batter. Those two moist, perfectly fried oysters were the best I had ever eaten.

As promised, while we had been gone, our sleeping mats had been set up in the middle of our tatami mat covered room. That bed made the term "climb into bed" unusable. When ready for bed, Sandy and I got down onto our hands and knees and rolled over onto the bed.

The next morning, after crawling from the bed, I sat and stared out the window of our room. The local fishermen, in reality oyster farmers, had started their workday early. A few boats motored from the small harbor while others, already loaded with conical piles of oysters, headed to my left. On our way to the Ryokan the previous afternoon, out the window of the transport van, I noticed a small metal clad building. Protruding from one wall was a running conveyor dumping oyster shells onto a large pile below it. Now it all made sense. That is where the boats were taking the oysters to be processed. Seeing, and now understanding, the oyster aquaculture process, caused me to recall the previous night's dinner featuring those freshly harvested oysters and the pleasure of eating them.

Our stay at the Ryokan on Miyajima was the perfect place to begin our visit to Japan. It provided a laidback slow start to our trip. Whereas the balance of our trip would expose us to the hustle and bustle of city life in Japan. Departing Miyajima, we headed an hour north, via a local train, toward a place steeped in sadness and hope – Hiroshima.

The morning after our arrival, we walked the busy workday streets filled with people, toward Hiroshima's Peace Memorial Park. Just before a river bridge, we turned left into the park area. Directly in front of us, stood the damaged remains of a building now commonly called the A-Bomb Dome. This destroyed shell of a four-story concrete building, with a dome of exposed rusty steel, was left standing after the blast, and today it is a stark reminder of the destruction caused by the atomic bomb. As I walked around to photograph the building from different angles, I began to suffer from some American guilt. We dropped the bomb, but they started the war. How should I feel?

We then walked along the calm riverside toward a solemn memorial to the 140,000 people who lost their lives in the first nuclear bomb attack. The memorial is a stone arch that is positioned so that when I looked through the opening, off in the distance I again viewed the remnants of the A-Bomb Dome building. Although the memorial is in Peace Memorial Park, it seemed impossible to think about peace initially.

To fully understand the human cost of the first nuclear bomb attack, we joined visitors from all over the world to somberly shuffle through a museum filled with graphic reminders. Inside were photographs of the city, and its inhabitants, before and after the blast. The tattered and burnt remains of possessions and clothing, along with graphic photos of victims of the nuclear attack, filled glass display cases and the walls of the museum. On our way out I noticed and read something displayed on a large plague. The writing, from the testimony of Akiko Takakura, a survivor of the atomic blast, touched me and reinforced the fact that common people are the victims of war started by leaders and politicians.

Black, black rain.
Huge drops.
People craned their neck
To the sky
With their mouth wide open.
Hot bodies, so very hot,
They wanted water.

Therefore, it was okay for me to feel sad. The people who died in the blast did not start the war with the U.S., and I could grieve their loss. Then, I began to think about the need for ongoing peace in the world. That is the intent of the museum. My visit to Hiroshima's

Peace Park strengthened my resolve to stand up and demand peace when politicians and governments talk about war.

We left the museum emotionally drained and hungry. We walked unfamiliar streets looking for a lunch spot to eat a dish called okonomiyaki. Often referred to as a Japanese pancake or omelet, it is made with a thin wheat flour batter mixed with cabbage, noodles, a small amount of meat or seafood, some chopped vegetables and topped with a special sauce and mayonnaise. Cooked on a flat top grill, it looked like a two-inch-thick pizza, loaded with every possible pizza topping when it was set in front of me. Of course, we all ordered the oyster version, and searched through the massive pile of ingredients to locate and savor the three large oysters hidden within. It was pure comfort food that I enjoyed, so on the way out I shouted "oishi" (delicious) to the cooks. I walked away satisfied, over-full and vowing to eat a light dinner.

Next on our itinerary was an extended five day stay in Kyoto. Our train arrived at Kyoto Station which, like all large train stations in Japan, was more than a transportation center. This massive complex included a shopping mall and a restaurant hub. It is hard to describe the scope and scale of these mega-stations. This one contained a shopping mall full of specialty stores and upscale anchor department stores. One section had nothing but restaurants. A small food store, within the station, is where we shopped every evening for yogurt and fruit for our breakfast. Another example that still makes me salivate; we had a choice of four high-end French bakeries in the shopping complex.

Our newly constructed hotel, located just a few blocks away, had only been open for seven months. It was big, beautiful, and had a spacious lobby decorated with Japanese art and artifacts. During our stay we found the customer service over the top. I noticed what I thought was a Spanish flag lapel pin on the suit of the young man checking us in. I asked, "Is that a Spanish flag?"

"Yes, I am from Spain, but moved to Japan to work. The Spanish economy is not doing so well," he said.

Because of my interest in European soccer I asked, "What football club do you support?"

"Barcelona, of course," he said while grinning.

After my soccer buddy handed us our room keys, he accompanied us up the elevator and all the way to our rooms to ensure we were satisfied with the accommodations. Another indicator of their customer focus was evident every time we entered or left the hotel. The area next to the large sliding glass doors, leading in and out of the lobby, was always staffed with two people. On multiple occasions one of them was the middle-aged hotel manager, who greeted us with a bow and the offer to help in any way.

One evening, because it had started to drizzle, Sandy and I decided to dine in at the hotel's upscale white tablecloth Italian restaurant. I sipped my Campari and orange juice while looking for something unique on the menu. I decided upon and ordered the risotto Milanese. Sandy settled on a pasta dish with fresh seasonal vegetables. The risotto, served in a large shallow white bowl, looked like the sun. The bright, saffron-infused yellow rice dish topped with a generous amount of shaved Parmigiano-Reggiano cheese was flavorful, creamy, and luscious. It was the best preparation of that dish I had ever tasted, so while settling the bill I asked our waiter to compliment the chef. He asked me to wait a moment while he invited the chef from the kitchen, so I could personally thank him. Out walked a European chef, who during our conversation, told us he had been born and raised in Milan, the birthplace of risotto Milanese. I did not ask, but the recipe for that golden risotto flavored with fragrant saffron may have been his Italian mamas'.

One of my food-related objectives, while in Japan, was to eat a bowl of ramen at a highly rated ramen noodle shop. An internet search revealed a Kyoto top-ten shop was within walking distance of our hotel. Looking up from a map app that guided us to the location, we saw a line in front of the noodle shop. We took our place at the rear of the line, and as it moved forward, we found ourselves peering through an open window into the kitchen. Boiling water and steaming pork broth created a surreal misty scene. Visible through the steam stood a stack of wooden trays filled with pre-portioned coiled fresh ramen noodles and two cooks, wearing red bandanas, making ramen magic. When it was our turn to enter the restaurant, I knew my ramen dream would come true.

The place was small with about eight tables for four and a few seats at a counter. The hostess seated us at one of the small tables. As I looked around it was clear they served joy as well as soup. Smiles filled the faces around us as they slurped their noodles and drank the broth.

This shop served only one type of ramen and had fifty years of experience making and serving it. It was a pork broth-based ramen, filled with noodles and topped with slices of freshly roasted pork and a mound of chopped scallions. When the bowl was set in front of me, I took a photo before mixing the scallions into the broth with my chopsticks. I then secured a bundle of noodles with the chopsticks and slurped them up. The rich gelatinous pork broth and the chewy texture of the noodles made it clear this was the ramen of my dreams. Eating that bowl of steaming hot soup, and the buzz provided by a large refreshing bottle of cold Ashai Super Dry beer, made me feel ecstatic. As we settled the bill, I used a translation app to confirm the word for delicious in Japanese. We stood up to leave and I intention-ally walked by the open kitchen so I could shout, "Oishi!" Knowing smiles filled the faces of the cooks as they nodded to another satisfied customer.

We filled our five days in Kyoto with visits to temples, shrines, markets, gardens, and museums. The many temples and shrines we visited, or just passed while walking, provided a contrast to the churches and cathedrals I have visited in Europe. Rather than crum-bling old stone structures in need of repair, the wooden temples, and shrines with sloping tile roofs, both Shinto and Buddhist, appeared to be well maintained. I could not tell one from the other, for they all seemed similar. Common elements included surrounding gardens with skillfully pruned pine trees, flowering trees, contemplative rock and raked gravel beds, and reflective ponds or pools of water, often with Koi fish. The temples and shrines varied in size, but tradition has preserved their architectural style and look. I liked the open, natural feel and their manicured grounds. When I walked around and through them, a calming peaceful easy feeling came over me. Wasn't that the title of an Eagles song? Anyway, what I felt, felt good. In contrast, my feelings when entering the large, often dark, and dreary, cathedrals of Europe is different. I am always intellectually impressed by their architectural and historical significance. Yet, despite their massive size, driven by the prideful and unchecked belief that bigger is better, they fail to touch me emotionally.

One common feature we observed in parks, gardens and shrine locations were blooming plum trees. We had hoped to catch the beginning of the cherry blossoms, but our timing was off by a few weeks. The planting of plum and cherry trees at those locations relate to the springtime cherry blossom festivals that occur all over Japan. Their blossoms signal a rebirth that the whole nation celebrates, much like Easter is celebrated in the West. The trees we observed, planted in groupings or along walkways, were of many different varieties. They appeared well cared for, with wooden structures supporting old heavy limbs, and some looked to be incredibly old. I read about one cherry tree that is over one thousand years old. I, along with many locals, had my camera out shooting way too many photos of the blossoms from all different angles and in different light. We all felt caught up in the excitement as we viewed the beautiful blooming trees.

We now headed for our final stop in Japan, Tokyo, a busy and sometimes hectic city of fourteen million people. We had begun our trip by experiencing the slow pace of Miyajima Island and now headed for a much different experience, the hustle and bustle of Tokyo.

We boarded a high-speed train and sat back to watch the countryside and cities flash by. The route from Kyoto to Tokyo was along the flat eastern seaboard of the country. Looking east from the train, we occasionally caught glimpses of the coastline and harbors filled with boats. To the west a mountain range was always present. Also taking advantage of the flat coastal land, small scale farms that raised rice and vegetables, lined the route for much of the trip. Most small-scale agricultural operations such as these, had been gobbled up by industrial farming in the United States decades ago. That made me think that the farm to table food movement, touted by some restaurants in the U.S., must be commonplace in Japan.

As the landscape flashed by, I pulled out my phone to check our current location using a map application. Identified on the map, to the west and north of our location, stood Mount Fuji. As we continued forward, we began to peer out the window hoping we would get a sighting from the train. This revered mountain, which is really a volcano, is a symbol of Japan and is ever present in their visual arts. Then as the train cleared some large hills it came into view. The almost perfectly formed conical shape, topped by a snow-covered cap, sits alone on a large flat plane of land. When it came into view, I excitedly handed Sandy my cell phone. From her window seat she snapped picture after picture trying to capture an image without a power transmission pole in the frame. She succeeded, and we have a digital memory of an iconic Japanese natural wonder even though it was not on our travel itinerary.

Our destination in Tokyo was the Uneo Station. It was another huge complex with shopping and dining opportunities. After exiting the station, we followed an overhead walkway that took us over some roadways and got us close to our hotel. As I walked in, I could see this hotel was nothing like the spacious new seven-month-old hotel we stayed at in Kyoto. This was an older place with a small lobby full of luggage and people. Our room was small and reminded me of hotel rooms we had stayed at in Paris. But off course, since this was Tokyo, it was more expensive than the room in Kyoto. After checking in and stowing our belongings, we met our friends in the lobby and then headed out to urban hike the area.

Within a few blocks of the hotel, we found a market area with pedestrian-only streets. The food stalls, retail outlets, and restaurants attracted hordes of Sunday afternoon shoppers, so we found ourselves walking in a sea of humanity. In many other countries, this might cause travelers to tightly clutch their wallets, purses, and passports. Not necessary in Japan. Never once did I feel unsafe.

European travels had taught me to be vigilant and aware of my surroundings, especially in crowds or when using public transportation. In Italy, Spain, and France, I had a death grip on my personal possessions. But at this point, after ten days in Japan, I completely trusted the Japanese people around me. This trust was developed through experience. For instance, when on crowded subway trains in Kyoto and Tokyo, my cell phone was most often in an open small pocket on the side of my pants leg. The top of the phone stuck out slightly and was very visible, and yet, no one touched it. My wallet, in an open rear pocket just as it would have been at home, never attracted pickpockets. I had come to understand that in this culture, built upon respect for others, no one would even consider stealing my possessions. I felt safe in Tokyo and all of Japan.

Before leaving on our trip to Japan, Sandy had signed us up for a cooking class in Tokyo. Our instructor, Yoshimi, who had worked in the corporate marketing world, and traveled internationally for work, was now raising children, and decided to do something different. She taught her cooking classes in a small Tokyo rental apartment but lived in a town south of Tokyo. On days when she had clients she commuted via train into Tokyo. As soon as class ended, she commuted home and arrived before her school age children. Yoshimi spoke excellent English and taught us more than the four recipes we prepared and ate together. She focused on dining etiquette, food history, and Japanese culture as much as food preparation. How to properly hold and use chopsticks was valuable information that we could have used at the start of our trip. For instance, stabbing a piece of food with a chopstick mimics a Japanese funeral ritual, so avoiding that action while eating in restaurants would be a good idea.

The four dishes we made included okonomiyaki (the dish we had eaten in Hiroshima), cold cooked spinach with a sesame seed and soy dressing, tofu with a fresh tomato salsa and miso soup. Most Japanese cooking is based on simple preparations using fresh ingredients. The tofu dish, which I really loved, was a great example of that style of cooking. Because of my lifelong passion for cooking, I went into the class expecting to have fun, but not learn any new techniques. Although when we prepared the cold spinach dish, Yoshimi taught me how to solve a common problem. Cooked spinach has a kind of metallic taste that makes your teeth feel funny, like the smooth enamel that coats them has been removed, when you eat it. To elimi- nate that taste and sensation we learned to wash the just cooked spinach under cold water before removing the excess water, by squeezing it. To complete the dish, the other ingredients, soy sauce, ground roasted sesame seeds and a little sugar, were added to the spinach. It now had a clean, delicious flavor.

Eating in Tokyo restaurants provided some memorable experi- ences. Often when Japanese menus had been translated into English, they became confusing. For instance, as the four of us stood outside of a ramen noodle shop looking over a large menu board, we commented on an item titled, "Best ass meat barbecued pork ramen."

"Mark, do you think they mean the ham portion of the pig's ass?" I asked.

"I don't know." He responded. "I guess the only way to find out is to order a bowl and see if it tastes good or offal."

At another restaurant, everything was prepared and served on wooden skewers. After being seated, the waiter handed us the English menu. The "English" on the English menu was confusing at best. As we looked over the menu an item titled "Beef Tendon" stood out.

"That is probably small chunks of beef tenderloin, but the trans- lation is confusing," I noted.

"Let us order that." Sandy said.

We selected a few other items and when the waiter returned to take our order, we tried to clarify the meaning of beef tendon. The animated waiter used all his pantomime skills to demonstrate what we might be ordering and eating.

He repeatedly pointed to his neck while repeating, "Mooooo, tendon, mooooo, tendon."

It felt like a game of charades. When these formerly inedible pieces of neck tendon, which had been slow cooked for hours, arrived in front of us we just stared. They came skewered, of course, and covered with a secret sauce. Our cooking school instructor had pointed out that there are at least thirty words just to describe the texture of food in the Japanese language. I am certain one of those words must have been created just to describe the soft pliable texture of cooked beef tendon. The long and slow cooking process had made what had been inedible into something delectable. The intense beef flavor was over the top and the sauce complimented the beef.

Another restaurant reminded me of a neighborhood bar. As I entered and looked around, the furnishings, tables and chairs, lighting fixtures, and even the staff seemed a bit weathered and worn. The hostess guided us up a narrow stairway and seated us in an open area. Nearby, two groups of salary men in their work suits, ate and drank. Their boisterous laughter and camaraderie confirmed all we had heard about Japanese salarymen going out after work to drink and enjoy themselves.

Our waitress did not speak English, but she gave us the English menu. One of the items listed, "Flat row of grilled anchovies," got me excited.

"Do you guys remember the food store we walked through yesterday?" I asked.

"Yeah, why?" Someone responded.

"I saw these packages of perfect three-inch-long bright silver and black anchovies in that store, and look here on the menu, flat row of grilled anchovies. We have to order them!" I said excitedly.

As we continued to discuss the menu, and select additional items, my mouth started to water as I thought about those oily little fish grilling over hot coals. When a plate with what appeared to be four crackers with poppy seeds arrived, I did not immediately make the connection to my order.

"What is that? We did not order crackers," someone said.

I picked up the plate for a closer look and then said, "Oh, those are not poppy seeds. Those are little fisheyes."

Hundreds of exceedingly small anchovies had been pressed and glued together with something (fish slime?) to create wafer thin fish crackers. The grilling must have been a quick pass over some hot coals to crisp them up. The mild tasting crispy "flat row of grilled anchovies" was the seafood equivalent of beef jerky.

Before we departed from that restaurant we noticed, or I should say smelled, someone smoking. I did not understand the rules regarding cigarette smoking, but I did make some observations. I never noticed anyone smoking while walking on the streets or when using public transportation. But we did pass many outdoor designated smoking areas filled with smokers. This apparent restriction on smoking wherever one wanted, also seemed to be exempt in some restaurants and a coffee shop we visited.

One afternoon, Sandy and I needed a caffeine lift after walking the streets in a section of Tokyo full of shops selling cookware. We found a small, old, and established coffee shop down a side street. Because the Japanese have been historically smaller in stature, when the hostess seated us, we barely fit into the chairs and struggled to get our legs under the table. This was old furniture, and this was not Starbucks. As I sat at our tiny table in the rear of the shop, I watched an older gentleman prepare the coffees with milk we had ordered, while thinking to myself this place has the look and feel of an old neighborhood bar. Then just as we began to sip the delicious creamy coffee, someone near the front of the shop lit a cigarette. Within the next five minutes three other people, who had just entered the shop, did the same. Was this a designated smoking area? The coffee was good, but we quickly gulped it down before holding our breath and making our way to the exit. Rather than be offended, we laughed at our ignorance of the local language and the rules regarding smoking.

After two weeks in Japan, a country so different from ours, all four of us agreed that the highlight of our visit was experiencing the unique culture of Japan. A culture built upon respect for one another made it unlike any other place I have visited. I felt so comfortable and welcome in that trusting and respectful environment that I plan to go back.

COLD SPINACH SALAD

Ingredients

½ lb. fresh spinach
3 T toasted white sesame seeds
1-1/2 T soy sauce
1 T water
1-1/2 t sugar

Preparation

In a skillet, toast the sesame seeds over medium heat until they start to pop and begin to brown. Remove seeds from pan, reserve 1 teaspoon, and grind the balance with a mortar and pestle. Put ground seeds into a serving bowl and add soy sauce, water, and sugar. Stir until sugar is dissolved.

Add the spinach to a pan of salted boiling water and cook for 1 minute. Remove spinach to a colander and place under cold running water to both cool and rinse the spinach. Squeeze spinach to remove moisture, place on a cutting board and rough chop. Add spinach to serving bowl containing dressing and stir to combine. Garnish with the whole toasted sesame seeds and serve room temp or chilled.

After eating your salad, and you have poured your second glass of sake, while waiting for the chicken teriyaki to finish cooking, please notice your teeth do not feel funny because you rinsed the spinach. Think of and thank Yoshimi, our Tokyo cooking school instructor, for that tip.

9

ENGLAND

THE HOME OF FOOTBALL

I have visited England on at least ten occasions, most of those trips being work related. In many cases the work trips allowed me to interact with locals and experience the culture to a greater degree than a tourist.

Like most European countries England has a lengthy history. English football (soccer for us yanks) is a big part of English culture and has a history going back to 1863. Football clubs throughout England have long histories and generations of fans that are emotionally tied to their club. For example, a North London based club, the Tottenham Hotspurs, recently replaced a 118-year-old stadium, called White Hart Lane, with a new one that seats over sixty thousand fans.

My first exposure to English football occurred when I was a young lad. A show titled; "Wide World of Sports" was a Saturday afternoon staple on the ABC network. Exotic, for the U.S. market, sports like rugby, soccer and Formula 1 racing were occasionally featured. I distinctly remember watching a soccer match from London's Wembley Stadium. What intrigued me most during the match? The fans. They actively participated and helped to influence the match outcome by singing and chanting almost non-stop.

Fast forward four decades plus, and I am in England consulting when an English work associate and friend named Jon, who possessed two Manchester United season tickets, invited me to join him for a match at Old Trafford. To prepare for the experience I visited a sporting goods apparel store and purchased a Manchester United logo jumper.

That evening, as we walked toward the football stadium, we passed many pubs overflowing with fans drinking beer. Jon explained that to avoid the high cost of drinking in the stadium, most fans fueled up at the pubs before going in. Also, the expensive beer purchased in the stadium could not be taken to your seat, it had to be consumed below the stands in the concessions area.

Our seats were located near one of the goal ends. I felt excited as the teams filed onto the pitch and the match began. Soon the fans seated behind the goal began to sing in unison. Childhood memories of televised soccer matches flooded my mind. The singing fans, in full voice, used standard songs from their repertoire, or created new ones, to deride or cheer on a player, or the opposing team, on the pitch.

Here are a couple of examples of what you might hear at an English soccer match. Near the end of a match, during a long losing streak, the home team fans might sing this to their opponents, "Your nothing special – we lose every week! Your nothing special - we lose every week!" Or, when a home team goes down by four goals the fans might chant to their opponents, "You only scored four, you only scored four."

Before that match at Manchester United's Old Trafford Stadium had ended, I knew soccer was my kind of sport. It is often referred to as "the beautiful game," and I get that. It is a game of finesse, skill, and creativity rather than brute force. Soccer is like a chess match where the soccer pitch replaces the chess board and the players on the pitch must constantly make decisions. Soccer quickly replaced football for me. Football in the U.S. is a game where players try to injure each other for twelve minutes while running plays they have practiced over and over. To watch the twelve minutes of actual playing time, you must sit in front of the television for three hours while enduring endless commercials and annoying announcers. Soccer matches have two forty-five minutes halves that are pretty much non-stop action. When injuries, or time wasting by players occurs, the referee adds some time at the end of the halves. So, in less than two hours you have seen at least ninety minutes of play.

U.S. sports fans often say they do not understand soccer, or it is too slow and there is not enough scoring. I usually ask them if they watch hockey, a violent game with low scoring. If they do, I inform them they then understand soccer for it is just slow hockey without the violence.

The reserved English have a reputation of being prim, and proper. I had the chance to debunk that while consulting at a manu-facturing facility in the northeast of the country, in Newcastle. At the start of my two-day workshop, I informed the participants that they were about to experience the best workshop they had ever attended, and at the end of the event they would be so excited they would be doing high fives and group hugs. One of the managers quickly pointed out, "We are British, there will not be any group hugs."

Two days later, after four small teams of workshop participants had reported out on their assigned improvement projects, I asked them all to stand up for a group photograph. I organized them into neat rows, with the tallest people in the middle, until they looked prim and proper.

After I snapped a few photos I said, "Okay let us have some fun. Put your arms around someone, it is time for a group hug."

They looked at me like I was crazy. Then as I repeatedly shouted, "Come on lads," like I was cheering at a soccer match, one person, and then two, and then multiple people broke into laughter as they hugged someone. The photo I snapped was marketing gold. They really did attend the best workshop ever, and I have photographic evidence to prove it.

On multiple occasions, I stayed at the same B&B while doing business in the small town of Glossop, located east of Manchester. The guesthouse, located just outside of town, sat in a bucolic setting not far from the Peaks District National Park. As I walked back and forth, between the worksite and the B&B, I passed pastures full of sheep and an old stone Anglican church. I overheard locals making fun of each other by saying, "You have never been over the bridge." Meaning, they had never left Glossop to go anywhere. It was a laid back and relaxed area of England, and the proprietors at the B&B made me feel welcome.

Each morning, when I went down for breakfast, she would be waiting to ask what I would like and then prepare my breakfast meal from scratch. Although I am a coffee drinker, I would ask for the English breakfast tea. It just seemed to be the proper drink based on my location.

Then as she set the tea of my table she would ask, "Would you be having the full fry this morning?"

If I thought I might have to spend the balance of the morning using a team of horses, pulling a steel plough, to till the pasture across the street, I would say, "Yes."

The "full fry" consisted of two fried eggs, fried bangers (pork sausage), fried rashers (thin cut ham), fried black and white pudding (blood sausage), fried mushrooms, a fried tomato half, canned beans and toast. But on most morning, my response would be "Just two poached eggs on toast please. I want to save room for a scone." I never asked her, but the scones had to be made fresh every morning. They had a slightly crisp exterior and a soft moist interior. Split, and then generously spread with butter and strawberry jam, it became the highlight of each breakfast.

While on another business trip, my host Jon thoughtfully arranged a hotel in a town near Stonehenge so that I could visit and view the historic site. We arrived late in the afternoon and stopped at the site museum, which is down a lane from the actual archaeological site, to purchase entrance passes. The staff informed us the designated viewing area was closing soon and ticket sales had already stopped for the day. So being resourceful lads, we drove to the archaeological site, parked the car near some construction equipment, and struck off across a field occupied by grazing sheep. Doing that allowed us to view the stone circle from a location outside of the fence line that surrounded and protected the historically significant site. As we stood in the sheep dung littered field, we had a fantastic view of the monolithic site. It was near sunset and with each passing minute the light changed and provided new photo opportunities. And since the official viewing area inside the fence had closed, no people despoiled the view of Stonehenge as we took our photos.

As we turned to leave, we both needed the WC that was inside the fence, so we relieved ourselves along the fence line while the flock of sheep watched. Not sure if the sheep keep repeating baaa, or baaad, but they kept repeating something.

On a trip to the northeast of England, Sandy and I found ourselves in York in early November. Dominating the city's skyline is the massive York Minster, or cathedral, which was consecrated in 1472. We set out for it after checking in to our hotel. We paid the entrance fee and then viewed yet another large cathedral. The architecture was impressive but the interior, since it was an Anglican cathedral, was plain and seemed as cold as the November weather outside. Near the rear of the building, rows of chairs had been set in place for an evening orchestral concert. Listening to music performed in a massive cathedral appealed to us since we occasionally attend orchestral concerts by the Chicago Symphony Orchestra, so we purchased tickets.

We then spent much of the afternoon strolling the narrow streets lined with some medieval era buildings with exteriors containing crisscrossed wooden planks, tourist shops and restaurants. Watching the time, we selected a restaurant for an early dinner of local lamb chops, and when finished we walked through the chilly autumn air to the cathedral for the concert. The skies were darkening as we stepped inside and sat in the small wooden chairs. Soon the orchestra filed in, warmed up and then began to play. The beautiful music bounced and echoed throughout the cavernous structure. As I sat their marveling at the sound, I thought I heard explosions outside. I wondered what was going on. Interspersed randomly throughout the concert, the explosions continued. Is was only after we departed into the chilly night that, after asking a local, we found out it was Guy Fawkes Day, a day celebrated with bonfires and fireworks. Guy Fawkes had been born in York, and later led a failed assassination plot against the King and some members of parliament. As a result, since 1605, his effigy has been burnt over bonfires on November 5th.

While in the Manchester area of England on another work trip, a work associate said he and a friend would be driving to Edinburgh, Scotland on Saturday, to have a look around. He asked if Sandy and I would like to go along. A chauffeured trip to another country sounded wonderful so we agreed. We departed early on Saturday and spent the next few hours watching the rolling countryside of northern England and then Scotland flash by from the back seat.

As we drove into town, my first impression was that it seemed to be a dull, gray city. Many or most of the old historic buildings were gray stone structures that had discolored. They now appeared a dark splotchy gray or even black. Maybe it was the result of three hundred years' worth of coal soot. After an hour of walking around the city, including a stop for a coffee and a scone, it began to rain.

To escape the drizzle, we ducked into an empty bar. The bartender looked up as we entered. He seemed happy to see us as he said, "#&%*, @%$# *&% & $#% &*&?"

I could not understand a word he had said because of his accent, but I responded like I had, "Two scotch whiskies please." And before he could ask which scotch whiskey, I said, "You pick the whiskey, you are the expert."

He nodded, poured our whiskies, and set them on the bar. Grabbing our drinks, we sat at a table near the windows. Watching the raindrops make concentric circle in the puddles, that had accumulated on the stone paved street, made me a bit gloomy. Each sip of scotch increased my melancholy, and if I had ordered a second, I am sure I could have written a sad poem or a gothic novel.

When the rain subsided, we walked the town. We stopped and viewed some of the historical sites, including the large hill-top Edinburgh castle, and visited some of the gift shops. No matter who we interacted with, I had a difficult time understanding what they said. The Scottish accented English that they spoke, required close concentration and lip reading. I am not particularly good at either of those, but I really enjoyed listening to them talk.

It was now late afternoon and we had agreed to meet my co-worker and his friend at a preselected restaurant near where we had parked that morning. The restaurant was in an old house, so it had many small dining rooms. The menu board outside listed some classic Scottish fare along with interesting new items. Once seated, I studied the menu trying as always to find something unique and local. A preconceived notion that I should order Haggis was quickly forgotten when unique jumped right off the page as I read, Loin of Springbok, listed amongst the entrees. To the best of my knowledge, Springboks do their springing on the plains of Africa. I wanted to ask our waiter if I understood this menu item correctly, but then I remembered I would not be able to understand him. I assumed that Springbok must be farm raised as deer are in the US. I decided to pass on the offal, oatmeal concoction cooked in a sheep's stomach, known as Haggis, and ordered the Springbok. The four-inch-long piece of loin was cooked perfectly, medium rare, tender, and mild in taste. When I make a trip to Africa, I will correct my cultural misstep by ordering Haggis.

Over the fifteen years or so that I have visited England, I observed the traditional English pub food change for the better. Items like the Ploughman's Lunch, which consisted of bread, butter, cheese, onions, and pickles, have been replaced with menu items like Thai curries. This change is the result of both an elevated interest in good food and the influence of England's immigrants. Many restaurants that years ago only served stodgy fare, now have a variety of interesting local and internationally inspired offerings.

After a day of business just outside London proper, I joined my English work associate Jon, and some of the workshop participants at a nearby pub for dinner. Hunger, and drinking a pint on an empty stomach, drove me to quickly look over the appetizer portion of the menu. Whitebait, one of the menu items, had me puzzled. After asking the Brits at the table, I learned they were small, 1-2 inches in length, deep fried fish. Probably sprats, small young cousins of the herring. They informed me you ate the whole thing, head, fins, entrails, and bones. Sounded delicious to me, so I ordered them. They tasted like fishy French fries, crispy and crunchy, and I would order this example of traditional pub food again.

On another occasion, someone from a work site invited me to a group dinner. As I walked into the restaurant it was obvious that it was not posh, as the Brits would say, and it had been a few decades since the worn brown wood interior furnishings had been updated. It was in a working-class town, and this was a working-class restaurant.

As I looked over the menu, the lamb shank offering caught my attention. I love lamb shank when it has been seared and then braised for three to four hours. When served, the meat falls from the bone and every drop of the umami rich cooking sauce must be dredged up with crusty bread. I could not wait for it to arrive. "Someone at the table asked, "What did you order?"

I smiled and said, "The lamb shank, I cannot wait to tuck into it."

When the shank was served, I noticed some nuanced differences from my past dining experiences. They included size, texture, smell, and TASTE. My first bite, and resulting facial contortions, confirmed it was a god-awful dish. The huge shank formerly belonged to an old mature sheep, not a lamb. It was mutton. Rather than meat that fell from the bone, each morsel of the gamey tasting meat had to be pried and chiseled from the bone. Did I mention it smelled and tasted extremely bad? It took more than one pint of ale to remove that taste from my mouth and I sent the dish back hardly touched. All the people in the world who say they do not like lamb, must have also been fed tainted tasting mutton. Yuck!

To guarantee a tasty meal while anywhere in England, I would seek out an Indian restaurant. I am familiar with Indian food, so I could order dishes I already knew that would be spicy, flavorful, and delicious. Indian restaurants are so prevalent in England, that a few years back a dish called chicken tikka masala became the most popular, dare I say national dish of England. Tender cut up pieces of chicken are stewed in a spiced tomato and yogurt sauce that is finished with the addition of heavy cream. I have read chicken tikka masala was created by a chef from Bangladesh who worked at a restaurant in Scotland. He used Indian cooking techniques to create a dish for the palate of his customers from the UK.

So just as that chef had to adapt, so do travelers when visiting new counties. England is a perfect place for new travelers to begin "Bumping & Snacking" because of its many similarities to the U.S., our knowledge of their history, and most importantly, a shared language.

CINNAMON AND SUGAR SCONES

Ingredients

1 cup cold whole milk
¼ cup sugar
½ t salt
2 cups all-purpose flour
1 cup whole wheat flour
2-1/2 t baking powder
1-3/4 sticks butter, divided
Demerara sugar
Cinnamon

Preparation

Pre-heat the oven to 375 degrees. Line a large, rimmed baking sheet with parchment paper.

Combine, in a small bowl, the cold milk, sugar and salt. Stir until sugar and salt have dissolved. In a large bowl add both flours and the baking powder. Stir to thoroughly combine. Cube 1-1/4 sticks of cold butter into ½ inch pieces. Add the butter to the flour mixture and using your fingers or a pastry cutter, mix the butter into the flour until only small pea sized pieces of butter are visible. Add the milk mixture and stir until just combined. Scrap onto a floured countertop and knead just enough to pull the dough together. Do not overwork.

Using a rolling pin, roll the dough into a 8" X 16" rectangle. Soften, but do not melt, the remaining ¼ stick of butter. Spread about 2/3 of it over the top of the rolled-out dough. Sprinkle the dough with sugar and cinnamon. Fold the dough in half to make a 4" X 16" rectangle. Spread the remaining butter over the top and then sprinkle with sugar and cinnamon. Cut the rectangle into quarters and then cut each of the four 4" X 4" rectangles into two triangles.

Place the scones on the prepared baking sheet and bake for about 20 minutes, or until the bottoms are browned.

You have options. Instead of cinnamon and sugar, just before adding the milk to the flour mixture, mix in blueberries, raisins, dried cherries, or chocolate chips. The possibilities are limited only by your imagination.

As soon as they come out of the oven, split one and slather it with good quality butter and strawberry jam. As you take your first bite, close your eyes and envision the rolling English countryside.

10

UKRAINE

HISTORY INFLUENCES A COUNTRY'S CULTURE

U kraine is a country I never envisioned visiting. Despite my genetic link to the region, my mother's parents emigrated from what is now Slovakia, all the former Soviet eastern European countries turned me off because of their repressive authoritarian political past. I want to travel where I can find joy. Then, out of the blue, in 2012 I received an offer to speak at a conference in Ukraine and I said yes. My travel expenses would be paid by the organizers, plus I would earn a handsome fee, so why not go?

Before leaving, I dedicated some time searching the internet to educate myself. I discovered Ukraine is located between Poland and Russia, formerly part of the Soviet Union, and had gained its independence in 1991. Much or most of the internet information was about the city of Kiev, the largest city in the country. This information stirred my interest, for Kiev seemed like a place worthy of a visit, but that was not my destination. Instead, I would travel to the eastern part of the country, close to the Russian border, to the city of Donetsk. This industrial town was in a region known for coal and steel production. So long before I departed, I knew visiting beautiful cities and magnificent historical sites would not be part of my itinerary. My opportunity would be to witness and experience a country with a culture quite different from mine.

There were no non-stop flights from Chicago to Donetsk. My flight plan took me from Chicago to London, London to Munich, and then Munich to Donetsk. I made the decision to take my time on this trip, so I arranged a hotel room in both London and Munich. That would ensure I would be rested and would not have to suffer through a zombie day when I arrived in Ukraine. After I cleared passport control at the Donetsk airport, a stern looking driver, holding a placard with my name written on it, was waiting for me. I had been told in advance that he would transport me to my local contact's office. During the ten-minute drive, I got my first views of the city. The architecture was Soviet era at its finest, mostly dull buildings without ornamentation.

My contact, a safety professional who quickly pointed out she was Russian, not Ukrainian, had attended Tulane university in the United States. Her English language skills were excellent. That and her organizational skills made my four-day visit trouble free. After a brief meeting to review and confirm my activities over the four days, I was driven to my hotel by my driver, who had waited for me.

The multi-story hotel, which was also the site of the conference, was newly built and across the street from an impressive recently constructed soccer stadium. At night, the stadium was bathed in beautiful indigo blue light. It was the home of FC Shakhtar Donetsk, a top team in the Ukraine soccer league. The hotel and the stadium seemed other worldly and out of place when contrasted with the other buildings in the area. Owned by the richest oligarch in the Ukraine, both the hotel and stadium were constructed for a recently held European soccer tournament that had been co-hosted by Poland and Ukraine. The company sponsoring the safety conference, at which I was to present, was also owned by the same Ukrainian.

After walking into the lobby containing chrome and vinyl covered furnishings, the indifferent unsmiling staff, dressed in black suits, methodically checked me in. I quickly stowed my possessions in my room and went urban hiking to see some of the city.

I soon noticed that every visible store sign was in Cyrillic script, so I had no idea what services or products were being offered. For instance, this is the word for restaurant in Russian – ресторан. The Ukrainian people also seemed different. As I passed them, they did not look up nor did they make eye contact. The word stoic must have first been used in this part of the world to describe the expressions on the faces of the people. The facial muscles that control smiling had to be atrophied on everyone I passed during my walk. Maybe it was illegal to show your teeth. Then a few days later, when someone at the safety conference referenced the local coal miner's historical attitude about life, I began to understand the absence of facial expressions. He stated, "You are born, you work hard, and then you die." The people I passed on the streets had obviously been in the hard work phase of life.

As I continued my walk, I observed the architecture. Noteworthy was a large onion domed Orthodox church that, like large churches in old neighborhoods all over the world, had seen better days. In the small area I walked, I did not see any single-family dwellings, only two-or three-story drab concrete apartment buildings. Survivors of the Soviet era I guessed. They were joyless structures. Eventually I came to an area that appeared to have some newer construction. Located there was a Nike store, and in the distance, I sighted the newly installed golden arches sign of a McDonald's restaurant. I wondered if the locals smiled as they ate their first Big Mac.

My circular walking route brought me back toward the new soccer stadium and a large park that surrounded it. A line of old drab green Soviet era tanks and artillery pieces identified the area as a memorial park. Then I passed a tall sculpture of a soldier in uniform standing alongside a man in coal miner's apparel, which memorialized both those who gave their lives on the field of battle or deep underground in the areas numerous coal mines. Another sculptural monument, of what I believed to be a soldier, showed him suspended in air and rising upward after death. There was nothing uplifting in the park. It was a place of sadness and remembrance.

As I walked by the empty soccer stadium, I noticed the stadium store was open and team logo apparel was sold inside. I looked around and before leaving purchased a T-shirt and baseball style cap. The orange T-shirt reminded me of a Soviet Era poster for it featured the image of a man with one clenched fist raised above his head. In 2016, as I was marching in a Chicago science march organized to protest the election of a man who discounted the value of science, I wore the FC Shakhtar T-shirt because to me the image symbolized resistance. During the march, a young man approached me with excitement in his eyes. He has sighted my shirt and, to him, the image symbolized home, for he had grown up in Donetsk. We talked and marched together for a few blocks before I wished him well on his immigrant journey.

The team logo hat turned out to be too small, so when I returned home it took up residence on a coat hook with some other hats. Then just last week, during a semifinal match of the 2020 Europa League tournament, I gave it away. As I watched the start of the match with an eight-year-old grandson, FC Shakhtar took the field and I suddenly remembered the hat I had purchased eight years earlier. I retrieved it, gave it to Declan, and it fit perfectly.

I said, "Declan, you are the only boy in the United States with a hat like that."

He was beaming.

With my souvenir clothing in hand, I walked back to the hotel. Near the elevators, I passed a tall stout man, wearing a black suit, standing along a wall in the hallway. He emotionlessly observed everyone who passed and reminded me of my vision of a secretive KGB agent. I wanted to ask him if he could recommend a good place for dinner, or if my room was bugged, but I was not sure he spoke English. After four days I began to view him as a living sculpture, for he was always standing in the same place.

I do not think eating out was a common practice in Ukraine. I had not seen, nor did I recognize, any restaurants on my walk except for the McDonalds. So, I decided to eat at the hotel restaurant. Of course, they served pizza, but I ordered the rabbit. The full loin, with Frenched rib bones attached, a rear leg, thigh, steamed cracked wheat and a lovely mushroom cream sauce had all been elegantly arranged on the plate. Sitting alone in the empty dining room, I slowly ate my meal and was pleasantly surprised by the quality of the food.

The next morning, I was up early to eat breakfast, for I was scheduled to go on a road trip. The hotel staff directed me to a restaurant located one floor below the lobby level. The lack of windows in the space made it a dark uninviting space. When I walked in, I was seated, ordered coffee, and was then directed to the buffet breakfast. As I loaded my plate with scrambled eggs and bacon, I noticed some small thick pancakes, so I added two to the plate. I did not see any syrup, so I topped them with cherry preserves. As I began to eat the overcooked scrambled eggs that resembled hard yellow pellets, I was disappointed. Then I cut into and had my first bite of a pancake. The dense, moist, almost cheesy texture made them unique. They were anything but light and fluffy. The cherry preserves, which added some tart sweetness, perfectly complimented the dense pancakes. I finished them off quickly and went back for two more. Now feeling a bit sluggish, I headed up to the lobby to depart.

Since the conference started the following day, I had the day free and had accepted the offer to travel south to the city of Mariupol to visit the Lenin Iron and Steel Works. My primary contact had asked if I wanted to tag along, since she planned to escort another visitor who had requested a site visit. The three of us climbed into the rear of a small mini-van and our driver headed south on roads that made me appreciate those back home. The 113-kilometer journey was a two-hour trip on a slow-motion roller-coaster ride. The roads undulating surface combined with the soft bouncy suspension of the van made me want to raise both of my arms and holler, "Weeeee," on a few occasions. It was November and the landscape was devoid of color and life. My host and interpreter noted that the plowed dreary fields we viewed along our route had been, just a few months before, full of sunflowers which are a major cash crop in Ukraine.

While traveling, my host shared some information about the site we would visit. The steel-making facility was founded in 1897 and the plant's blast furnaces had been disassembled and temporarily moved to Siberia when the Germans invaded during WWII. She also informed me that this massive plant produced plate steel, primarily for shipbuilding, and employed 60,000 people.

As we drove into a rather drab run-down part of Mariupol, I thought to myself, this is a one hundred-year-old mill town, and this is how it should look. Cities that have heavy, dirty industries as their economic base are rarely attractive. Then we turned left into the entrance of the massive steel mill complex. At the entrance stood a statue of Lenin, the plants namesake, that had probably been there for decades. After a safety orientation, and dressing in the appropriate safety apparel, I was given a personal tour of two mills. The first, a complex where melted steel was converted into ingots, and the second was the rolling mill where the ingots were rolled into steel plate.

The first stop, the melt shop, contained huge vessels in which scrap steel was melted using electrodes. Sparks flew from the large vessels of molten steel as they were tipped and poured to cast large rectangular ingots. Following my tour, the general manager of the melt shop met with me in a quiet training room. Through my translator he described his facility as world class. He did all the talking. As his dialogue was translated, I just nodded to convey understanding. When he finished, we departed the meeting room, but he suddenly stopped by a mirror near the exit door. Stenciled on the bottom part of the full-length mirror was the following sentence written in Russian, but translated for me, "You are looking at the person most responsible for your safety." I have seen this same safety reminder all over the world, so I did not think it was anything special. But then he laughed heartily as he reached to the top of the mirror and pulled down a window shade that had the image of Stalin painted on it. I laughed with him and wondered if the painted shade had been located there since the Stalin era, when Stalin executed seven hundred thousand people and imprisoned one million more. Now there was another reason not to smile.

The second stop, the plate mill, is where the cast ingots formed in the melt shop were transported. After being heated until red-hot in reheat furnaces, the ingots were pulled through a series of hydraulic roll stands to gradually reduce their width and thickness into steel plates. To reduce the large ingots down to one-inch thick steel plates required a mill that was about a quarter mile long. For our safety we walked the length of the mill on an overhead walkway. It was dusty and dark, and I was happy when the tour finished.

Following the tour, we stopped to eat lunch at what looked like a dining room for mill staff. We took seats at a small square table, the only one in the large room. Immediately, a lady in a floral print apron and a gray headwrap, who looked like she could have been my Slovak grandmother's sister, began bringing out small plates of food. She continued until the entire surface of the table was covered. Choices included pickled everything, fish, and sautéed pork steak. I have learned that fresh fish, which has been handled properly, does not taste fishy. I estimated the fish served to us was at least two weeks past that point. A child who was served and tasted that fish would say, "I do not like fish," for the rest of their life. I ate the pork steak and then poked and picked at some of the pickled vegetable dishes, to feign interest in the food. When the meal ended, I asked my host and translator to express my gratitude for the food I had been served. Internally, I was happy that the meal had ended. It had been a unique culinary experience that challenged my willingness to eat things that did not appeal to me.

The impressions I had formed during my brief visit to Ukraine were questioned at the conference, when a few local people who spoke English asked, "So, what do you think of Ukraine?" They asked in a hushed tone, and only when one on one. They seemed very sincere and interested in how I, as an outsider, viewed them and their country. "Interesting and different because of your political past," seemed to be the honest answer. Being their guest, I instead replied, "I am really enjoying my visit. I just wish I had more time to get to know you and your culture better."

During the afternoon of the second day of the conference, the attendees had a chance to tour a steel mill that produced large diameter pipe or go on a bus tour of Donetsk. My contact, the one who hired me to present at the conference, asked me to visit the pipe mill. She noted the steel mill management team had expressed interest in hearing my opinion of their facility.

Since I had worked for a large steel company early in my career, the production processes in the mill were familiar. Plate steel was rolled and formed into rounds and then the seam was welded to produce pipe. My real interest was the chance to assess the work culture. How people thought, acted, and interacted while at work, is what I wanted to witness.

The managers of this mill had taken ownership of an old Soviet era facility and obviously had worked hard to modernize it. I observed an organized and clean facility which validated some level of success. The workforce, those performing the physical work of forming, welding, and grinding, had their noses to the grindstone. As I watched them, they failed to engage with the visitors in any way, no eye contact, and no conversations. This is typical when a top down directive style of management is used in a workplace. This somehow seemed appropriate in Ukraine, because of the top down directive political system they had all lived under during the Soviet era.

After the tour, one of the senior mill managers asked what I thought of the facility and I responded by saying, " I applaud your efforts to clean up and organize an old facility, and I hope I have the chance to return in the future so I can see how you have progressed." I did not mention the unempowered workforce I observed or their directive style of management. They were all victims of the past.

The next day a driver, provided by my host, shuttled me to the airport to start my journey home. Sitting in the airport departure lounge, I reflected on my experiences and thought about what I had learned. It seemed to me the country's culture, built by a political system that restricted freedom and instilled fear, seemed to influence all the people I met. It was impossible to read anyone's body language, for they always had on their poker face. To gain someone's trust always takes time. In Ukraine it must take a long time. If I had a few weeks, and some quality vodka, I am sure I could have made some friends.

SYRNIKI (CHEESE PANCAKES)

Ingredients

16 oz (around 2 cups) farmer's cheese
4 eggs
¾ cup all-purpose flour
3 T sugar
1 t baking soda
1 t white vinegar
½ cup raisins or dried cherries (optional)

Preparation

In a large bowl, mix the crumbled cheese, 4 eggs, ¾ cup flour, and sugar with a hand mixer. Combine vinegar and baking soda in a small bowl. When it fizzes, mix it into the cheese mixture and continue to mix with the hand mixer until batter is uniform. Stir in optional dried fruit if using.

Heat a skillet and add some olive oil to lightly coat bottom. To a small bowl, add ¾ cup of flour. Scoop heaping tablespoons of the batter into the bowl of flour. Cover dough with flour and then using floured hands, shake the excess flour from the dough and pat them into thick patty shapes. Cook them about 3-4 minutes per side or until each side is nicely browned.

Serve with toppings. Fresh fruit, jam or jelly, sour cream or powdered sugar are a few options.

If you are unable to control yourself and eat more than three of these cheesy pancakes plan on an afternoon nap.

11

PHILIPPINES

EXOTIC AND POOR

The taxpayers of the United States financed my first trip abroad. Sweet deal, huh? When it was clear that I would be drafted into the army, and then very possibly given the opportunity to serve in a combat situation in Vietnam, I headed to the local military recruiting center. After weighing my options, I enlisted and committed to serving four years in the U.S. Air Force.

Soon after that decision, I found myself boarding my first ever flight for the trip to basic training. When finished with basic, I received orders for my first duty station, an airbase in Shreveport, Louisiana. Then, after two years at Barksdale, AFB, I received orders to report to Clark AFB in the Philippines for an eighteen-month tour of duty. Feeling excited and apprehensive, I headed home for a week of leave, before making my way to California.

My flight for Clark AFB left from Travis AFB in northern California. My first overseas flight was on a commercial airliner contracted by the US military to fly troops overseas. Because I was traveling to the other side of the world, two refueling stops, in Hawaii and Guam, were required during the twenty-hour flight.

Once the plane landed in the Philippines, it was clear I had traveled to a place vastly different from home. I disembarked from the plane, via metal stairs, and was soon standing on the concrete tarmac. A scorching hot sun radiated heat up from the concrete and the humidity level made it feel like August back home in Illinois. I squinted while peering up at a bright blue sky filled with enormous white puffy clouds. Then up ahead, fronting the passenger arrival terminal, I could see a row of elegant palm trees. I had been transported to a faraway and strange land.

Following my orientation, I was assigned my place in an airbase barracks. The barracks was a long single-story building. It was divided into sections, or cubicles, by rows of lockers, and within the cubicles were beds. I was assigned a bed and a locker. This would be my home for the next eighteen months.

I was also informed that for five dollars per week, I would have access to the shared services of a Filipino house boy. He would make my bed, wash, and change the bedding, wash my clothing, shine my shoes, and maintain the cleanliness of the barracks. This meant I only had to report for work, five days per week for eight-hour shifts, and that was it. Sweet deal, I thought. I soon recognized that my houseboy, and hundreds of other Filipinos, entered the base daily to perform the low-skilled jobs that keep the base functioning.

My house boy was not a boy, but a grown man who looked to be in is early thirties. In addition to taking care of many of my needs, he helped me understand that different people have different realities. My first lesson occurred when Neil Armstrong was about to set foot on the moon for the first time. A friend, who had purchased a small twelve inch black and white television, set it up on a table in his cubicle. As a few of us hovered around the television anticipating the astronaut stepping from the lunar module and onto the surface of the moon, my houseboy walked by.

I excitedly called him over and said, "Watch this, he is going to step on the moon!"

He quickly stated, "Not possible," while shaking his head. Then, while looking at me like I had just arrived from the moon, he walked away.

My workplace on the airbase was alongside the busy airfield where military airplanes of all shapes and sizes landed and took off. One morning as I walked from the office building to a refueling truck, a group of groundskeepers sat eating their lunch nearby. Eight small, wiry, darkly tanned men sat squatted in a circle. As I watched them, they opened their banana leaf-wrapped lunch packets of rice and fish and used their fingers to eat. In my line of sight, directly behind them, an example of modern technology, an F-4 Phantom jet fighter, taxied by on the tarmac. This juxtaposition reinforced the reality that we came from two different worlds.

The work I performed in the Philippines, refueling airplanes, mirrored the work I performed while stationed in Louisiana. The airbase, designed and setup to be a slice of America in a foreign land, occupied twelve square miles. Many on-base amenities provided for the day-to-day shopping and entertainment needs of the airmen stationed there. At a base exchange I could purchase food, clothing, cameras, stereo equipment, and the latest rock and roll albums. An airmen's club, a place to hang out with friends, is where I went for musical entertainment and drinks. Sitting up front, while listening to a jazz quartet and sipping a glass of scotch whiskey, was an enjoyable evening. Outdoor activity options included golf, swimming, tennis, trap and skeet, and horseback riding. I could have spent my entire eighteen-month tour of duty on the base without ever leaving. But an interest and curiosity about what lay beyond the airbase main gate always pulled at me. As a result, friends and I often left the sterile environment of the airbase to explore a world much different from our homes in the U.S.

Whenever I exited the base main gate to enter Angeles City, the smell of things to come attacked my olfactory senses. The unmistakable aroma of raw sewage accompanied me as I departed the pristine base with manicured lawns, and paved roadways lined with palm trees, and entered a scruffy city with open sewers and dirt roads. First to greet and accost me as I exited were the money changers, holding large rolls of cash, who offered Philippine pesos for U.S. dollars. The time of day often dictated where and how I might spend the new wad of pesos in my pocket.

During the day I could visit skilled tailors and shoemakers who occupied open front retail stores along the main street of town. The baggy military issued fatigues that arrived with me in the Philippines soon hung in my barracks locker collecting dust. I replaced them with custom tailored form-fitting uniforms made by skilled tailors. I also purchased and wore a matching custom-made hat, with side embroidery that depicted two small flowers and the words "Flower Power." Wearing that hat allowed me to stage my own daily war protest while refueling planes supporting the Vietnam War.

I certainly did not need, nor did I ever think I would own, custom handmade dress shoes. Yet soon after standing and watching craftsman convert flat pieces of leather into beautiful leather shoes, I found myself standing barefoot on a piece of cardboard while a cobbler traced the shape of my feet. A few weeks hence I picked up my black winged-tip shoes.

During those daytime visits to town, it became clear that most of the people who lived around the base struggled to get by and lived very poorly. The economic viability of the town, and its residents, depended on the discretionary income of the personnel stationed on the airbase. This fact was highlighted each night when the town took on a different aura.

The products and services offered after dark revealed the darker side of Angeles City. As friends and I walked down the street both the loud music emanating from open front shabby bars, and the prostitutes who worked there, beckoned us to enter. Music drove my decision making. Some of the cover bands who regularly played the bars contained extremely talented musicians. Within weeks of a new album release they would be skillfully playing the hit tunes from it. After a few local San Miguel beers, I would close my eyes and believe I was listening to the Beatles, Jimi Hendrix,

Cream, and the Doors perform live. The musicians had that much talent.

After our night of rock and roll, we began heading back toward the base main gate. As we walked, street vendors would shout, "Balut, balut." I never consumed enough beer to have the courage to eat one of those boiled duck eggs that contained the fully formed duck embryo. Instead, to absorb the beer and fill my stomach, I often purchased a small bag of bread rolls from a vendor. Made with milk, and sweetened with sugar, the tender still warm balls of bread finished the night like a dessert ends a meal.

My walking excursions into town provided a different view, but not an accurate view of the Philippines and its people. The airbase influenced and tainted the town and residents of Angeles City. Within a few months of my arrival, friends and I began to plan weekend getaways to explore the real Philippines.

Manila, the capital and largest city on the island of Luzon, where our U.S. airbase was situated, was our first travel destination. We packed some civvies and boarded a local train for the fifty-mile trip to Manila. As the train approached the outskirts of Manila, from my window seat I observed more than one gated community. They were like fortresses with concrete block walls topped with barbed wire and protruding shards of glass. Then as the train began to slow the housing became very dense and different. I now peered into huge slums of makeshift ramshackle housing. Open sewers, discarded trash, and scores of dirty, poorly dressed young children added to the sad scene. The contrast in housing was a visual socioeconomic lesson about the disparity of wealth. I grew up in a large family without discretionary income but peering into those massive slums redefined my definition of poor.

During our time in Manila we arranged to take a boat to the Island of Corregidor, a site of military significance during WWII. We sat on bench type seats in the back of a jitney, a local shared ride vehicle, to get to a small bay. Jumping from the back of the jitney I could see the area was a dirty backwater of Manila Bay. In the stagnant smelly water were three small outrigger canoes. One of them would transport us across Manila Bay to Corregidor Island. As I climbed into the narrow canoe, I felt like I was heading out on an exotic adventure. Then, the boat operator started the noisy, smelly engine and we were underway. As we chugged across the large bay, with the water no more than six inches below the sides of the boat, I noticed there were no life preservers. This was exotic and risky, I thought to myself.

After a twenty-minute trip we disembarked from the canoe. For the next two hours we walked around and viewed the remains of buildings, massive gun emplacements, and the large tunnel where thousands of U.S. soldiers sought refuge before the Japanese took control of the island. Looking back from this point in time, I now realize I visited that WWII site just twenty-three years after the end of WWII. As a nineteen-year-old, twenty years seemed like a lifetime.

Tours, organized by an on base service and a local bus company, made seeing the Philippines easy. On one excursion, I visited the Manila American Military Cemetery, where over 17,000 American soldiers are buried. I exited the bus at the entrance of the cemetery and walked to a large monument erected to honor those who lay in rest. I climbed the stairs to the monument and from that vantage point I looked out, and as far as I could see the terrain was covered in geometric rows of white marble crosses. No joy, only lessons to be learned, can come from visiting such a sad place. It was a sobering experience that reinforced my rationale to avoid the draft, and two years in the Army, by enlisting in the Air Force for four years. Visiting these WWII sites instilled in me the obligation to question the reasoning of politicians who drag our country into wars on foreign soil.

On our return trip from the cemetery, we stopped to observe a local cultural happening, a Sunday afternoon cockfight.

Stepping from the bus, I could see a four-sided weathered open wooden structure about the size of a small house. It was a little stadium with wooden bench seating, about eight rows high, on all four sides of a dirt floored cockpit where the fighting cocks would do battle. Filipino men, holding their colorful prized roosters in one hand, while stroking their back with their other hand, stood around waiting for their chance at fame and riches.

Before entering the arena, I first smelled, and then observed, a food stand where two whole pigs spun on wooden spit poles over beds of hot coals. Lechon, or roasted whole pig, is a Filipino special occasion dish. As pork fat dripped onto the hot wooden embers it filled the air with an irresistible smell. Passing, I stopped and stared at the deep mahogany red skin of the roasting pigs. I had never seen anything like this. I wondered if they would be cut up and served before our bus departed. I hoped so.

It appeared that going to cockfights is what Filipino men did on Sunday afternoons for the only women observed on my way to the seating area were two women processing the losers in a small stall, below the stands. They dunked the dead roosters, who had lost their fighting spirit, into a vat of boiling water before skillfully plucking and eviscerating them. The smell of wet, hot feathers and chicken entrails dampened my appetite.

Our bus driver had informed us that we would see fighting cocks, not just any barnyard rooster, in action. They had been bred, raised, and pampered by their owners until the age of two. He even claimed that some men took better care of their fighting cocks than their children. As I passed by some men holding their roosters, they reminded me of people who carry their small dogs. Just like dog owners, these men stroked the backs of their animal to calm them.

I stopped to watch one man prepare his bird for the upcoming fight by carefully tying two upward curved metal spurs, or small knife blades, onto the rear of the rooster's legs; right where the natural bony spurs are located. By nature, fighting cocks are aggressive and want to fight each other for dominance. They display their hostility by flying at each other while lashing out with the spurs on the back of their legs. Adding a three-inch razor-sharp metal spur, alongside their natural one, turns them into killing machines.

After walking into the seating area at cockpit level, I climbed some stairs and took a seat near the top of the small stadium. Then, when two men entered the cockpit holding their birds, the place erupted with shouting. Suddenly everyone in the seating area began yelling and making hand gestures to place bets with numerous bet-takers. After the betting finished and the pesos had changed hands, the bird handlers moved to opposite sides of the cock ring. A man who served as a sort of referee then signaled them to release their birds.

Once set onto the ground, both fighting cocks stretched by elevating their heads to reveal their full splendor. Their feathers caught the sunlight and became an array of iridescent blues, browns, and blacks. Atop their heads, the brilliant blood red comb and wattles seemed to pulse. They were edgy, and they knew what was up for almost immediately they saw each other, and the fight began. With their neck feathers flared outward, they ran toward each other, while flapping their wings to get airborne. Unlike a boxer who leads with gloved hands, these fighting cocks lead with their feet. As they flew toward their opponent their legs lifted upward until the bottoms of their feet almost faced the sky. Then, while airborne, they violently thrust their legs down, trying to jab the three-inch-long metal spurs into their opponent before they dropped to the ground. When they hit the ground, both birds retreated, and then almost instantly ran toward each other to repeat the attack. This repetitive sequence of violent acts happened so quickly the birds were a blur. Over and over, they thrust their metal weapons at each other until one of them lay on the ground bleeding, seriously injured, and unable to continue. When it ended, I gasped for air. I had been totally mesmerized.

The fight had lasted less than thirty seconds. The loser's handler, who had moments before proudly set his bird down to do battle, picked up and carried the now limp bird below the stands to be stitched up or plucked and readied for the stew pot. The winner's handler walked over and picked up his still bristling and strutting fighting cock. He then proudly stroked the back of his bird to bring him down from a fighting cock's version of an adrenaline rush.

Not every place I visited with friends on our weekend excursions had historical or cultural significance. One location, a beach front resort on the Lingayen Gulf, made me completely forget about the military while spending time there. The resort, located on an endless stretch of white sand beach, resembled a 1970's one-story motel. To be truthful, it really was not a resort by today's standards, for there were no amenities or activities provided. It really was just a motel, with food service, located on an amazing stretch of tropical beach. The people who owned and operated the place were friendly, kind, and happy to see us. The food was good, mainly because it was not from the base chow hall, and it was served by smiling staff. The view left and right, from my resort lounge chair, revealed only palm trees, gentle waves slapping the sandy shoreline and the bluest of skies filled with billowy white clouds. This idyllic location provided a place to escape from work and just relax. Friends and I would spend our time bodysurfing, laying on the beach or just doing nothing.

Since we did not have a car, and there were no restaurants around, we ate all our meals at the resort. At breakfast, when I saw someone eating a bright orange-fleshed oblong shaped fruit, that I had never seen before, I asked what it was, and the waitress said, "It is papaya, would you like to order that?" I did. My first bite revealed a texture like a melon but a taste that was completely new and unusually good.

A Filipino dish I ordered for lunch, and loved, were small fried eggs rolls called Lumpia. They contained ground pork, shrimp, and vegetables. A plate of Lumpia, and a cold bottle of locally brewed San Miguel beer, made a great beach lunch every day of my stay at the resort.

One afternoon, we hired an outrigger canoe to transport us out to some coral reefs located off the beach in front of the resort. The service also provided the masks and snorkels that would be required to view the reefs and the fish species that populated them. As the low draft boat skimmed over the turquoise blue water, I thought I saw something break through the surface and glide forward before disappearing into the deep. This caused me to focus on the water's surface just ahead of the boat's bow.

"Look, flying fish!" I shouted to my friends.

Again, and again, small flying fish broke through the surface. The bright sunlight reflected and refracted off their translucent wings creating small rainbows of color that lasted until the fish submerged below the waves.

As the boat slowed and stopped over the reefs, my friends and I donned masks and snorkels before entering the placid water. Not being a swimmer, the reason I joined the Air Force rather than the Navy, I stuck close to the boat and clung to the outrigger while peering downward. What I observed looked unworldly, beautiful and unlike anything I had ever seen. Colorful coral and fish filled my downward view. I wished I could dive down for a closer look, but my inability to swim kept me dangling from the outrigger.

On Sunday afternoon, when we boarded a train to return to the airbase, I reflected on the fact that getting away from the airbase exposed me to a different side of the Philippines. The locals here at the beach had been friendly, helpful, and smiled readily. Or, even more noticeable, they paid us little heed as they went about their business. They seemed untarnished and real. As I watched flooded rice paddies and fields of tall sugarcane flash by the train window, I contrasted them with the people of Angeles City. The airbase, and the wealth that flowed from the main gate and into the community, had corrupted many of the people who lived there. I began to understand that the ever-present, in-your-face hucksters and prostitutes outside the main gate did not represent most of the people of the Philippines. They represented an anomaly to the kind, gentle and helpful people I had interacted with during my weekend away from the base.

A different view of Angeles City revealed itself when I went into town for a Good Friday procession. The Spanish, who had colonized and then ruled the Philippines for over 300 years, forced the Catholic form of Christianity on its inhabitants. Some of the current day faithful, I had been told, would parade through town on Good Friday either carrying large crosses or practicing self-flagellation.

Bloody spectacles attract onlookers. I stood amongst them along a dusty dirt road with my 35mm Pentax SLR camera in hand, waiting to record the unique event. Looking up, while waiting for the procession to appear, I thought that the crystal clear sunny blue skies seemed like part of an inappropriate stage set. Cloudy and gloomy seemed more appropriate.

The crowd ahead of me began to tighten up as they shuffled forward toward the roadway. They raised their heads, and all peered to the right, indicating they had a view of the oncoming procession. Soon enough Filipino men began to parade by. Most of the marchers had white clothes over their heads, and many wore a symbolic crown of thorns. Some strained to carry large wooden crosses on their shoulders while the trailing end of the cross left a zig-zag track in the dirt roadway. Other marchers kept a sort of macabre rhythm as they beat their own backs with a flog. Attached to the handle of the whip were multiple cords. Each cord had a triangular wooden block dangling from its end. As they approached, I watched their forearms and hands move left and then right causing the wooden blocks to rhythmically slap their backs. Then, as they began to pass my position, I could see their bloodied backs. Each time the wooden blocks struck their back; blood trickled from small self-inflicted cuts.

Occasionally they stopped, knelt on the roadway, and bowed their heads in silent prayer. As I stood there transfixed by the bloody show, I remembered the camera hanging around my neck. I raised it, peered through the viewfinder, and snapped some photos to record the actions of people I could not comprehend.

A unique opportunity to closely interact with a Filipina occurred when I enrolled in an art class. The University of the Philippines offered some on-base courses, including the watercolor painting class

I signed up for. Taking an art class, something I had never done before, seemed risky, but the instructor quickly put me at ease. A talented watercolorist, who readily shared her knowledge, guided me and the other students through multiple projects. She was about sixty years old, gentle, kind, and talented. I sat mesmerized as she painted demonstration pieces in just a few minutes, using free flowing stokes of brushes dapped in watercolor paints. It seemed effortless for her, and that bolstered my confidence. It was an inspiring learning experience, and like all artistic endeavors which focus your mind on creating something, a great escape from reality.

My reality, that I joined the Air Force to avoid the draft and duty in Vietnam, resulted in the opportunity to learn about a country and its people. I learned that the people of the Philippines were different from me because of their socioeconomic conditions, and the political systems that governed their lives.

A military recruiting message I remember went something like, "Join the military and see the world." After my time in the Philippines, I thought the statement should be changed to, "Join the military and begin to understand the world."

LUMPIA (EGG ROLLS)

Ingredients

1 pkg spring roll wrappers (8-inch square)
16 oz fatty ground pork
4 oz raw shrimp, minced
2 cloves garlic, minced
1-inch piece of ginger, peeled and minced
2 t soy sauce
1 egg, lightly beaten
½ t black pepper
4 oz cabbage, thinly sliced

Preparation

Cut spring roll wrappers in half producing 4" X 8" rectangular shapes. Cover with a damp paper towel to keep them pliable.

In a large bowl combine the balance of the ingredients. Using your hands, mix and combine the ingredients to ensure a well-blended mixture.

To assemble, lay a wrapper with its narrow side in front of you. Place one heaping teaspoon of filling two inches from the bottom edge. Lift the bottom of the wrapper and place it over the filling and then roll the lumpia up within 1 inch of the top. Use your finger to wet the top edge before you complete rolling the lumpia to seal the roll. Lay the finished lumpia on the seam and continue rolling until all the filling has been used.

In a high sided skillet heat ½ cup of vegetable oil over medium high heat. When hot, add the lumpia 5-6 at a time. Cook for 3-5 minutes or until golden brown on all sides. Drain on paper towels.

Serve lumpia with sweet chili sauce. For a true Filipino experience, purchase some San Miguel beer, pour one into a chilled glass, and enjoy it with the lumpia.

12

PORTUGAL

GO FOR THE EGG CUSTARD TARTS

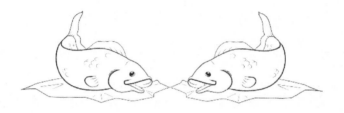

Portugal suddenly made it onto our list of places to visit in 2018 when a client invited me to spend a week training their staff. Sandy decided to accompany me and immediately began researching a ten-day stay following my work week. Then, after we had booked our flights and accommodations, the client backed out of the deal. They agreed to reimburse me for the airfare, and Sandy and I decided to travel to Portugal anyway.

The trip just happened to coincide with the 2018 World Cup soccer tournament. On our second evening in Sintra, a small town outside of Madrid, the Portuguese national team was scheduled to play their archrivals Spain. When I asked where I might view the match in a setting with some local residents, a hotel clerk made it clear that taverns and sports bars did not exist in Portugal.

"People will be watching the match at home. But many restaurants will have the game on their television," he informed me.

Since I really wanted the experience of watching the match with Portugal fans, I suggested to Sandy that we eat out and dine close to the match start-time. Based on our hotel staff's recommendation, we made reservations at an upscale, Trip Advisor four-star rated, restaurant just around the corner from our hotel.

After arriving at six o'clock, a courteous staff member, dressed in suit and tie, guided us to our table in an empty dining room. As I looked around the large high ceiling room, I noticed that not only were there no other diners, but there was also no television, so I questioned our waiter.

He responded, "The kitchen staff are from Brazil and could care less about Portugal soccer."

I wanted to say, "But I care."

While we ate, I hatched plan B.

The meal started with sliced seared foie gras on toast and finished with a coffee caramel flan. It was all delicious, but I was distracted. And, since we ordered and finished a bottle of wine with the meal, I was also a little lit. As we prepared to leave, I recalled that the prior night we had dined at a small family run restaurant which had a television in the dining room. To get there required a ten-minute uphill walk along a tree lined winding road. So, I suggested to Sandy that we walk there, have a drink, and watch the second half of the match.

"I am tired, but why don't you go," she said.

We split up. She walked back around the corner to our hotel while I headed toward the restaurant.

After a wine buzz assisted brisk walk, I entered the small family run restaurant. There were about a dozen tables, and diners filled about half of them. While trying to catch my breath, I mentioned my wife and I had dined there the night before and asked, "Can I just order a drink and watch the match?"

"Just give me a minute," was the response.

While I waited, I watched the owners, two brothers, darting back and forth between tables and occasionally glancing up at the television. They both wore unusual brimless hats that were the colors of the Portuguese flag. Red, green, and yellow. One of them then removed a chair from a table, slide it against the wall next to the cash register, and invited me to sit.

I said, "Obrigado (thank-you), Beirao, por favor."

The previous night, I had ordered an after-dinner aperitif. When I had asked for something uniquely Portuguese, the brothers suggested Beirao, which is produced in Portugal. Served over ice, the caramel flavored liqueur, when mixed with fresh lemon juice, was both flavorful and refreshing.

When my drink arrived, I sat back, sipped my Beirao, and watched the balance of the match. Portugal had twice taken the lead only to have Spain score goals to tie the match. Then late in the game, Spain scored again to take the lead. The two owners, and the other diners watching the match, looked deflated. The buzz went out of the restaurant. Then Ronaldo, one of the best soccer players ever, who is Portuguese, yet plays professionally for a Spanish club, was awarded a late game, 88th minute, free kick. It was a moment that promised a fairy tale ending for Portugal. A tie, against the stronger Spanish side, would be something to celebrate. Restaurant service ceased, the two brothers stood transfixed in their supporter's hats, the diners stopped eating, and everyone, including me, watched while hoping for a miracle ending.

Our hopes and dreams came true when Ronaldo, the Portuguese born soccer hero, curled the penalty kick past the defending Spanish goalie to tie the match. The two brothers went crazy. They screamed, shouted, and raced around their restaurant. As they passed me, I stopped them, put my cell phone camera in selfie mode and took a photo of the three of us. The photo shows a brother on each side of me screaming and smiling. Experiencing that Portuguese sporting moment, while sitting in a restaurant in Portugal, is something I will always remember.

Following our stay in Sintra, we hired an Uber driver for the fifty-minute trip to Lisbon. Our new hotel, located on a corner in the busy downtown area, had a small lobby and small guest rooms. All over the world, big cities have small room for big prices. We stowed our gear in the room and headed out for an urban hike. The old part of town, our destination, is located on a hillside. As we made the long ascent up the retail store lined street, we would stop and window shop in order catch our breath. Shortly after we crested the hill and began to descend, I smelled something I had dreamt of eating. Grilled sardines.

Over the years, whenever someone asked me if I had traveled to Greece, I would say "No, but when I do, I plan to sit along the Aegean coast eating grilled fresh sardines while sipping Ouzo." I still have not made it to Greece, but while planning our trip I read that sardines are part of Portugal's food culture. So, I followed my nose to turn my food fantasy into reality.

As we walked toward the aroma, I busied myself taking photographs of yellow street cars, reminiscent of San Francisco's, flowering trees covered in pink blooms, and a panhandler with a small dog, holding a small red tip can in his mouth, on his shoulder. Then on the far side of a crowded plaza, smoke signals led me to a steel grate with rows of fresh silver and black sardines cooking over hot charcoal. Their dripping juices hit the hot coals and vaporized into thick aromatic smoke. I breathed in the heavenly aroma, snapped a few photos, and then asked the staff for two seats. The seating, small metal chairs at a communal table, was outdoors with shade provided by tall old trees and large red umbrellas. When our food arrived, Sandy enjoyed her bowl of caldo verde, a local kale soup, while I peeled back the skin and flesh from six seven-inch-long grilled sardines, and washed down the delicate grilled fish with an ice-cold Sagres beer.

"Take Greece off of our list of countries to visit," I said to Sandy as I settled the bill.

"What, why?", she responded.

"Because my grilled sardine dreams have been fulfilled here in Portugal."

Another specialty food served all over Portugal is the Pastel de nata, or egg custard tart. They are small round custard filled pastries that look like miniature custard pies. I became aware of them before we departed home when I searched the internet to learn about the specialty foods of Portugal. They made it to my mental list of "foods I must eat" while there. Then as we continued our walk, we noticed a pastry shop with window displays full of them. We stopped, purchased two, and then oohed and aahed with each bite. Based on their small size, smooth luscious egg custard and crispy crust, it was easy to overconsume them. During our stay in Portugal, four of the six hotels at which we stayed, included them as part of the breakfast buffet, which is why the previous sentence is oh so appropriate. Although, I would always stop eating them when the wait staff gave me dirty looks.

A business acquaintance, Manuel, who lives in Setubal, a coastal city located south of Lisbon, invited us to share lunch and visit his "neck of the woods." I know that is a cliché, but that is what he said! We made the decision to use public transportation, which meant we would have to switch trains for the final leg to Setubal. As our train pulled into the station where we needed to change trains, I pressed the button located by the exit doors and naturally expected them to open so we could get off. They did not. I pressed the button again and again, and one last time as the train started to pull away from the station. Since I did not know any Portuguese swear words to respond to the situation, I instead tried to remain calm.

We departed the rail car at the next stop through a different exit door. We then walked through the small rail station and to the street outside, where I opened the Uber app on my smartphone and summoned a car. A few minutes later, we left for the Setubal train station in the back of somebody's sedan.

As Manuel, our host, pulled up in front of the station we jumped into his car. He then drove us out of the city and up to the top of the tall bluffs that run all along the coast north of Setubal. There we visited the remains of a local historical site, the Forte de Albarquel. The clifftop location provided great views of the coast and expansive white sand beaches below. He then told us he had arranged lunch for us at one of his favorite small family run restaurants in town. He chose it because they prepared local specialty dishes that he wanted us to taste. As we entered, Manuel introduced us to the owner of the small eight table place who greeted us warmly. Soon a bottle of local red wine, produced with a blend of Negra Mole and Castelao grapes, which thrive in the sandy southern coastal region of Portugal, was poured. After we raised our glasses and shouted, "Saude," the first dish arrived. A large platter of delicate little clams that had been quickly sautéed in white wine, along with aromatics like garlic and parsley, was set in front of us. Eaten with crusty bread to mop up the sauce, it was the type of dish I could pick at, while drinking wine, for an entire afternoon. The sauce tasted of the sea and fresh herbs.

Next, the owner proudly set a large casserole dish filled with seafood rice on our table. His version of the Portuguese specialty, which is like a soupy risotto, featured monkfish, monkfish liver, tomatoes, onions, garlic, and bay leaf cooked in a seafood broth. It was a soul satisfying dish, the Portuguese equivalent of comfort food. One ingredient, the fish liver, was a new eating experience for me. Eating the liver reinforced my belief that you should try everything, but you may not be that fond of some things you try.

After our leisurely lunch, Manuel drove us north along the coast. We parked at a high point along the coastal cliffs to enjoy and photograph the expansive ocean views. After Sandy took a photo of Manuel and me, we both thanked him for sharing his knowledge of the local culture, historical sites, and local food with us. He then drove us back to the train station.

We will always remember his kindness and generosity. He lives in a beautiful "neck of the woods," and invited us to return as we said our goodbyes in front of the train station.

After our three day stay in Lisbon, we hopped a train going north. The next stop on our itinerary was a small coastal beach town called Nazare. We arrived mid-afternoon via a local bus caught at our train departure point. As we pulled our luggage toward our beachfront hotel, it was evident that this historical fishing village was now a tourist destination. The beautiful beachfront area was lined with gift shops and restaurants.

The morning after our arrival we walked to a city market housed in an old spacious warehouse building. As I walked up and down the aisles with the local shoppers, displays of fresh fish, meats, vegetables, flowers, and bakery products made me wish I lived in Europe where these markets are commonplace. We appeared to be the only western travelers in the building. By now that was not a surprise, for wherever we traveled in Portugal we did not see many western tourists or travelers. I had read that that was the case, and our first six days, in which we visited five different locations in Portugal, confirmed it.

Always on the lookout out for unique and local food offerings in markets, when I saw an elderly lady selling balls of fried dough at the end of an aisle I stopped. Unable to ask about them in Portuguese, I used open hands, hunched shoulders, and a puzzled look instead. She reached behind her counter, lifted a large orange fleshed squash, pointed at it and then to the fritters.

"Fritters made with squash; I am going to get a few," I said to Sandy.

I pulled out some cash and purchased four. As I bit into the first plum-sized, orange-colored sugar-coated fritter, I was hooked. The deep-fried, moist pastries must have been made just before she left home for the market. After Sandy and I finished them off, I walked back to her stall. She displayed a sincere and knowing smile as I gushed sign language compliments about their goodness.

Since we had booked two nights in Nazare, the next morning I walked back to the market hoping to eat a healthy breakfast of squash fritters. Being Sunday, the market was noticeably different. Many of the vendor stalls remained closed or empty, and the hum of commerce witnessed the previous day had gone silent. I searched all the aisles but could not locate her.

When we returned home, I searched for and found an online recipe for Filhoses De Abobora (squash fritters). I know they will never be as good as the ones eaten in the Nazare market, but I will make and eat them again. And as I bite into the first warm fritter, I will fondly remember the smiling face of the lady who made and introduced me to them in Portugal.

On the next segment of our Portugal trip, we spent the good part of a morning on a train going up the Doro Valley. There, in a small riverside town, we rented a car to explore the region where the grapes used to make Port wine are grown. Port wine is a fortified wine that has been produced in and around the city of Porto for over five-hundred years. As we drove around the Doro valley, the area reminded me of other wine growing regions I have visited, Napa in California, Chianti in Tuscany, and Adelaide in Australia. They are all rural and dotted with small towns.

We checked into a rather worn old hotel, in another riverside town, and the next morning caught a ferry boat up the Doro river. The sloping hills that ran down to the river, on both sides of the valley, were completely covered in vineyards. From the boat, while sampling port wine, we observed the advertising signs of large port wine producers, like Grahams, Dow and Taylor dotting the hillside vineyards.

One of the reasons we rented a car for two days was so that the next morning we could drive east to the Spanish border. There we visited a museum, and then with a guide descended a trail down to the Doro riverbed in a remote area. Our objective was to see the simple drawings of animals that had been scratched into vertical stones alongside the river over 10,000 years ago. These drawing were discovered about the same time a large construction project, to dam the Doro river and flood the area, had begun. Due to the public outcry to protect this historically significant site, the dam project was scrapped, and the museum was funded. As I viewed an ancient carving of an antelope, it made me realize that the length of my life-time, in its total, is insignificant, and I must keep traveling and living life to its fullest while I still can.

After leaving the museum, we drove back to the town where we had rented the car, dropped it off and walked to the train station to purchase tickets to get to the next stop on our itinerary, Porto. While trying to communicate with the clerk in the ticket office, a local man intervened to clarify, in Portuguese, what we had asked for. It turned out the clerk was trying to inform us of the fact that we would have to switch trains, down the line, to get to Porto. Now it was clear we would also have to purchase our tickets at that distant station for the final leg of the journey. We then purchased our tickets, thanked them both and headed for our train platform.

The gentleman, who had interceded on our behalf, boarded the same train, and sat near us. When we arrived at the first stop, he immediately guided us to the ticket counter, explained in Portuguese that we needed two tickets to Porto, and then directed us to the correct platform. We felt as if we had our own personal travel agent and thanked him over and over for his kindness. He smiled an unassuming smile, shook our hands, and then disappeared.

Our train arrived mid-afternoon in Porto. Just before stepping out onto the street we stopped in the exit vestibule to admire multiple historical scenes made from painted and fired blue and white tiles. After turning on a map app, we realized our hotel was located directly up a steep hill from our current location. We stopped to window shop, code words for "catch our breath," as we struggled to walk uphill to the hotel. Turning a corner, we could see it was located on a city center plaza with locals going about their daily business, a few vendors selling street food, and a lovely old church with blue and white tile decorations on the exterior.

Porto is an old port town built on hilly terrain. Its claim to fame is port wine. All the major producers of that fortified wine have their bodegas (cellars) located here. Producers like Sandeman, Graham and many more, are positioned along the riverfront and up the hillside. During one of our three days in Porto, we paid the fee to tour through the Sandeman bodega to both sample and learn about the differences between the sweet, fortified tawny and ruby port wines. I have been drinking and serving these complex sweet wines after dinner parties for decades, with or as the dessert course, so it was fun visiting a bodega.

Old European towns always have large old stone churches. In Porto they are symbolic remnants of Portugal's glorious past when they sailed the world, established colonies, and gained superpower status. As we visited the church at the rear of the plaza, just outside our hotel doors, we noticed a flyer for a classical guitar concert to be held that evening and purchased tickets. We arrived and walked into a rather dark church. With the lights off, the only light entering the church were the last remnants of daylight, from a cloudy and overcast day, that bled through the old church windows. The barely visible guitarist, wearing black, entered and took his seat up front. As he began to play hauntingly beautiful music, a single spotlight illuminated his hands as he skillfully worked the strings to play classical pieces and pop hits such as "Yesterday," by the Beatles. I sat transfixed in my seat until the concert ended and the lights were switched on to break the magical spell.

On my 'must eat' list while in Porto was a famous sandwich that originated there. It is named the francesinha, or little Frenchie. The word "little" and this sandwich really have nothing in common. Eating one of these 1,300 calorie concoctions for an early dinner caused me to sadly pass up the egg custard tarts at the next morning's breakfast buffet.

An online search located a small restaurant, just two blocks from our hotel, that specialized in francesinhas. When the young university student waitress took my order and asked, "Would you like French fries with the sandwich?", the answer seemed, well obvious. What else would I eat with a sandwich called the little Frenchie? When it arrived at the table, I moved my chair back and stood up to get a complete view. Two more steps backward and I was able to get the entire sandwich framed within my cell phone's screen for a foodie photo. Looking back, I guess I could have used the "Panorama" setting.

Feeling like I was back in my high school biology class dissecting something, I began to prod and poke the large, layered concoction, to discover its make-up. Between two thick slices of square white bread was a butcher shop assortment of meat. Roast pork, cured ham, beef steak and Portuguese sausage. Slices of melted yellow cheese completely covered the square shaped architectural structure, which had also been doused with a beer and tomato sauce and topped with a fried egg. Sitting on a full-sized round dinner plate it looked like a large yellow box floating in a pool of sauce, surrounded by French fries. Sandwich, 1300 calories, fries, 400 calories. Hmm, since I had already eaten breakfast and lunch, I may have exceeded the recommended calorie intake for the day. But I did show some restraint. Five French fries remained on my plate as I waddled from the restaurant.

Portugal should be on everyone's travel list. It is less crowded and touristy than its neighbor Spain, and therefore the people we interacted with were less jaded. Most everyone was genuine and helpful. I did gain weight during my visit to Portugal and blamed those egg custard tarts. I would suggest their tourism commission adopt this phrase to attract travelers. "Come for the egg tarts but stay for the friendly and helpful people."

PASTEL DA NATA TART (EGG CUSTARD TART)

Ingredients

Crust:

1 cup all-purpose flour
¼ cup powdered sugar
¼ t salt
½ cup unsalted butter
¼ t vanilla extract

Filling:

3 T all-purpose flour
1-1/4 cup milk, divided
1 cup plus 2 T sugar
1 cinnamon stick
2/3 cup water
½ t vanilla extract
6 large egg yolks, whisked

Preparation

Heat oven to 350 degrees. In a mixing bowl combine the flour, powdered sugar, and salt. In a small saucepan melt the butter. Add the vanilla to the butter, stir and then add to the mixing bowl with the flour mixture. Stir mixture to incorporate the butter evenly into the dough.

Press the dough, using your fingers, into an 9 or 10 inch tart pan with a removable bottom. Ensure the sides are thicker than the bottom. Place the tart pan onto a baking sheet and bake for 10-12 minutes or until the crust is set. Cool the tart shell.

Raise oven temperature to 450 degrees. For the filling, mix ¼ cup milk with the flour until smooth. Add sugar, cinnamon, and water to a saucepan. Bring to boil and cook, without stirring, until an instant read thermometer reads 220F.

In a second saucepan scald 1 cup of milk and then whisk it into the flour mixture.

Remove the cinnamon stick from the syrup, and pour, in a thin stream, into the hot milk and flour mixture. Add the vanilla and whisk the mixture for a few minutes to cool it. Next, add the beaten egg yolks and gently whisk until well combined. Pour the mixture into the tart shell and bake for 15-20 minutes or until the custard top begins to brown.

Cool on a rack. Cut into wedges and serve with fresh fruit.

*Warning: The small tarts in Portugal were addictive.

13

AUSTRALIA

A LONG COMMUTE

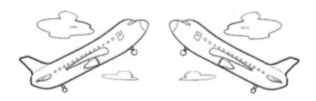

W hy would anyone want to endure twenty hours of travel, eighteen of those hours on an airplane, to go anywhere? Well, because that is what it takes to get to work in Australia. I have traveled to and from Australia for consulting work eight times since 2010. My travel always begins with a four-hour flight from Chicago to LA. Then a minimum two-hour layover in LA followed by a 12 to 14-hour non-stop flight to Australia. Of course, my flight crosses the international date line, which means a day of my life temporarily disappears.

To help myself understand that the trip really is not that difficult, I simply reflect on the first Europeans who made the trip. They sailed from England and spent the next three months on wooden ships, probably barfing their guts out, before making landfall at Botany Bay. So, as I sit in my seat watching movies, drinking red wine, and eating multiple meals, I tell myself, "Stop whining, and enjoy the journey."

Australia is the country that most reminds me of the United States because of our common language, and the fact that, compared to European countries, we both have short histories. Geologically it is incredibly old. An Australian mate once said, "It is an old worn out country. No majestic peaks like you have in Rockies, only worn out nubs on top of our hills."

On a few of my business trips my wife Sandy accompanied me, and we stayed to vacation after I had completed my work. On our first trip to Australia together, in 2011, we booked four nights at a hiking lodge near the Great Ocean Road located on the southern coast of Australia. On each of our four days, we section hiked a portion of the Great Ocean Walk trail, with a guide, before returning to the lodge to eat and sleep. The trail first opened to the public in 2006 and the lodge owner recognized a tourism business opportunity.

A man in his late thirties, who left a role in the corporate world to start this new venture, picked us up at our hotel in Melbourne and drove us to the hiking lodge. After checking in, we headed to our room to unpack. It was in a prefab modular building, that was rectangular, understated, and was a nice fit, architecturally, in the wooded setting. The sliding glass door entry to our room faced a natural wooded area providing a great view of a peaceful and serene setting.

One of the staff at the hiking lodge, a Vietnamese immigrant chef, prepared all the meals. The food he prepared always contained some bright Asian flavor elements like chiles, fresh coriander, ginger, citrus, and shallots making it interesting, flavorful, and delicious. He and the other staff served our breakfast, usually a hearty bowl of oatmeal, and evening meals featuring entrées like fresh local lamb and seafood, in a common space where we sat with the other lodge guests. Our pre-made lunches, that we enjoyed on the trail, consisted of a plastic container filled with a grain like brown rice or quinoa, combined with vegetables and herbs, along with fruit and a granola bar.

Another hiker, a retired school principal from the Sydney area, had also requested a guide. So, along with our guide, a young Australian lady, he joined us and became our hiking companion for four days.

The first morning, after eating breakfast, our guide distributed hiking gear that included backpacks, raingear and gaiters, protective fabric covers to seal the area between our pants bottom and the top of our hiking boots. Our guide informed us the gaiters would keep sand and gravel out of our boots. Then, along with Katie, our guide, we all piled into a van and headed to the trailhead.

The Great Ocean Walk trail covers sixty-five miles of varying terrain. At times, the trail bends along the high cliff tops overlooking the Southern Ocean. At others, it meanders along the sandy beaches below. We planned to hike six to nine miles daily. This meant we would walk approximately half of the trail's total distance during our four days of hiking.

Australia is a land with one hundred different species of poisonous snakes, twelve of which can kill you. As I put on my gaiters each morning, I wondered if they might also protect us from slithering creatures. I never found out, for we did not encounter any snakes during our four days on the trail. Although I did come across a bloodthirsty hazard. Leeches!

While slogging up a steep section of the trail, that took us from beach level to a cliff top, our guide Katie calmly said, "Hang on Bob, you have something on your leg." She then reached down and pulled off three leeches who had attached themselves to my calves.

As I continued to make the step climb, I commented, "They used to call that bloodletting. I wonder if it will make my tired legs feel any better?"

"If it does, I want some leeches as well," said my Australian hiking mate.

The weather was springtime cool and mostly sunny for the first three days of hiking. On Day Four I switched from shorts to long pants for the weather forecast predicted high winds and rain blowing off the Southern Ocean. Sandy, keenly aware of the fact that Antarctica was the next land mass south of our current location, elected to stay at the lodge and drink hot tea.

Our hiking guide, upon hearing that Sandy had backed out, looked at me and my Sydney hiking partner and asked, "So mates, do you still want to hike today?" We gave her the answer she may not have been hoping for.

"Sure," we said in chorus. "What's a little wind and rain?"

We donned full rain gear and jumped into the van.

Hiking along the ocean on sunny clear days offered great views and the warmth of the sun. When we stepped from the van to begin our last day of hiking, we knew this section was not only the most difficult, based on the hilly terrain, but also the longest. Under gray skies, we trudged forward along the high cliff tops while horizontal rain, driven by forty mile per hour gusts off the Southern Ocean, pelted us. At the end of our nine-mile hike, I began to get a sense of what hypothermia meant and felt like. My teeth were chattering, and my body was shaking as I climbed into the warm van. The steaming hot cup of tea, poured from a thermos by the van driver, was the best cup of tea I have ever sipped.

Following our hiking adventure, the lodge provided transportation back to Melbourne, where we spent the night in a B&B, and then on Sunday morning left to catch a train for Adelaide.

My golfing buddies have given me the nickname, "One beer Bob." It is appropriate since I rarely drink while on the course, but will have just one good craft beer in the clubhouse after playing. Well, as I stepped onto the late Sunday morning train in Melbourne, I decided to have a beer because it was my birthday. When I asked, a member of the train staff informed me they could not sell beer until we crossed the state border, and entered the state of Southern Australia, because sales of alcohol are restricted on Sunday in the state of Victoria. I tried to sound like an Aussie when I replied, "No worries mate."

Staring out the train window, as we traversed the outback, I saw a lot of sheep and something I never expected to see, rabbits. The train passed a few fields that literally had hundreds of rabbits feeding on the foliage. As I dreamt of a delicate rabbit stew flavored with fresh thyme, my wife went to the dining car, and to my surprise came back with a bottle of pale ale. Apparently, we had crossed the border. As I sat there sipping my birthday beer, a Kiwi (a person from New Zealand) sitting near us, who had overheard that it was my birthday, walked up, wished me happy birthday, and handed me a beer. Twenty minutes later the train manager, who had filled my wife's beer order at the bar, walked up, said, "Happy Birthday mate," and handed me a beer. "One beer Bob" was overwhelmed with beer and gratitude. The Aussies and Kiwis are a friendly lot who are quick to chat you up and include you in social gatherings.

While on a business trip to Melbourne my host, and friend, Victor asked, "Would you like to go to a footy match?" He explained footy, or Australian Rules Football, was a uniquely Australian sport that was a cross between rugby, soccer, basketball, and U.S. football.

"Sounds entertaining," I said, "Count me in."

Two nights later, I met Victor and his friend at our predetermined meetup location, the Member's entrance at the MCG (Melbourne Cricket Grounds). The MCG is a massive round multi-use stadium that seats over 100,000 sports fans. I was impressed that his friend, an MCG member, had access to this special entrance. Impressed until an old guy, in a wide brimmed Australian outback-style hat, stopped me on the way in and noted, "You cannot enter."

"What did you say?" I responded.

Once again, he stated, "You cannot enter. You do not have on a collared shirt. Members must have collared shirts."

My host quickly interceded, "He is from the United States. He had no Idea about the collared shirt rule."

The old guy in the hat stood his ground. "Does not matter. No entry without a collared shirt."

He then pointed out that I could go to one of the many concessions outside the stadium and purchase a footy logo shirt with a collar. I grabbed a ticket, told my mates I would meet them inside, and hurried to purchase a shirt. This was a quarterfinal match and the concession stand sold apparel for the two teams about to face each other. I choose the Geelong Cats shirt, simply because I thought it looked better. After pulling off the tags, I slipped it over my collarless shirt and was now a Cats fan. I then walked past my antagonist, found my seat, and cheered wholeheartedly for the Cats even though I did not fully understand the rules of the game.

At a break in the game Victor asked if I would like a meat pie.

"Meat pie?" I asked.

"Yeah, that is what we eat at footy matches," he noted.

"What about hot dogs, have those?"

"No, but I could get you a sausage roll," he responded.

"I will try the meat pie, please."

He returned with a calorie laden, pastry lined pie filled with bits of tender beef suspended in a lot of beefy gravy. It reminded me of my mother's Sunday pot roast with mashed potatoes and gravy, tucked into a crust. I enjoyed it, but the food I preferred most while in Australia was seafood.

My work in Australia often finished on Friday, and my flight for home departed on Sunday morning. This left Saturday free to urban hike around Sydney. I began my hike by strolling through the Royal Botanic Gardens, that fronted the Sydney Harbor, and ended near the Sydney Opera House. More than once, I encountered fruit bats roosting in large trees. These twelve-inch long bats spend the daylight hours sleeping, while hanging upside down and intermittently flapping their wings to cool themselves. Occasionally they emitted a screeching sound, which is what first attracted my attention. The first time I walked over to a tree to see what was making the racket, I could not believe what I was seeing. I had only seeing flying fox fruit bats on television and had no idea I would encounter them in Sydney.

Near lunch time, I would always reset my hiking path to take me to the Sydney Fish Market. This sprawling indoor market, located right on the harbor, had the largest displays of fresh seafood I have seen in my travels. The main building of this fish market housed many restaurants along with vendors selling fresh fish. As soon as I arrived, I scanned the broad selection of fish and took photographs. While doing that I searched for the specific fish I wanted to eat for lunch. Once found, I asked the fish monger to prepare the red snapper I had selected for cooking. When finished he placed my prepped whole fish in a plastic bag and handed it to me. I walked about twenty feet and passed it to a cook at a nearby food stall. After relaying my preferred cooking method, I told him I would return in about ten minutes, before walking away to purchase my side dish: a cold beer. I returned with a craft beer, brewed by Little Creatures Brewery, picked up my pan-seared snapper, and looked for outside seating. Then as I sat there in the warm sun, overlooking the fishing boat lined harbor, I squeezed lemon juice over the delicate fish and tucked into my simple and delicious lunch.

On another business trip, I flew from Melbourne to Brisbane and arrived midday. By the time my taxi dropped me off at my uninteresting suburban hotel, I was ready for lunch. The hotel staff, when asked, directed me down a street, toward town, where they said I would find some restaurants. Many large towns have a "Chinatown" area, but I stumbled upon "Indiatown." I walked past numerous large Indian restaurants and was drawn to a ridiculously small place because of a chalk board sign, hanging from a horizontal piece of rusted steel angle iron, in front of the place. On it was written, Masala Dosa.

A masala dosa is a large, almost crepe like, pancake made from a batter of soaked, pureed and slightly fermented rice and lentils. Before the cooked dosa is rolled up and served with dipping sauces, its center is most often filled with crushed potatoes and peas spiced with chili, turmeric, and fenugreek. As I stood there dreaming of this delicious Southern Indian vegetarian dish, a lady in a sari approached me from inside. When I asked about the availability of the dosas, she responded with a head waggle that could have meant yes, no, maybe, or something completely different.

Then she said, "No, but we are serving a thali plate, would you like that?"

I responded with an enthusiastic, "Yes!" and turned to follow her.

A thali is both a round metal serving plate and the name of a meal served on the plate. A thali meal is a balanced meal composed of many small dishes that provide the taste of sweet, salty, spicy, bitter, sour, and astringent to the person eating the meal. The meal is often served in small metal dishes set onto the thali plate and can be meat based or vegetarian.

As she led me into the long narrow restaurant, I immediately noticed it contained no tables. The seating, benches with a narrow table surfaces, reminded me of picnic tables that had been sawn in half lengthwise and the halves pushed against the walls. As I took my bench seat, I noticed two older Indian men leaning over their thali plate meal and eating with their fingers. I felt excited. This was going to be an authentic Indian dining experience.

A second sari-clad middle-aged lady approached and set a vivid green banana leaf in front of me. My authentic Indian plate, I thought. Then, the lady who had greeted me at the door approached carrying a large stainless-steel tray holding many small containers of food. She set the tray down and rotated the banana leaf 180 degrees so that the stem end was facing to my right. Later, I read that the stem, or larger end of the banana leaf, is positioned to the right because the rice will be set at that end of the leaf and it takes up a lot of space. The rice is on the right because those who eat with their hands, which is the custom in India, always eat with their right hand.

The first item she spooned onto the leaf was a salty condiment commonly called a pickle.

She then looked at me and asked, "Do you know why the pickle is served first?"

I replied, "No, why?"

She explained, "Pickle is very salty and will make you salivate, which will prevent you from choking on your food."

Next, she spooned something into a small plastic cup and as she set it on the leaf she commented, "And this is your dessert. It is served next because we should always remember that life is sweet."

I sat transfixed. She had, with the food, drawn me into her culture. Five more vegetarian dishes were spooned onto my banana leaf followed by a large pile of fragrant basmati rice topping with a sauce flavored with a garam masala spice mix.

Before departing, she looked at me with a twinkle in her eyes and softly asked, "Would you like a fork?"

"Yes, please," I responded.

As I sat there enjoying a wonderful meal, I began to understand I was not in a restaurant. No menu, except for the chalkboard sign outside, existed. I felt like I was sitting in her kitchen eating food she had prepared for me. I felt cared for and dare I say loved, which is an uncommon experience in a restaurant. When finished, I returned the joy she had given me by telling her how wonderful the food and dining experience had been. She displayed a shy smile while her head waggled in appreciation.

This is the fourth book I have authored. The first two are technical books that relate to my consulting business. The courage and inspiration to write something with a broader appeal occurred to me on a flight from Melbourne to Sydney. As I took my seat next to a woman, I asked her, "How is it going?" In the States, I would have asked her, "How are you doing?", but I was in Australia. Funny how some nuanced differences in language usage had rubbed off on me. She turned out to be as chatty as me, so we talked for the duration of the flight.

She told me she had attended a non-fiction writer's conference in Melbourne to try and find a publisher for a manuscript she had completed. She had written about a heinous crime. After obtaining all the police records, she wove her story around those factual documents. I explained that I had written a couple of technical books, which is why I was in Australia working, and had often thought about writing about some childhood experiences. She encouraged me to join the organization, Creative Non-Fiction, that had sponsored the conference.

When I returned home, I did join and then about six months later began to seriously write a memoir about growing up as a baby boomer. For the next year I wrote and re-wrote the manuscript before self-publishing, *BoomHood – A Baby Boomer's Free-Range Childhood*. Funny that a lady on a plane in Australia inspired me to write a memoir. When you travel inspiration is all around you.

My most recent trip to Australia was in the fall of 2019. As I sat at the Sydney airport, waiting for my flight home, I decided to spend, rather than carry home, the Aussie dollars in my wallet. After looking over the pastry selection in a coffee shop, I decided to purchase a few to take home and share with Sandy, who had not accompanied me on this business trip.

I asked the clerk, "Are any of your pastries uniquely Australian?" He responded, "Yes, lamington cakes." "Great, I will take two to go please."

I carefully placed the paper bag, containing the two small cakes, at the top of my backpack and headed home. I arrived there about two hours after I departed Sydney, for I gained back the day I had lost crossing the international date line. It was late afternoon when I walked into the house. After a light dinner, I pulled the lamingtons from my backpack, and we enjoyed our Australian treats made of sponge cake that had been enrobed in chocolate and coconut.

Yes, it is a long trip to Australia. But it is a vast country with much to see and do. I hope to return to explore some of the outback and visit the friends I have made while working there. I now consider them my mates.

LAMINGTON CAKES

Ingredients

5 T butter, softened
1 cup sugar
½ t vanilla
3 eggs at room temperature
1/3/4 cups all-purpose flour
3 t baking powder
½ cup milk
4 cups powdered sugar
1/3 cup cocoa powder
1 T butter
1 t orange zest
½ cup boiling water
¾ cup unsweetened coconut flakes

Preparation

Heat oven to 350 degrees. Grease an 8 X 8 baking pan and line with parchment paper, leaving the edges overhanging to facilitate removing the cake.

In a small bowl, whisk the flour and baking powder together. Using a hand mixer, beat the butter, sugar, and vanilla together until light and airy. Add eggs, one at a time, and continue to beat until the batter is smooth.

Add half of the flour and fold to combine with the batter. Add half the milk and do the same. Repeat with the remaining flour and then the milk.

Pour the batter into the baking pan and bake until a toothpick inserted in the center comes out clean after 22 – 26 minutes.

Let cool for 5 minutes and then lift out by the overhanging parchment paper. Place on a rack to cool completely.

Cut cake into sixteen 2-inch squares using a serrated knife. Place on a plate and freeze cake squares for one hour or longer.

For the chocolate dipping sauce combine the powdered sugar, butter, cocoa powder, orange zest and boiling water. Mix until smooth.

Place the coconut in wide bowl.

To finish the cakes, using two forks dip each one into the warm chocolate sauce to completely coat. Lift them from the sauce and let the excess drip into the bowl before placing them into the coconut. Rotate them to ensure all sides are coated. Place the finished cakes on a rack for 2 hours or until the chocolate has set.

Good luck waiting two hours. The melted chocolate that covered my fingers proved I could not.

14

NEW ZEALAND

GREAT SAUVIGNON BLANC

Before starting some work in Australia in 2014, my wife and I flew to New Zealand for a six-night stay. We decided, when planning the trip, we did not want to try and see both the north and south islands that make up New Zealand. It would be too hectic. Instead we made Auckland, the largest and most populous city in New Zealand, our home base for the entire stay, and took day trips to explore the central area of the north island of New Zealand. To get around, rather than rent a car, we chose to use alternate forms of transportation like ferries and buses.

The high-rise accommodations that we booked, before our departure, turned out to be a nice one-bedroom apartment with a small kitchen. Having a kitchen allowed us to purchase breakfast items at a local grocery store and eat in before we headed out each day. Our city-center location meant an easy six block walk would get us to Auckland's harbor. There we had access to ferries that could transport us to nearby islands.

The morning after our arrival, we walked through the busy downtown area, not unlike other large cities, toward the harbor which was lined with restaurants. When our ferry arrived, we

climbed aboard for a forty-minute trip to Waiheke Island. Our itinerary, a tour of three wineries with lunch at the last one, began
when our pre-arranged guide, a middle-age man and permanent
resident of the island, picked us up, along with six other guests, at
the island's ferry landing. The sparsely populated hilly island was
quaint, and our guide provided a narrative on the islands history as
we drove between wineries. One fact I recall is that much of the
virgin forests that covered the island, were cut, and used for the
main masts on wooden sailing ships. All the wineries we visited
produced Sauvignon Blanc wine. I have learned that any one
winery tour is just like every other winery tour. They all make wine
the same way.

It is the wine tasting that still attracts me to wineries. I always
marvel at their sales technique. I am given samples of wine, sometimes for free and sometimes not, and then as I start to get a buzz on,
they offer to sell me wine. It works remarkably well. At domestic
wineries, I always seem to buy a case, but when I am 7,000 miles
from home, I do not. On this tour and tasting, I really fell for the
Sauvignon Blanc variety of wine. So much so, that my wife and I split
a bottle every night while dining out during our stay in New Zealand.
It has also become my go-to white wine choice because of its dry,
slightly acidic, grassy, and stone fruit (plums, peaches, and apricots)
flavored taste.

The following day, a second ferry trip took us to Tiritiri Matanga
Island. This small island was a unique place for multiple reasons.
There were no cars, only hiking trails, and no permanent residents.
As we walked up the trail, from the ferry landing toward the small
commercial area containing a cafe and gift shop, we caught our first
view of the island's lighthouse. As I photographed one of the most
powerful lighthouses in the world, a black and white stripped missile
shaped structure, a few large flightless Takahe birds appeared. They
paid little attention to us visitors as they roamed the grounds looking
for things to eat. I, of course, pursued them, trying to get the perfect
photo of a very unusual chunky bird that was the size of a large

chicken. It had purplish-blue-green feathers and a large beak topped with a red section above the eyes.

Before continuing our explorations, we went to the café and ordered flat whites (coffee with milk) and took seats at a small table to enjoy them and the silence. Silence is so rare in a world where the hum of vehicular traffic is almost always in the background.

Feeling rested, we hiked trails to a few different locations on the uninhabited island and ended up on a secluded beach all by ourselves. Sandy and I sat there for an hour watching the gentle waves lap the shoreline. A few shorebirds marched back and forth on the beach looking for a meal, while I tried to capture them in the perfect photograph. As we began our walk back towards the dock to catch the return ferry, the purpose of this lovely island became clear. To slow people down and let them enjoy nature. It had worked.

A fond New Zealand food memory is of a salad ordered at a fine dining restaurant in Auckland. The harborside eatery had outdoor seating that provided a wonderful view of the sailboats that lined the harbor. The salad, which I ordered for my starter, was composed of both cooked and raw beets. Colorful fresh beets, red, yellow, and candy-striped varieties, had been sliced extremely thin using a kitchen mandolin. They, along with some fresh greens and paper-thin slices of crispy croutons, were plated on a pure white plate and dressed with a light vinaigrette. When the plate was set in front of me, because we were seated outdoors, the brilliant clear sunlight illuminated the beet slices like pieces of stained glass. That rainbow-colored salad tasted even better than it looked.

I had heard about New Zealand green mussels for years. These large mollusks are endemic to the island and a large aquaculture industry ensures a steady supply. Early in our trip, we ordered them at a waterfront pub. The huge mussels arrived at our table in a metal bucket with their cooking liquid made of white wine, cream, fresh herbs and of course, the juice the mussels release when their shells opened during cooking. I had ordered mussels elsewhere in the past and before I felt satisfied, only empty shells remained. Not this time.

We feasted on the plump mussels and the broth, that we mopped up with crusty bread. When we could not eat any more, some of those meaty monsters remained in the bucket, proving you can make a meal of mussels.

Another tasty treat, not found back home at the time, was discovered in a food store while purchasing items for breakfast. Rhubarb yogurt. I have always loved the taste of rhubarb desserts because of the perfect combination of tart and sweet they deliver. My love for that flavor combination began when, as a child, I would dip stalks of fresh rhubarb, pulled from the garden, into a cup of sugar. My love affair with rhubarb continued my whole life. Each spring when rhubarb breaks through the ground to announce the spring season, I make at least one rhubarb crisp. So, the next morning, when I mixed some granola with that rhubarb yogurt, I honestly believed I was eating a dessert.

To explore another area away from the city of Auckland, we signed up for a one-day bus tour, which included a visit to some geothermal hot springs and a Maori cultural site. Every time I agree to take a bus tour, taking the tour reinforces why I do not like bus tours. After visiting the geothermal springs, which I found unique and geologically interesting, we headed to a Maori cultural center, a place intended to help the Maori preserve their cultural heritage and practices. As I sat and watched the loincloth clad middle age Maori men, and a few women, perform their dances, which included the ancient war dance, the haka, I saw joyless dancers, dancing for money. I left feeling sad that these staged performances existed, and I felt guilty. Tourists perpetuate these cultural re-enactments, and today I had sat there as a tourist.

A few days later, we packed up our possessions and took a cab to the airport. While waiting for our departure flight, I looked through a shop that contained sports apparel, and tried on an All Blacks logo jacket. The New Zealand national rugby team, the All Blacks, is a big deal to the people of New Zealand. The team, named the All Blacks because their uniforms are black, have a worldwide reputation for being winners. The jacket fit perfectly and was nicely tailored, so I purchased it as my New Zealand trip remembrance gift.

The following year I was wearing the jacket while walking in Times Square, in New York City. A young African American man, who was hawking tickets to a play, read the logo on my jacket, All Blacks, and asked me, "So, do you like black people?"

I do not think he knew what the logo represented, but I made eye contact and responded from the heart, "Of course I do."

In the fall of 2019, I found myself back in Auckland for two days of work. My gracious host Peter, who had taken me to dinner on the two previous nights, asked me to join him again on my last night. He had selected a modern, upscale, and relatively new Italian restaurant. As we walked in, I was struck by the sound within the restaurant. The place was full of young professionals who were drinking, laughing, and sharing stories which created a vibe or buzz that brought life to the restaurant. I immediately knew what they already felt – this is an above average restaurant with exceptionally good food. I could not wait to eat.

We ordered a bottle of local red wine and both looked over the menu. Missing were the traditional pasta and tomato sauce dishes. Unusual items, like the one that interested both of us, roasted shoulder of locally raised lamb, filled the menu. The lamb dish was listed as a share plate, suitable for two people. Since we both loved lamb, we ordered it and then continued to enjoy the full-bodied Shiraz wine as we talked about life.

My expectations for this meal were a few slices of tender moist New Zealand lamb. What arrived caused both of us to exclaim, "Wow!" Sitting on a wooden cutting board was the entire shoulder of a lamb. It had been slow roasted to perfection for the meat looked like it was ready to fall from the bones. It reminded me of the best slow cooked beef pot roast, only better. The succulent meat had been garnished with a smear of green sauce composed of parsley, garlic, and olive oil. We both ate more than our fill and were sadly forced to decline the offer of a dessert menu. If the quality of a meal is judged by how many times the eater tells others about the meal, then this meal was indeed special. That lamb, accompanied by local kumara sweet potatoes and a lovely green salad, would make the 7,000-mile return trip to New Zealand a worthwhile effort. Oh, and if you go, also order a good bottle of Shiraz. It paired perfectly with the lamb.

ROASTED LAMB SHOULDER

Ingredients

3-4 lb. bone in lamb shoulder
Olive oil
Salt
Black pepper
4 cloves garlic slivered
Sprigs of fresh rosemary
1 cup water

Preparation

Heat the oven to 325 degrees. Place the lamb shoulder in a roasting
pan with high sides. Coat the entire surface of the lamb with olive oil
and then with a generous amount of salt and pepper. Using the tip of
a paring knife poke 10-12 small vertical holes into the top surface of
the meat. Insert into each hole a sliver of garlic and a piece of rosemary. Pour the 1 cup of water into the base of the pan before using a
lid or heavy foil to seal the top of the roasting pan.

Roast the lamb for 3-1/2 hours. Raise the oven temp to 425 degrees, remove the lid or foil, and cook the lamb for another 20 minutes to brown the top.

Let sit for twenty minutes. Serve with your favorite sides and a great bottle of red wine.

You might wonder where you can purchase a shoulder of lamb. An alternative to flying to New Zealand is to visit a local middle eastern grocery store that sells halal meat. They will take good care of you.

15

GERMANY

I LOVE MOHNKUCHEN

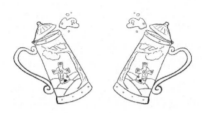

My friend Dusty, who first encouraged us to travel to Europe, has lived in Germany most of his adult life. During those years abroad, he would always return home for the month of December to catch up with family and friends. So, despite the physical distance for most of the year, our frequent get togethers while he was visiting, maintained and nurtured our friendship. As a result of our friendship, when Sandy and I have visited Germany, we did not tour Germany to see the sites. We have instead stayed at the home of our friends, Dusty and his life partner Ulla, located in Bonn. There, we would just hang out together, catch up on life and occasionally take a day trip via a local train. Not much different than our relationships with friends at home, except for the travel time to pay them a visit.

During a 2012 visit, we accompanied them to a festival of cultures. Immigrants from around the world, who resided in and around Bonn, gathered in a park to share the songs, dance, and foods unique to their cultures.

Since Dusty had spent time in Ethiopia, during a stint in the

Peace Corp, we found ourselves watching and talking to a group of Ethiopian and Eritrean men and women. As Dusty engaged the men in conversation, like they were old friends, I watched as the ladies prepared coffee the way it has been done in their homeland for hundreds of years.

In a flat pan held over an open fire, green coffee beans were stirred constantly to prevent burning. Once the beans turned dark brown, and shiny with oil, one of them used a mortar and pestle to crush them. Next, a lady wearing a long brightly colored, yellow, red and blue dress, along with a cream colored sweater and headscarf to ward off the cool morning air, poured the course ground coffee and water into the small opening at the top of a decorated reddish brown fired clay pot used only for this coffee ceremony. It had a round bulbous base, a vertical long narrow straight spout, and a side handle. Minus the handle, it stylistically reminded me of a vase used to hold a single rose. The pot was now placed over the hot embers of the open fire to boil the coffee. As Dusty continued to chat up the men, the rest of us, and the empty small white ceramic serving cups, waited for the coffee.

As I stood there, I envisioned people patiently waiting, in a long line of cars at a Starbucks drive-thru, for the coffee to boil. The attendant would then announce, "The coffee has boiled and will now be set aside for five minutes to allow the grounds to steep in the hot liquid and settle to the bottom." Obviously, this coffee ceremony was not about a quick cup of Joe.

When finished, the lady in the headscarf smiled as she poured the steaming hot coffee into the serving cups. I accepted mine in both hands, brought it to my nose and detected the smell of strong coffee and more. It also had the aroma of a cultural tradition where families gather to celebrate special occasions. Feeling fortunate, I thanked each of them, as they flashed brilliant smiles, for the authentic Ethiopian experience they had shared with us.

As we continued our walk through the park filled with food

booths and entertainment stages, I noticed a food stall full of ladies, all wearing red tops. Walking closer, I saw their quick to smile faces and a whole pig roasting on a spit, and I felt a connection to my past. Inside stood about fifteen Filipina women serving the foods of their country. I had been stationed in the Philippines for eighteen months while in the U.S. Air Force, so the familiarity of their smiling faces and lively banter drew me toward their booth. As I shouted the Filipino greeting, "Mabuhay," their faces lit up. Within two minutes, I was in the food stall surrounded by my new friends, so that Dusty could take a photo to record the special moment. After the photo session we purchased some lumpia, or spring rolls, that they were assembling and frying. As I bit into their crisp exterior and tasted that great flavor combination of pork and shrimp in the filling, I was transported back to the Philippines. As I walked away, I thought about how the world continues to shrink for those of us who see the world as one. One place, one people.

I have something in common with the German people, and probably many eastern Europeans. A love of mohnkuchen, or poppy seed pastries. Growing up, I enjoyed an eastern European poppy seed pastry (potica) my mother would make for the Christmas or Easter holiday. To recreate the taste of my childhood, a few years back I purchased a poppy seed grinder, that had been made in Czechoslovakia, and ten pounds of poppy seeds via the internet. Prior to buying the grinder, I tried using other devices to break or grind the seeds to extract their flavor. Nothing worked. In a food processor, the seeds that are the size of a pin head, spun as if caught in a tornado but survived the experience unharmed. My attempt at using a grain mill also failed when the small seeds just fell through the mechanical crusher. The grinder I purchased was purpose built to do the job. And it is quite a job. I enlisted family and friends to help rotate the little handle of the grinder for a total of five hours to dispatch my ten pounds of seeds. Their payment, for helping, came in the form of poppy seed potica.

On my first trip to Germany, my friend Dusty and I walked into a local bakery. I stood looking over their selection of sweets when I noticed a sweet roll that appeared to have a poppy seed filling.

"Hey Dusty, is that what I think it is? A poppy seed pastry?"

He responded with, "Yeah, that is mohnkuchen. It is sold all over Germany."

"No kidding," I said excitedly. "What does it take to become a German citizen?"

Dusty always attempted to deepen my cultural experiences, so he prodded me by saying, "Order one using German, I will tell you what to say."

I knew my German vocabulary consisted of hallo, ja, and kein, so I said, "Come on, just order it for me."

"No, you can do it," he continued.

So, as he whispered in my ear, like a ventriloquist standing next to a big dummy, I repeated the words, "Einer mohnkuchen geback, bitte." The clerk rewarded me with a delicious poppy seed pastry.

As I bit into the sweet buttery pastry filled with that unique earthy flavor of poppy seeds, I turned to Dusty and said, "You know, I was not kidding about German citizenship."

He looked at me and laughed.

A few years later, I was traveling to Ukraine and had an overnight lay-over in Munich. It was mid-afternoon by the time I had checked into my airport hotel. After receiving instructions from the hotel staff, I caught a local train into city-center for an urban hike. As I made my way down the Kaufingerstrabe, a wide pedestrian-only street, I saw the retail stores were closed because it was Sunday. In the U.S., stores are open every day of the week, but in Germany that is not the case. It appeared I would miss the Weihnachsmarkt experience by just a few days, for I observed workers erecting Christmas Market stands along both sides of the street. But not everything was closed. It was a cool late November afternoon and the smell of hot coffee coming from a coffee shop, with a display case full of pastries, drew me in. As I walked in, I glanced at the pastries and was immediately frozen in my tracks. There, on display, sat a tray of mohnkuchen. I resorted to sign language to point at and order a slice to go with my coffee. Stores closed; Christmas market not opened yet. I did not care, as I strolled down the leaf littered strabe eating mohnkuchen and sipping coffee.

As the sky began to darken, I caught a train back to the airport. When I disembarked, I followed airport signage toward my hotel. While passing an open area in between airport buildings I came across an area strung with overhead lights. Under the lights were vendor stands and joyous travelers walking through a small German Christmas Market. The smell of warm glühwein (mulled wine), grilling sausages, beer, and gingerbread filled the air. Strolling through the market, while eating a Nurnberg-style (very thin) bratwurst on a bun, I was happy to have not missed the Christmas market after all.

On another visit, we rode a train to Dusseldorf with our German friends and their dog. Germany is unique, for leased dogs are allowed on trains and in restaurants. Their dog, a Jack Russel terrier named Indie, like most terriers, had a feisty side. But since he was deaf since birth, he often seemed a bit aloof and at times calmer than most terriers.

Not far from the train station exit there was a food vendor selling sausages from a trailer. Ulla asked, "Have you ever had a currywurst?"

Being a bit of a smart-ass, I responded, "No, but I would prefer a currybest."

They both laughed and Ulla shouted, "You should try one."

So, Sandy and I shared and enjoyed the unique taste of a bratwurst topped with a curry flavored ketchup. As I was eating my half, I noticed Indie was quite attentive. He sat looking at me intently, and occasionally cocked his head to the side. If he were my dog, I would have thrown him a piece of sausage, but he was not, so I avoided eye contact while finishing my sandwich. Then as we walked away, Indie kept looked back and he seemed to give me the evil-eye.

We headed toward, and then strolled along, Dusseldorf's most famous shopping street, Konigsallee. There were few people since It was Sunday, and the retail stores were all closed, as is the custom throughout Germany. After about an hour of walking we all agreed to stop for a light lunch. As we ordered and ate, Indie curled up under the table and was calm until another terrier arrived two tables down. Like all dogs, he was territorial and fussed a bit until we departed.

Once outside we followed a tree-lined walkway along the Rhine river. The river was wide, like Mississippi river wide, with a strong flowing current and a few commercial boats, used to move goods up and down the river, anchored along the far shore. As we walked Indie was given a long lease so he could expend some of the pent-up energy the other dog had aroused. As we walked along, he rummaged around an area with large trees and returned holding one end of a foot-long stick in his mouth. He dropped it near me, as if asking me to toss it, so he could retrieve it. Sandy was quicker than I. She grabbed the other end of the stick and gave it a fling.

Immediately she said, while looking down at her hand, "That stick had mud on it."

Then upon closer inspection, and a whiff of something unpleasant, she shouted, "That is not mud, it is dog shit!"

The rest of us tried not to laugh, while she used tissues and bottled water to clean up.

As Indie scampered in front of us I thought I saw him glance back with a sly smile on his face. Can dogs hold grudges? Maybe I should have given him a bite of that sausage.

In 2010, after spending five days in Paris, Sandy and I took a train from Paris to Cologne. Our friend Dusty, who had taken a train from Bonn, stood waiting on the train platform when we arrived late in the morning. After hellos and hugs, we stowed our suitcases in an automated storage unit and went for a walk. Since this was our first visit to Cologne, we decided to look around and eat lunch before we all caught a train back to Bonn. As we exited the train station, the massive gray gothic Cologne Cathedral stood right in front of us, so we decided to pay a visit. Although built to impress, after visiting large cathedrals like this one in Cologne, I always leave unimpressed and thinking the construction money could have been put to a better use, like feeding the poor for one-hundred years. As we departed, we discussed our lunch options and decided to eat in a nearby restaurant that served traditional German dishes simply because we were in Germany.

I was familiar with the menu for it mirrored the offerings at German restaurants in the U.S. I had a taste for pork, and ordered the pork hock, with some sauerkraut and spaetzle on the side. I often try and match my drink with the cuisine, so I ordered a local Kolsch beer. I was expecting a gigantic mug of beer like those served at October-fest. Much to my surprise, my beer came in what I would describe as a juice glass. Just as I was adjusting my size expectations, the pork hock arrived. Holy hog, the previous owner of this hock must have been a giant. The mass of meat filled the platter, and some remained when I struggled to get up and leave.

Our German friends have practiced yoga for decades, so during one of our visits we went with them to their health club. We waited in a lobby area while they did whatever you do in a yoga class. When they finished, they introduced us to a couple of friends from the class as they walked through the lobby. One of them was a lady who had been born and raised in Columbia and then emigrated to Germany a few years before. I was aware of a Columbian chicken soup dish called sancocho, so I used that information to engage her in conversation. While we talked, my friend Dusty talked about a Columbian bread she had made and contributed to a yoga class get-together. She said it was a cheese bread, a specialty from Columbia called Pandebono. As she described the ingredients, two types of cheese, farmer's and feta, eggs, along with corn and tapioca flour, Dusty fondly recalled the soft chewy texture of the delicious bread. I wrote down the name, Pandebono, before she departed and told her I would make them when I returned home. I did, multiple times. The ingredients, mentioned above, are combined in a food processor. The moist dough is then formed into balls, about the size of a golf ball, and baked. The pandebono were, as Dusty said, soft, chewy, and salty. A perfect appetizer with a chilled glass of white wine or a cold crisp beer. Every time I have made them, I thought about, or shared the story with friends, of the Columbian lady who shared the recipe in Bonn, Germany.

MOHNKUCHEN (POPPYSEED CAKE)

Ingredients

1 cup butter, softened
1 cup sour cream
1-1/4 cup sugar
2-1/2 cups all-purpose flour
1 can (12.5 oz) poppy seed pastry filling
1 t baking soda
4 eggs, separated
½ t salt
1 t vanilla

Preparation

Heat oven to 350 degrees. Grease and flour a 12 cup Bundt pan. In a stand mixer bowl beat the butter and sugar until light and airy. Add the poppyseed filling and beat until well combined. Add the egg yolks, one at a time, and beat to incorporate before adding the next egg yolk. Add sour cream and vanilla and beat to combine.

In a separate bowl, add and whisk the flour, baking soda, and salt. Then, add flour mixture gradually to the mixer bowl containing the batter and beat well after each addition.

In another bowl, beat the egg whites until stiff peaks form. Fold them into the cake batter before pouring and spreading the batter into the prepared baking pan.

Bake for 1 hour or until a toothpick inserted in the center comes out clean. Cool for 10 minutes before removing from pan. Cool completely and serve with a dusting of powdered sugar. Call me when it is ready to eat. I would love to join you for a slice.

16

DENMARK, SWEDEN, AND NORWAY

CARING COUNTRIES

S candinavia has always appealed to me because of the way they look after their citizens. I am not sure if this general statement is true in all three countries that we visited, but the higher taxes paid by everyone provide guaranteed pensions, childcare, lengthy maternity leaves, medical care and other social benefits that take much of the worry out of everyday life. No place is perfect, but countries and governments that place the care of their citizens ahead of shareholder value, appeal to me.

Visiting these three Scandinavian countries during a single trip provided a throwback European travel experience. That experience, using a different currency in each country, reminded me of my travel in Europe prior to the establishment of the single currency European Union. Luckily, many or most transactions were completed using a credit or debit card, so having enough of the local currency became a non-issue. In addition, ATM machines made it easy to access the local currency when needed.

We began our adventure in Copenhagen, Denmark. To get to city-center from the airport, we took a train that transports airline passengers back and forth every twenty minutes. Exiting the railway station, I was taken aback by the number of bicycles jammed together in long lines in front the building. I occasionally have trouble finding my car in parking lots, so I wondered how someone would find their bicycle in the seemingly disorganized mess of bicycles. As we walked the half mile to our hotel's location, light traffic, and the absence of car parking lots near the station, confirmed that walking and bicycling appeared to be the norm in Copenhagen.

The hotel's business model aligned with a concept we observed in other Scandinavian cities in which we stayed. Old office buildings had been converted into hotels with small rooms, low room rates, and few staff. For instance, we were greeted by an iPad, for self-check in, when we arrived. This budget hotel concept was great because it reduced the cost of travel in countries known to be expensive for travelers. Our room was small, sparsely decorated and furnished, but adequate.

My first memorable food experience occurred early the next morning when we went down for the breakfast included in our hotel reservation. It was all self-serve, including cleaning up after yourself when finished. Reminded me of eating in a college cafeteria. The only staff I noticed replenished food items as required.

The breakfast offerings were distinctly un-American. No scrambled eggs, pancakes, sweet sugary breakfast cereals, oatmeal, or biscuits and gravy. Instead, set out on the counters, I viewed hard boiled eggs, muesli, hearty whole grain breads, cheese, sliced ham, and the star of the show, a large rectangular loaf of liver pate. I am a big fan of chicken liver pate and liver sausage, so I immediately made myself an LPJ (liver pate and jam) open-faced sandwich using a thick slice of multigrain bread and some strawberry jam. That concoction, with two cups of coffee mixed with hot milk, was a soul satisfying way to start the day. It was so good; I ate the same breakfast the next two days.

Keenly aware that I was visiting the home of Danish pastries, I kept an eye open for a bakery. After urban hiking a section of the city near a large attraction, Tivoli Gardens, we stopped mid-morning for a coffee and a Danish. The pastry shop, because of its proximity to the large tourist attraction, was most likely there to serve the tourists. It was spacious, but without many tourists inside it felt empty when we entered. We ordered two cinnamon Danish pastries and coffees. Sometimes a local food experience, eating something unique to a country or area while you visit, exceeds the quality of the food. The pastry was light and airy but was missing the flavor of butter. I would have liked more cinnamon as well. It was not nearly as good as the LPJ.

The following day, after taking a tourist boat excursion around the waterways of this city bordered by water, we headed to Tivoli Gardens, a large and incredibly old amusement park complex first opened in 1843. This amusement park was unlike any other. It was not Six-Flags. It truly was a garden with tree lined walkways that led us under trellises covered in blooming vines. Well-maintained blooming flower beds caused us to stop and stare. It reminded me of a Disney theme park except this was real. The amusement rides all appeared to be many decades old, but beautifully maintained. Walking through the area, the screams of children reminded me of how much my stomach dislikes amusement park rides. We continued our stroll and then stopped for cups of tea. At an outdoor stage we stopped and watched youthful ballet dancers perform. And of course, I took photographs. Tivoli Gardens was an enjoyable escape to the past.

Our next stop was Stockholm, Sweden. After a shuttle bus ride from the airport to a city-center bus terminal, we knew we had to catch a regional bus to get to our hotel. Our guidebook instructions told us the bus number, but we were uncertain about the bus boarding location, and where to get off once we were on. As we stood beside our luggage, studying a bus chart, a stranger offered their help. After he looked at our hotel's address, he guided us to the correct bus boarding and departure location. I shook his hand and said, "Tack," before he departed. We climbed aboard the bus when it arrived. I shared the map, with our destination noted on it, with the driver, and asked if he would tell us when to get off. He did, and as we jumped off, I shouted "Tack!"

Our hotel's location was across a bay from the downtown area of Stockholm. Most of the neighborhood surrounding the hotel contained new high-rise apartment buildings. Based solely on the number of new buildings it looked like an area that had been redeveloped. After our hotel check in, we went for a walk to find a place to have a light lunch. As we stepped into a local sandwich shop my eyes were drawn to a tray of pastries. Among the selection, I spotted a pastry that resembled a sailor's knot as large as my fist. The surface of the torturously wound and knotted half-dome shape was covered with what looked like crushed cardamom.

"Excuse me," I said excitedly. "Is that cardamom on this roll?"

The shop owner nonchalantly replied, "Ya."

Cardamom is an expensive spice. Ranked third after saffron and vanilla beans. Rarely used in baked goods in the U.S., it is a baking staple in Sweden. My familiarity with cardamom came from cooking Indian cuisine, so I always keep some in my collection of spices. It is a citrusy spice that has an alluring combination of sweet and spicy flavors. When I add cardamom to glazed baby carrots, diner guests always ask, "What's that flavor?"

My response is, "Just a minute."

I walk into the kitchen, grab a green cardamom pod from a spice jar, remove the black seeds from the pod and throw them into a small mortar and pestle. After crushing them to release their fragrance, I walk back into the dining room, hand them the pestle, and say, "Smell this, that is cardamom."

"Wow, that is a unique smell," is the common response.

I am not sure they understood I had just taken them on a cultural journey to India, where most cardamom is cultivated. For just a minute, we had been "Bumping & Snacking" together.

So along with our sandwiches, I convinced Sandy we needed to order the cardamom roll. As I ate that pastry, the uniquely fragrant smell and complex taste of cardamom created a lasting food memory.

I have no idea what sandwich I ordered and ate that afternoon in Stockholm, but I will fondly remember that cardamom pastry forever.

When we walked the neighborhood, young adults seemed to be everywhere. Over and over, during the day, we observed young men pushing children under the age of two in strollers. At first, we thought they might be unemployed or stay-at-home dads. When we mentioned this phenomenon to a Swede at breakfast the next morning, she explained that all couples receive eighteen months of maternity leave. They can split the leave time as they see fit. Mothers, if nursing their children, often take the first year and the fathers take the balance. I had heard about the social safety net provided by the high-tax Scandinavian countries, and here was evidence.

Museums are places of learning and are always on our itinerary. Visiting the Nobel Prize museum, located in central Stockholm, was a good experience. As we entered, the first thing that drew my attention was a powered rail system that ran above the central display area of the museum main hall. Suspended from clips on the ever-moving automated display were the individual photographs of every recipient of a Nobel prize. The rhythm of the display was hypnotic. I stood there looking up to watch the photos pass by. Most of the faces scrolling by were strangers to me, but two of my personal heroes, Mother Teresa, and Bob Dylan, made me reflect on their impact, and then smile as they passed by.

I found the backstory to the museum interesting. Alfred Nobel, who invented dynamite and other explosives, owned and operated armament factories. After reading his premature obituary, published mistakenly when his brother died, in which he was referred to as the "Merchant of Death," he amended his will. To ensure his legacy was something different than a story of a man who manufactured and sold weapons of war, he designated most of his fortune to establish the Nobel Prize. Annual awards are given to individuals in the fields of physics, chemistry, literature, medicine, and to someone who has worked to build peace. Sweden, a country that cares about its people is known around the world for the Nobel Prize, especially the focus on peace signified by the annual Peace Prize.

Some of the inventions or discoveries that garnered a Nobel Prize for their inventors or researchers, stood on display in the main building. Two struck me. In a small, illuminated display case, maybe eight inches square, sat an old weathered and worn medicine box, alongside a small glass bottle partially filled with a dried yellow powder. On the box was the word, "Penicillin." When thirteen, I contracted rheumatic fever and it was the prescribed penicillin that led to my recovery and prevented any long-term heart damage. Now that was a meaningful discovery that deserved a Nobel prize.

The second item that caused me to stop and read the display placard was a beautiful leather bound 1950's transistor radio. It was on display to recognize the inventors of the transistor circuit. Seeing that small radio, in the brightly lit display case, took me right back to the early 1960's, when I, for the first time, listened to portable rock and roll music.

On another day, we took a 45-minute train ride to visit a Viking museum. We departed the train in a small town with a three-block long commercial area. Knowing we had a twenty-minute walk to the museum, seeing some young Swedish mothers and their children sitting outside at a cafe enjoying pastries and coffees, caused us to take a break and join them. We entered, placed our order, and then sat in the bright sunlight enjoying our coffee and treats while eavesdropping on the conversations around us.

When we approached the museum site, we could see a long low building that overlooked an inlet leading to the Baltic Sea. It had been built to house the long narrow Viking ship on display. We paid the entrance fee to view the ship's wooden remains, which had been recovered from the muddy bottom of a waterway and then reconstructed in the museum.

Leaving the museum, we walked toward some Viking ship replicas floating on display in a small bay adjacent to the museum. One of them, a slight sailing ship equipped with long oars, was available for trips out onto the fjord. We signed up for the adventure and while we waited for the departure time, we chatted up an Englishman who studied Viking history as a hobby.

After educating us on the boat that held around twenty people, we all boarded, and he manned the oar in front of me. After the staff gave us instructions, we put our backs to work and departed the dock. Once clear of the harbor we hauled the long flat oars from the water, raised the sail, and the boat took flight. Everyone in the boat was excited, mainly because we did not have to row, but also because we were under sail. As I sat in cramped quarters enjoying the experience, I snapped a photo of our British mate, whose broad smile let me know he was enjoying the Viking experience. After about ten minutes, the sail was lowered, and the ten people manning the oars were instructed to put their backs to work to get us to the dock. As we disembarked and I stretched my sore back, our British mate asked, "So how did you enjoy that experience?"

"It was fun," I said. "But if I had been a ninth century Viking, I would never have signed up to be an oarsman on a multi-week pillaging voyage to the British Isles."

Following our Viking experience, we caught the train back to Stockholm and arrived hungry and ready for a late lunch. I had read about and seen pictures of smorrebrod but had never eaten one. Now, was my chance. We walked to an open-air market and found a place with a glass display case full of smorrebrod. I stood and watched the staff construct them. They began with a hearty piece of bread, smeared it with butter or mayonnaise, and then topped it with fresh ingredients in a thought-out composition. Small shrimp, sliced eggs, smoked salmon, liver pate, or thin slices of beef were just some of the main ingredient choices that they used to top the smorrebrod sandwiches. They also included colorful lettuce, spinach, arugula, tomato and sprouts in the food art compositions they constructed. After we enjoyed both a shrimp and a roast beef smorrebrod sandwich, it became clear that good quality ingredients, artfully arranged on a lovely slice of bread, should be visible and not covered with a second slice of bread. The opportunity to feast with your eyes, as you consume your smorrebrod, is part of the joy this open-faced sandwich provides.

Whenever we decide to visit what could be called a tourist attraction, we run the risk of sharing our time with large tour groups. Just after we entered a small museum in an old Swedish royal castle, a bus load of noisy Chinese tourists filled the small museum room. Their tour guide must have informed them in advance about the jeweled crown on display in a well-lit display case. They entered the museum with one thing on their minds. The loud crowd swarmed the case with selfie sticks, or companions holding cameras, to have their photo taken in front of the crown. A frustrated museum attendant repeatedly asked for silence, but the tour group ignored, or did not understand, the request. Most of them found no interest in the other remarkable artifacts on display. I found watching their behavior more interesting than the museum.

This Chinese tour group reflected the pent-up desire of a segment of the Chinese society. For the first time they had enough wealth, along with permission, to travel the world and experience the joy of travel. They, like most tour groups, were being ushered from one tourist destination to the next. My guess is they also sought out Chinese restaurants for their main meal. Some tourists from the U.S. eat at McDonalds while traveling in Europe, for the same reason. It gives them comfort. Tour operators ensure their guests see all the main tourist sites. But they fail to provide opportunities for their clients to interact with local residents, and through those interactions, learn about the local culture of the countries visited.

I also find it interesting to observe tour groups and try to guess, from afar, their country of origin. The contrast between Japanese and Chinese tour groups is striking. The Japanese are calm, reserved, and respectful. The Chinese are loud, unaware of social norms and always rushing to see the next tourist spot. The differentiating factors for tour groups from the U.S. and Western Europe is usually the style of clothing and shoes they are wearing. After making a mental guess about their home country, based on their attire, I will walk within listening range to hear them speak, to find out if I was correct. It is a fun travel game.

The final stop on our Scandinavian adventure was Norway. To get there we took the train from Stockholm to Oslo. Its route took us over the mountainous spine that separated the two coasts. The photos taken from the train all appear to be black and white photographs due to the snow and ice interspersed with the rocky treeless landscape at the higher altitudes.

After we arrived in Oslo, we walked about six blocks in a light rain to our hotel. By the time we checked in and stowed our possessions in our room the rain had stopped, and the sun was peeking out. We headed out to stretch our legs and see some of the harbor area. Along one section of the Oslo waterfront, are a line of sixteen old colorful red, white, and yellow buildings that are in everyone's photo collection if they have visited Oslo. They are Oslo's version of New York City's Times Square or San Francisco's Golden Gate Bridge. Lucky for me, when I found the perfect spot to take my photo, the passing dark rain clouds filled the sky above and behind the buildings, while the sun, low in the western sky, peeked out to illuminate the front of the buildings in bright light.

The next morning, we took a shuttle bus to the airport where we rented a car to spend the next five days exploring a fjord region. Driving back through Oslo on unfamiliar roadways with new traffic signs to interpret was a little tense, but once outside of the city the driving became easy for little traffic exists in this sparsely populated country.

Norway may lack traffic, but they do not lack tunnels. The combination of fjords and steep mountainous terrain meant tunneling through the mountains became a preferred method of road building. Some of the newer modern well-lit tunnels extended for six kilometers and accommodated four lane roads. Then there was that other tunnel.

On a beautiful blue-sky day, we drove and then took a ferry to visit a stave medieval wooden church that had been built between 1180 and 1250 AD.

Sandy paid the fee to see the inside, while I photographed the outside. Following the visit, we drove to a trailhead and hiked a steep winding trail to view a seventy foot tall cascading waterfall. It was a difficult, meandering uphill trail, but the views of the falls made it worth the effort. Following our descent, we sat along the fjord, marveled at the still reflective water, and ate apples and granola bars. We then climbed into the car and drove along a gently winding road that followed the fjord shoreline. By driving around the fjord, we planned to eliminate the long wait for a ferry boat which would take us across the fjord. Since it was a bright sunny day, I had on my sunglasses. Suddenly the road veered inland, away from the fjord, and entered a tunnel. Unexpectedly, I found myself driving with the headlights off, into a completely dark tunnel that had no lighting or lane markings. I jammed on the brakes, afraid to move forward.

I shouted, "Holy shit!", while fumbling to find the headlight switch and remove my sunglasses.

Luckily, it was a short tunnel, and soon the light from the exit ahead guided me forward.

Not long after the tunnel incident, we observed a large cruise ship making its way down the fjord.

"That is where all of the tourists are, on the cruise ships," Sandy commented.

"It is a shame they are missing the tunnels," I replied.

We arrived early in the small, picturesque town of Balestrand. We had pre-booked lodging nearby and a trip up a fjord on a local ferry boat. The town sat on a point of land that had deep, wide fjords all around it. Amazing views of mountains, and their trembling reflections in the calm fjords, had me busy with my camera while Sandy looked in a few gift shops. We met up and sat on a bench near a boat slip waiting for our ferry departure time. It was then that I noticed a small boat that had a sign referencing fjord angling. Just a few minutes later, a three-wheeled baby blue antique scooter pulled up near the boat. A sign hanging from a small platform on the front of the scooter read, "Balestrand Fjord Angling." The man who dismounted from the scooter climbed onto the fishing boat and began working on some fishing tackle.

I walked over to the boat and asked, "So what does it cost to fish and how long is the fishing excursion?"

"It is 350 kroner for a two-hour trip," he replied.

"Sounds like fun," I said. "But we have booked the ferry and it will not return until four this afternoon."

"No problem," he said, "I will be here waiting when the ferry returns."

So, when the ferry delivered us back to town, I went fishing on the fjord while Sandy drove back to our nearby hotel. My fishing guide, a tall lanky middle-aged man, grew up in town and pointed out his childhood home as we boated up the fjord. He also worked for the local school district teaching children outdoor and winter survival skills. Not a class I have seen on a school curriculum, but appropriate for wintery Norway.

After we had boated up the fjord, and away from town, he set me up with a spin casting rod and an artificial lure for bait. I have never fished in a more dramatically beautiful place. In the calm reflective waters of the fjord, the surrounding peaks appeared like mirror images floating around me as I cast the bait repeatedly.

While I fished, we continued to talk about families, work, interests, and life in general. When he learned that my consulting practice focused on process improvement and employee engagement, he shared some concerns about his relationship with his school district administrators and his future employment. They had been butting heads and he felt the need to talk about the situation.

After two hours of casting and good conversation, my arms were sore, and our minds were empty. I just sat back and enjoyed the views during our trip back to the dock. There were no fish to clean. But it had been a marvelous outdoor experience shared with a local resident. Like me, he was a hugger, so we gave each other a man-hug while I said, "Takk skal du ha og ha det." (Thank you and goodbye.)

When our time in the fjords ended, we drove back to Oslo and dropped the rental car off at the airport location. We then spent our final two days in Scandinavia exploring Oslo. We visited both an art museum to view the Munch painting titled, "The Scream" and a museum dedicated to the WWII resistance fighters who fought the Nazi invaders. During the morning of our last full day, we used the light rail system to get to the Vigeland Culture Park. The beautifully landscaped park is filled with over two hundred sculptures create by Gustav Vigeland (1869-1943). They are all studies of the human form created from either granite, cast iron or bronze. One stunning granite sculpture, a fifty-foot-tall obelisk, is composed of intertwining human bodies. I loved being in the middle of a park dedicated to art, with people who appreciate art, and I have the photographs to prove it.

On the last afternoon, as we urban hiked up a pedestrian-only shopping street, we spotted a large crowd gathered along a street in front of us. As we moved closer, we saw people wearing or carrying rainbow-colored items. Happenstance had provided the opportunity to stand with a few thousand people who were celebrating gay rights. As I watched the joy on the faces of those who paraded by, I commented to Sandy, "This is a fitting event to conclude our visit to three countries who give focus to caring about their citizens – all citizens."

SMORREBROD (OPEN FACED SANDWICH)

Ingredients

4 slices dark rye bread
3 eggs hard boiled, cut into ¼ slices
16 small shrimp, peeled and boiled
1 T Dijon mustard
¼ cup mayonnaise
3 T chopped dill, divided
Chopped chives
Salt
Black pepper

Preparation

In a small bowl mix 2 tablespoons of the dill, along with salt and pepper to taste, into the mayonnaise.

To assemble, lay the sliced bread onto a flat surface. Divide the mayonnaise between the slices and spread into an even layer.

Top the bread with the sliced eggs and boiled shrimp. This is your chance to be creative, make them look irresistible. Then garnish your artistic creations with the remaining chopped dill, chopped chives, salt and pepper.

17

ALASKA

GO, JUST TO VISIT BOB

I n mid-August 2018, I had a planned early September consulting
trip suddenly get cancelled. Sandy and I had talked about visiting
Alaska many times in the past but had never finalized our plans. So
now, just a few weeks before our September 3rd departure, we sponta-
neously planned a ten-day trip to Alaska. We quickly reserved our
flights in and out of Anchorage, before booking a rental car and our
lodging in five different locations, Anchorage, Girdwood, Seward,
Whittier, and Denali National Park.

We used Uber transportation to get from the airport to our chain
hotel lodging for our first night. Then, the morning after our arrival in
Anchorage, the largest city in Alaska, I went to the rental car facility
to pick up our vehicle. I had reserved a mid-size SUV thinking it
might be more suitable than a sedan if the roads were rough. After
completing the paperwork, the attendant informed me he did not
have a mid-sized SUV. He offered in its place, a monster of a vehicle.
An Armada. Any vehicle named after a fleet of warships got my full
attention. We walked over to it, and as I strained my neck to look up
at the oversized SUV I said, "Too bad we did not bring the ten grand-
kids on this trip."

I drove back to our hotel to pick up Sandy and our luggage. Before leaving our room, I told her, "Be prepared to see the largest motorized vehicle I had ever driven, excluding the 5,000-gallon fuel tanker trucks I drove while serving in the U.S. Air Force."

She replied, "You are exaggerating, it cannot be that big."

I was quickly exonerated when Sandy went out to the parking lot and walked up to the SUV.

Looking up, she shouted, "Oh, my God! How am I going to get up there?"

It took some doing, including a discussion about the possible need of a ladder, but she eventually settled into the seat that provided panoramic views of the Alaskan wilderness landscape.

For the first few days, as she made the ascent up and into the SUV, she repeatedly said, "What a waste. This thing is too big."

Near the end of our 10-day trip she commented, "We should get one of these."

I just smiled.

Anyone who researches or plans a trip to visit Alaska hears or reads about the danger bears may pose when hiking, long before they depart. While planning the trip, Sandy read a few stories about bear attacks and then watched a few YouTube videos to heighten her fear and concern. Taking an offensive strategy, to help ensure our safety, she ordered bells for our backpacks. She also read about bear repellant pepper spray and decided we should purchase a can. Since bear spray is packaged in a pressurized aerosol can, we could not bring it onto our flight to Anchorage. But on our first morning in Anchorage, after we both climbed into our giant SUV, we drove to a large sporting goods store to make the purchase.

Right up front, by the entrance door, was a display of bear spray.

"Positioned and waiting for the tourists to walk in," I commented sarcastically.

Of course, a note on the shelf for $30 and $40 sized cans read, "Out of stock." The only cans remaining on the display cost $60. After asking Sandy, about six times, to reconsider spending $60 on something I did not think we needed, she finally agreed with, or at least temporarily accepted, my rationale. I reminded her we would be hiking well used trails with other hikers around us, as opposed to hiking in the back country.

"We do not need bear spray," I said.

We left the store without making the purchase. I had gotten my way.

We then drove toward our first destination, a small town named Girdwood, an hour from Anchorage. Anxious to get out and hike, we stopped at two short trails while in route to stretch our legs. With ski season still a few months away, our lodging, a large ski resort complex, offered cheap room rates. After checking in, we took another walk near the facility and made dinner reservations. That evening, we rode a cable car ski lift to a restaurant located up on the mountain top that overlooked the resort. From this high perch, we had our first views of the beauty and grandeur of Alaska.

The next morning, we put on our hiking gear and drove five minutes to a local restaurant for breakfast. We ordered two items, huge pancakes with maple syrup and an omelet, and split them. While eating, I watched a customer order a cinnamon roll to go. It was the size of a softball and drizzled with frosting. So even though I was stuffed, I suggested that we get one to eat later after our hike. I made the purchase and then we drove a few miles to the trailhead. As I pulled the Armanda into a parking spot, I pointed out why we did not need bear spray.

"Look, there are five cars here, so there must be other hikers on the trail," I said confidently.

I opened the rear hatch of the vehicle so we could retrieve our hiking gear. As I slung my backpack over my shoulder, and grabbed my camera, Sandy said, "Wait, we have to put the bells on our backpacks."

As she handed me my bell she said, "You know, I read that Alaskans call them bear dinner bells."

We both laughed as we attached the bells to our backpacks and then walked, while jingle-jangling, about fifteen yards from the parking area and turning left onto the main trail.

After moving forward no more than ten yards on the trail, Sandy suddenly grabbed my arm and said, "Wait, wait, there is a bear on the trail!"

Sure enough, a black bear sow with three cubs, stood on the trail no more thirty yards directly in front of us.

"Shit, I have the wrong lens on my camera, my telephoto lens is in my backpack," I whispered, as we slowly backed up.

As we continued to shuffle backwards, the bears walked off into the woods and we soon resumed our hike. As we moved forward, now constantly jingling our bells, Sandy occasionally reminded me, "We should have purchased bear spray."

Because I am a writer, I viewed things differently. Since we did not purchase bear spray, the two of us had just created a wonderful, shared travel story. I kept those thoughts to myself.

After our hike we pulled the paper plate containing the oversized cinnamon roll out of the bag. The smell of sweet cinnamon goodness filled the air. Much to our surprise, and delight, the waitress had smeared about a quarter stick of butter onto the edge of the plate. Using a plastic spoon found in a coffee cup, we smeared butter onto each piece of the snail-like structure as we peeled off our next bite. Each mouthful was loaded with cinnamon, moist, chewy, and sweet with frosting. And the best part is that we ate it guilt-free, because of the calories we burned hiking and worrying about bears.

Two days later, we left the Girdwood area and drove two hours to the coastal fishing town of Seward. Inland reflective waterways, distant mountains and vast colorful prairies along our route caused us to stop several times. Often, we just stood and stared before photographing the amazing views. Arriving in Seward around mid-day, we located and checked into our hotel. It was a bit dated. The worn turquoise fabric on the lobby couches and chairs must have been classy back in the nineties.

After we dropped off our luggage in the hotel room, I suggested we take a walk since we had been in the car for a few hours, and then find a place for lunch. We followed a boardwalk along the dock area where we viewed, and I photographed, some fishing vessels. At one slip, where a boat had just returned, we watched fishermen disembark from the charter boat. The crew busied themselves unloading the catch into a wheelbarrow to get them to a fish cleaning station. Because I had looked through some brochures, and considered going on a charter, I could identify the flat white-bellied halibut, the long narrow black cod, and the bright red rockfish that they began to process. The largest fish were hung on dockside hooks under the charter service's sign. The fishermen then took turns posing with the catch, as friends or a crew member took photographs to preserve the memory. As they walked away, I photographed the fish to create my own memories of our time on Seward.

As we continued our walk, just past the docks, I saw people up ahead fishing along the shore of the inlet. A fishy smell, blown toward us by a light breeze, pulled me toward them. I am the kind of a person that enjoys watching people fish, just as much as fishing, because I am excited when they hook one and I do not have to clean the fish.

As I watched them yanking their fishing rods backward with force, I commented out loud, "I wonder what is going on; it looks like they are trying to snag fish."

Then a stout man, sitting on a large shoreside boulder, who looked to be in his mid-sixties, with hair and beard as gray as mine, responded. "They are snagging salmon. Every year hatchery-raised salmon fry are released from this location. As salmon do, when they are mature, they return from the ocean and congregate right here where they were released years earlier."

He continued, "Last week an annual fishing tournament was held with prizes awarded for the largest fish caught. Then, after the tournament, residents can snag and keep the remaining salmon."

"Interesting," I said. "Why snagging rather than fishing?"

"Well, the salmon were not born in a stream, so they will not enter a stream to spawn. They will just die right here in the inlet. So rather than waste the resource, the state allows snagging. These fish are an important food source for local people."

"Thanks," I said. "What is your name?"

"Bob. What is yours?" he asked.

"Bob," I said.

Turns out this guy, named Bob, was a local so we continued to talk. We learned that when he was in college, a friend who traveled to Alaska to work at the North slope oil fields, called and told him he would earn over $100,000 that year.

Bob said, "I quit college the next day and went to Alaska."

Decades later, he now owned and operated a tour service. He had a small fleet of mini-buses and a crew of drivers that hauled tourists around the state.

As we continued to talk, since Bob was a local, Sandy asked, "What is your opinion about carrying bear spray while hiking?"

"You should. It is your last line of defense," he said with conviction.

Before Sandy could tell me "I told you so", Bob asked, "Do you want some? This is my last week of operation and I will have to buy new cans next spring."

So we followed Bob to one of his minibuses. He located the can of bear spray in the back of the vehicle and gave it to us. A generous gesture from a genuine and nice man. We really hit it off. If I lived near Bob in Alaska, I knew we would be friends.

Our day and a half in and around Seward were spent hiking some of the local state park trails. We then drove back toward Anchorage to stay in the small fishing town of Whittier. It was a town dominated by a harbor full of fishing vessels. The reason for our stop in Whittier was to see some nearby glaciers.

We checked into one of the two hotels in town. It was a three-story wooden structure that sat right on the inlet, next to the harbor entrance. We used the elevator to haul our luggage up to our second-floor room. As soon as we entered, Sandy noticed an odd smell. We searched for the source of the unpleasant musty aroma but could not locate it. She then headed down to the lobby front desk and asked if we could be moved to another room. With no vacant rooms available, the hotel manager tried to placate her by offering to spray something to mask the smell while we were out of the room.

The hotel had a rustic wood-paneled restaurant and bar that overlooked the inlet waterway. We found seats and ordered drinks. We so liked the beautiful views from our table that we asked for dinner menus. We ordered and ate fresh local seafood, salmon and halibut. Unable to resist a dessert made with local fruit, we ordered and split a crisp made with wild cloudberries and blueberries. After settling the bill, since we were both tired from our day of travel, we headed up to our room.

Just as our room door swung open, Sandy said, "The room still smells!"

So, when we turned in for the night, we decided to sleep with the window open, even though the temperature would drop into the forties overnight. Since the window opened inward, the drapes also had to be left open. Next the magic occurred.

About two o'clock in the morning Sandy poked me and said, "Wake up, I think I see something."

I rolled over and mumbled, "That is great."

Fifteen minutes later she shook me and said excitedly, "Wake-up, I really see something. I think it is the northern lights!"

I crawled from the bed and stared out of the open window. Yes, something wavy and weird swirled in the distant sky. I then became interested and grabbed the new DSLR camera I had purchased just one week before we had departed for Alaska. For the next fifteen minutes, I experimented with different settings to try and capture a clear image of the unexpected light show. Finally, I figured out that by selecting the manual mode, which allowed me to control the length of time the shutter stayed open, I could capture the swirling green images. A long exposure meant the camera had to be held steady. A tripod would have been ideal, but I relied on bracing myself and the camera against the window frame.

"Look at this," I said over and over, as I took photo after photo.

Because our room overlooked the harbor and the boat docks, I captured some surreal images of the northern lights whirling above the distant mountains, while the nearby harbor and boats provided perspective to the photographs. The ever-changing light show meant every photograph was unique.

Sandy had always wanted to see the northern lights, or aurora borealis. Because of the unpleasant musty smell in our room, and the subsequent decision to leave the drapes and window open, her dream came true. That happenstance night provided lasting memories for both of us.

We had purchased tickets for a mid-day boat trip up the inlet to see a glacial field that terminated at water's edge. With the morning free, we walked toward the small commercial area beyond the harbor. On our way back to the hotel, a pickup truck pulled up alongside, and the passenger window went down.

The driver called out, "I do not want to alarm you, but there is a bear across the street in that boat trailer parking area."

We said thanks and walked a little faster back to the hotel. I then suggested we get in our monster SUV and drive into the parking area, with camera ready, to see if we could locate and shoot pictures of the bear.

As we turned onto the dirt access road leading to the parking lot, I lowered my dirty window so I could get a clear photo if we located the bear. I saw a man walking up ahead of us, and as I passed him, we both looked at each other at the same instant.

He shouted, "Bob!"

I shouted back, "Bob!"

Yes, it was Bob, the Alaskan tours operator who had given us the bear spray in Seward three days earlier.

"What are you doing here?", I asked.

"Well, my brother-in-law called me last night and asked for my help. He placed shrimp pots in the inlet at the start of the shrimping season and the season ends tomorrow, so they must be removed. The guy that was supposed to help him with the boat backed out at the last minute, so I got the call."

He continued, "We just finished, and I walked over here to get the truck and trailer so we can load up the boat."

I said, "Hop in, we will give you a ride."

As he directed us to his vehicle, I asked, "What kind of shrimp are they?"

"Just stop by the boat ramp, I will show you the shrimp," he said.

I drove back to the hotel; Sandy went to our room and I walked along the harbor to the boat ramp.

As I walked up, Bob said, "Bob, this is brother-in-law, Bob."

That is correct, three Bobs.

Bob then climbed up onto the boat, reached into a cooler and held up a large reddish-brown shrimp. "This is a Spot shrimp."

"It looks just like all of the shrimp I have cleaned in my lifetime, but I have never seen a fresher shrimp," I commented.

"Yeah, they are really good eating," he said, as he bent over to return it to the cooler.

"Before you put it back in the cooler, hold that shrimp up again. I want to get a photo."

He did, and I have a photo of Bob looking at and admiring the shrimp rather than the camera.

When Bob came off the boat, we shook hands and said our good-byes. Alaska is known to have a very sparse population, and yet, I ran into the same Bob in two locations one-hundred miles from each other. It is a small world after all. Sorry Walt.

Denali National Park, a wilderness location I had dreamt about visiting for many years, would be the final stop on our ten-day trip. The next morning, we packed up the Armada, left Whittier, and began the five hours plus drive north.

After passing through Anchorage, we saw and decided to stop at a grocery store in Wasilla. Since we had no idea what in the way of food and supplies would be available in and around Denali, and the prices might be doubled due to the remote location, we decided to purchase some fruit, granola bars and other snacks that we could take with while hiking.

As we walked toward the store I said to Sandy, "You know, Wasilla is where Bob lives, right?"

"Yeah, I remember him saying that. Do you think we will see him in the store?", she asked, and then laughed.

"I think our odds are really good," I responded enthusiastically.

So, as I walked around the food store, I kept an eye out for Alaska Bob. No Bob sightings were reported by either of us, so we purchased our groceries and headed north.

The fall colors intensified as we drove toward Denali. If a tree was not a conifer, and therefore covered in green needles, it had leaves that shone some shade of bright yellow. The closer we got to Denali National Park, the more often we pulled onto the shoulder of the road and jumped out to take photographs. Unspoiled views revealed themselves at every twist and turn, or elevation change, in the road. Distant scenes of mountains, close-by streams lined with yellow leaved aspen and birch, and treeless broad plains with multi-colored tundra plants as far as I could see made me say, "Wow!"

Wow quickly became my favorite word. "Wow look at that view. Wow, how lucky are we to be here to see this. Wow, this is unbelievable."

The furthest we, or anyone, could drive a personal vehicle into the wilderness of Denali National Park was fifteen miles. All visitors are required to take a bus, operated by a corporate service provided, to go beyond that fifteen-mile point. Therefore, we signed up for a four-hour bus trip that would depart the next morning. It would take us sixty miles into the park following the only access road.

Early on a chilly fall day, we piled onto a bus with a group of tourists and headed into the wilderness armed with our cameras and provided box lunches.

The wilderness portion of Denali, as defined by our driver/tour guide, had been left untouched by man, except for the road on which we traveled. This meant no construction of roads, buildings or trails and no wildlife management. Untouched natural beauty is all that we would witness. Looking out the bus window, I watched mile after mile of treeless flat tundra and snow topped distant mountains pass by. When the driver or a passenger sighted a distant caribou, grizzly bear, or mountain goat, the bus would stop. Then, looking like an eighteenth-century wooden battleship with canons protruding from its sides, the open windows of the bus had cameras with long tele-photo lenses jutting out of them to capture the distant image. When the shutters stopped clicking, the bus continued down the gravel road.

The corporate influence on the Denali bus service was very evident when I opened the box lunch they had provided. It was filled with individual snacks, think junk food, wrapped in foil or plastic packaging. The packaging seemed environmentally sinful consid-ering our wilderness location. Why not just an apple along with a sandwich or two wrapped in paper?

The bus made a few stops so we could get out to take photos and stretch our legs. Because the weather had remained cool and cloudy, the warm bus almost seemed inviting when we were instructed to climb back aboard. Except for this overcast day, we had experienced exceptionally sunny cool fall weather during our ten-day visit. So, on the one day I had the opportunity to photograph the wilderness tundra, the gray skies set a mood different from what I had antici-pated. Instead of sunlight-illuminated tundra and mountain vistas, I captured a landscape filled with the muted colors of brown, gold, yellow and red tundra plants on display in front of distant snow-covered peaks, under gray moody skies. It was breathtaking.

On our last day at Denali, just before sunset, we drove about ten miles into the national park. No other cars were in sight as I pulled off the road and onto the shoulder. I shut off the engine and the two of us stepped out into complete silence. I was in the wilderness and it felt eerie. No people, no noise, and within a short while, no sunlight. We waited and watched as daylight faded and complete darkness enveloped us. The quickly dropping temps drove Sandy back into the car. I stood shivering in the cold while looking up at a wonderous sight. Millions of stars, and I am not exaggerating, appeared above us. I repeatedly set my camera, with its lens facing directly up, on the car roof and took long exposure photographs of the star filled sky. I felt awestruck while previewing the slightly blurred digital images filled with stars and the cloudy whitish haze of the Milky Way and other distant galaxies.

Those night skies topped a wonderful ten days in Alaska. The tourist season and our trip ended during the same week. The next morning, as we drove back to Anchorage for our flight home, we discussed a return trip.

CINNAMON CARDAMOM BUNS

Ingredients

2 packages of instant dry yeast
½ cup warm water
2 T sugar
2 cups boiling water
3 T butter
1-1/2 t salt
3 T sugar
2 cups all-purpose flour
3 large eggs
4 additional cups of all-purpose flour
1/3 cup melted butter
1-1/4 cup sugar
3 t ground cinnamon
1 t ground cardamom

Preparation

In a small bowl combine the dry yeast and sugar with the warn water. Stir to dissolve the yeast.

Meanwhile, in a stand mixer bowl, combine the butter, salt, sugar and boiling water. After the butter has melted add 2 cups of flour and beat, using the dough hook attachment, at high speed for 5 minutes. Then add the eggs and beat to combine. Pour in the yeast mixture followed by the additional 3-3/4 cups of flour 1 cup at a time. When all the flour has been incorporated, continue to beat for 5 minutes until the dough is soft and smooth.

Transfer the dough to a large bowl, cover with a kitchen towel, and let rise for about one hour or until doubled in bulk.

While the dough is rising, butter a 9X13 X 2-inch-deep baking pan and set aside.

Scrape dough from bowl onto a floured countertop and let it rest for 15 minutes. Then cut the dough into twelve equal pieces.

Add the cup of sugar, cinnamon and cardamom to a shallow pan and mix until well combined. Melt the butter and pour into a pie dish.

On the floured countertop, use your hands to roll and form each of the twelve pieces of dough into an eight-inch log shape. Roll the logs of dough in the melted butter and then the cinnamon/cardamom sugar mixture to completely coat them. Pull and stretch the dough lengthwise until you can tie each piece into a simple knot shape.

Lay the dough knots in the prepared pan and let rise for 45 minutes or until doubled in size.

Pre-heat the oven to 375 degrees.

Bake the cinnamon buns in the center of the oven for 25-30 minutes.

Cool on a rack just long enough to ensure the caramelized sugar exterior on the bun you grab does not burn your fingers or your mouth when you take the first bite.

18

HAWAII

IT IS BLUE

Traveling to the island of Maui has become an annual trip to escape a portion of the Midwest winter. Our first visit was for our honeymoon, a long, long, long time ago. Then about ten years ago, right after Christmas, we discussed going someplace warm for a week or two in early January, to get away from the Chicago area weather. We planned to use our accumulated air miles to purchase our flight tickets. As I searched possible flights to Florida or Arizona, which would require 25,000 air miles for each round-trip ticket, I noticed for 35,000 miles we could fly to Maui. I talked Sandy into going back to Maui and we have returned for the last eight years.

Maui has two types of scenic beauty. The first being the artificial man-made form observed at every resort along the beachfront. Closely cropped manicured lawns, spotted with beautiful coconut palms and flowering plants, run along white sandy beaches. This is the Maui tourists see while staying at the large hotel complexes located along the popular beaches. It is not real. It is a view defined and created by landscape architects and maintained daily by multiple crews of hard-working landscapers.

Contrast that created prettiness with the real natural beauty of the island. Always in view is the unimaginably vast and beautiful blue Pacific Ocean. Along the shoreline, every light blue color available on an artist's palette has tinted the water. Then as your eyes look farther out, the color of the ever-deepening water turns to a deep dark blue. Every time I observe that kaleidoscope of blues, I want to sing the Elvis Presley classic tune, Blue Hawaii.

Much of the island's shoreline is a labyrinth of weathered black lava rock. Behind the coastline is a different kind of beauty. Simply turning and looking away from any shoreline causes your head to raise, for the mountains and ancient volcanos automatically draw your gaze upward. The towering peaks cut through the passing clouds to drain their moisture and send it rushing down the mountainsides. Often a light misty rain, floating down from the peaks toward the coastline, combines with the clear tropical sunlight to create rainbows so brilliant that I am forced to stop and stare. The foliage, on the surrounding mountains and hills, can be vibrant greens, or golden yellows and browns depending on the season and rainfall. Maui is so much more than beaches and resorts.

It is not just people who go to Maui to escape winter. During the month of February, when we visit, thousands of humpback whales are also visiting the Hawaiian Islands. They come to give birth and mate, before making the long journey back to the waters along the Alaskan coast. To observe them only requires me to look out to sea from any shoreline vantage point and wait. The sighting of a blow, a breach, the back or tail of a whale will soon confirm they are ever present.

A friend, Julian, who lives on Maui and owns a boat, often invites us to join him on the water. The excursions are both to observe the whales and to try and catch a mahi-mahi for dinner. I will always remember the first trip out on his boat. From the water, the view of the mountainous and lush island of Maui, and the surrounding islands of Molokai and Lanai was spectacular. While the view took my breath away, Julian inserted a CD of his favorite Hawaiian music into the boat's CD player. When the first song began, a song by

Keali'I Reichel, I felt a sort of euphoria as goosebumps covered my arms. The combination of the natural wonders all around us, and the hauntingly beautiful and appropriate soundtrack, created a unique moment I will never forget. The whales I have spotted, and the occasional mahi-mahi I caught, all produced memorable boating moments. But none of them compare to that goose bump moment.

In addition to the whales, green sea turtles are abundant around the Hawaiian Islands. While sitting along the shoreline, I can see their heads as they occasionally surface to take a breath of air. Although I do not snorkel, friends who do have had close encounters with them as they feed on the seagrasses and algae along the shoreline. My preferred method is watching them sleep.

The shoreline in front of the small condo complex where we stay is mostly large lava rocks with a few small sandy sections. At low tide, as many as thirty green sea turtles will haul themselves out of the water and onto a small sandy beach for a nap. Without a worry in the world, the completely relaxed turtles find a comfortable spot in the sun, close their eyes and sleep. I often just sit on the shoreline, no more than fifteen feet away, and observe them. If I practiced meditation, this would be the ideal spot. Watching turtles sleep is so calming it makes me drowsy. It is the Hawaiian version of counting sheep.

One day as I sat observing the turtles, I watched two young Hawaiians, maybe in their late teens, moving toward me as they gathered something from the large lava rocks along the shore. One young man would scamper and climb onto the rocks that stood amongst the breaking waves, while the other stayed back out of harm's way. While climbing from rock to rock, he would occasionally stop and use, what looked like a butter knife, to pry something from the surface of the rocks. Occasionally he would get close enough to the second young man to unload, from his pocket, whatever he had been harvesting into a small cooler.

When they came close, I asked the one holding the cooler, "What are you gathering?"

He responded, "Opihi."

"What is that?" I asked.

He then explained they were small sea mollusks.

"Do you eat them raw?" I asked.

"You can, but we usually cook them on a barbeque grill. Do you want to try one?" He asked.

"Yes," I said excitedly.

He removed a round conical shaped shell from the cooler and used a second shell to scrape the meaty bit from the first shell. He handed it to me, and I put it in my mouth and chewed. It tasted like a sea salt flavored gummy bear.

As he started to walk away, I said, "Thanks for letting me taste one. That was a great Hawaiian experience."

He nodded and then continued up the beach, while keeping an eye out for dangerous rogue waves, so his friend, who continued to look for and harvest Opihi, would not be swept off the rocks.

During our stay on Maui we prepare and eat most of our meals in the condo.

Seafood is often center stage. The fish we purchase and prepare comes from Costco. We usually get to pick from a selection of local fresh fish that includes mahi-mahi, ono, monchong, and opah. A favorite preparation, that I often cook for guests while in Hawaii, is fish poached in a Thai green curry sauce. Purchased curry paste, combined with canned coconut milk, is the sauce base. To it I add fish and many different vegetables like squash, green beans, eggplant, spinach; or sweet potato. The choice depends on availability. Garnishes include fresh coriander (cilantro), fresh basil, and a squeeze of lime juice. Everyone loves the preparation served over jasmine rice, because of the bright flavors the curry paste and fresh herbs add to the dish.

A couple of Hawaiian specialties that I enjoy are poke and musubi. A poke bowl from a local food store, just a ten-minute drive from our condo, makes a delicious and filling lunch. It contains diced hunks of fresh raw ahi tuna, that has been marinated and spiced with a variety of ingredients, served over white rice. Another food store, to which I often walk, is where I buy musubi. It is a rectangular block of white rice, topped with a slice of spam that has been sautéed with teriyaki sauce, and then wrapped with a sheet of nori (dried seaweed). It is found in the deli area under some warming lamps. I tell the cashier not to bag it for as soon as I exit the store, I pull off the plastic film wrapper and bite into the warm Hawaiian snack food. It is sweet, salty, and comforting.

Getting to the other side of the island, where the Costco and all the other large stores are located, requires a forty-five-minute drive. I never mind the scenic drive and sometimes wish it were longer. Mist covered mountains and beach views line the route for most of the amazingly beautiful drive.

Every Saturday morning a large swap meet, where vendors sell fresh produce, food, and tourist gift items, is held near the community college on the other side of the island. Once or twice during our stay we will drive there just to visit a food truck that serves shave ice. Not to be confused with a snow cone, which starts with crushed ice, shaved ice is used for the Hawaiian version. The small mountain of shaved ice is then topped with a syrupy topping, or toppings, of your choice. Hapa, a Hawaiian term referring to someone of mixed race, is also the name of my favorite shave ice topping combination. The two syrups, flavored with coffee and coconut, when poured over the lighter than air ice, allows me to believe I am eating something not only delicious, but almost calorie free. I am easily fooled by deliciousness.

We have found, after returning to Maui for multiple years, that we are content just taking it easy and enjoying the beauty that is all around us. There are many activities for tourists on the island, and during our first few visits we participated in them. Now, we just kick back and relax in blue Hawaii.

MAHI-MAHI IN A GREEN THAI CURRY SAUCE

Ingredients

1 jar Thai green curry paste (Thai Kitchen brand)
2 T canola oil
1 can coconut milk
½ cup water
4 six ounce mahi-mahi fillets
2 medium sweet potatoes
2 limes
3 T fresh basil, chopped
3 T fresh cilantro, chopped
Basmati rice

Preparation

Microwave the two sweet potatoes for about 5-6 minutes or until until tender. Cool, peel and cut into chunks.

Cook the basmati rice by following the packaging instructions.

In a straight sided pan big enough to hold the four pieces of fish lying flat, add the oil and heat over medium heat. When hot, add 4 T of the purchased curry paste, and sauté for 3 minutes. Add the can of coconut milk and the water to the pan and whisk to combine. Bring to a simmer and cook for 4 minutes to slightly reduce the liquid. Turn the heat to medium low, lay the fish fillets in the coconut milk, and cover the pan to poach the fish. After 10-12 minutes check the fish using the tip of a small knife to see if it will flake. When the fish is done, squeeze in the juice of half a lime and stir in 2 tablespoons each of chopped basil and cilantro.

To serve, place some basmati rice in the bottom of a flat-bottomed serving bowl. Arrange sweet potatoes around the rice. Top the rice with a fillet of fish, and then divide and pour the coconut milk sauce over the four servings. Garnish each dish with lime wedges, chopped basil and cilantro.

19

THE CARNIVORE CLUB

AN ALTERNATIVE TO INTERNATIONAL TRAVEL

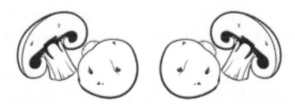

T he ability to touch people, in a way that makes a difference in their life, is a unique skill. My friend Mike had that ability.

Mike, a professor at a local university, grew up within forty miles of the campus. That is not the norm. Full-time university teaching positions are rare, so those seeking them must be willing to pick up and move. More than likely, this vagabond lifestyle began while they worked on their advanced degrees, so historically, moving has been part of working your way up the academia life ladder. As a result, many of Mike's colleagues, when they were offered and then accepted their positions at his university, had to relocate. That move severed, or at the least impacted, their relationships with current friends and required them to develop new ones when they arrived. Mike understood how a sense of loneliness might impact those new professors. He often reached out, by inviting them to lunch, so they had a connection on campus.

At the time when Mike started to plan his retirement, by reducing his course load and backing away from academia, he understood he, too, would lose, or impact, his connections with people on campus. He never said so, but I believe he had a plan to not only maintain, but to strengthen and build relationships with some of his peers, despite his retirement. He accomplished this by starting a "men's lunch club."

He began by inviting two colleagues to join him for a Saturday lunch at a Chicago hot dog stand. The place, Hot Dougs, was famous for gourmet hot dogs and French fries cooked in duck fat. Since the owner had announced the imminent closure of his business, a long line of patrons joined Mike and friends as they waited for their hot dogs topped with unusual ingredients such as foie gras. Despite the wait, the three of them enjoyed the outing and planned another one the following month.

Over the next few months, as the Saturday lunchtime outings continued, Mike extended an invitation to join the club to a few more university peers, and me.

The core group of attendees are as diverse as the cuisines we have eaten. Mike, the founder of the club, grew up in a western suburb of Chicago and spent his career teaching English literature. He was a talented, witty conversationalist who loved to read, cook, travel, and follow not only Chicago sports, but also the Tottenham Hotspurs in the English Premier League.

Dominic has a thoughtful personality and calm demeanor that reflect his area of expertise, theology. His love for teaching is evident in his eyes when he tells stories about his students. A lifetime NY Yankee fan, he entertains us with stories about his Brooklyn Italian heritage childhood, and experiences related to multiple semesters spent teaching in Rome.

Mike, a composer and the music department chair, spent his childhood in Oklahoma. He has a playful wit and when he says, "Now, listen," we do. He is always involved in a variety of creative musical projects, like having one of his compositions performed at Carnegie Hall, and has an interest in cooking and eating new and unusual foods.

Mark, a history professor, shares stories from his childhood in Georgia. He is a passionate educator who uses creative techniques to engage his students in history and has taken his two sons on immersive learning vacations to out of the way places like Uzbekistan.

Dick, a retired English professor, splits his time between Chicago and Florida.

He grew up in the Roseland area, located on the far southside of Chicago. He is a wonderful storyteller, and an outspoken social justice activist, but his claim to fame is that he introduced the carnivores to Malort, a uniquely Chicago liquor, at a famed Chicago bar, The Green Mill.

Pramod, who teaches English, tells stories of a childhood spent in an indigenous village in Nepal that are both entertaining and inspirational. He stays grounded by planting and maintaining a large garden and connected to his cultural home by writing a column for the Kathmandu Post.

Jamil, a member of the English department, is passionate about his specialty, Gothic literature. In 2007 he taught for a semester at Bethlehem University, near where his father was born, and now organizes and leads student experiential study-abroad trips to London each spring.

Mardy who in addition to his English instruction, is an administrator at the university. His shared sensibility ("Now, wait a minute."), along with an engaging and outgoing personality, make him a natural conversationalist. He was raised in central California.

Arsalan, a deep thinker, delves into philosophy with his students and was raised on the far north side of Chicago. Having cultural roots in Pakistan allows him to influence and expand our worldview.

I guess it is obvious that everyone I briefly described is an intellectual. Then there is me. My roots are midwestern, Minnesota and Illinois, and my career was in manufacturing management. Our differing socio-economic, cultural, and professional backgrounds all contribute to remarkably interesting and engaging lunchtime conversations.

For multiple years this diverse group has explored the world by using food as our portal. Our genuine attempt to eat at different and unusual restaurants is made possible because we reside in the Chicago suburbs, and have easy access to a myriad of restaurants. Our food inspired travels have taken us, figuratively, around the world. You name a cuisine; we have probably eaten it.

Early on someone called our lunch group the "carnivore club" and the name stuck. A possible explanation is that initially we dined at restaurants where meat was featured. For instance, a Mexican restaurant that served only goat or a meal at a Serbian restaurant that included so much meat, we all considered vegetarianism for the next two weeks. Another possibility is that two of the members, musical Mike and Mardy, are sons-of-butchers. No, read it again, it is "BUTCHERS!"

I like to pair what I drink with the cuisine I am eating, when possible. A search of a Puerto Rican restaurant's website revealed that they did not have a liquor license but allowed patrons to bring in alcoholic beverages. So, the day before our lunch gathering, I purchased two six-packs of El Presidente beer. I could not find a Puerto Rican beer to accompany our lunch, but El Presidente is brewed in the Dominican Republic which is only about sixty nautical miles from Puerto Rico. Close enough, I thought.

As we walked into the long narrow room, with tables for four filling the area in front of a bar running along the long wall, a waitress, when seeing the beer, immediately went and filled two buckets with ice and inserted the beers. We then ordered a selection of dishes and washed down our meal of mofongo, lechon, tostones, and empanadas with ice-cold beer. As we finished up, we noticed two beers remained in a bucket. Nearby sat two young Puerto Rican men enjoying their meal.

I caught their attention and asked, "Would you two like a beer with your lunch?"

Their eyes lit up, and both said, "Sure."

"Where did you find El Presidente beer?", one of them asked.

The name and location of the liquor store was passed on and the conversation between our tables continued for a several minutes.

Soon after, when we finished and stood up to leave, they said goodbye like we were old friends.

When we visited a small storefront West African restaurant, we relied on the owner to help us order a selection of food. He explained the simple ingredients and preparation technique for the some of the dishes he recommended. Then when the food arrived, he visited our table to see if we liked them. After finishing the meal of long cooked stews and vegetables, we sat and talked. The owner once again came by and asked if we would like to try two specialty health drinks. Receiving positive responses, he brought out small plastic cups of each. One was a bright red hibiscus tea and the second, my favorite, was brightly flavored with fresh ginger and "Good for your digestive system," he noted. As we each shook his hand on our way out, we felt a connection to him and his culture via the food and drink. He had welcomed us like guests and guided us through the meal.

One Saturday we journeyed to the far northside of Chicago to dine at a Chinese restaurant that specialized in preparing and serving Peking duck. As we entered the cavernous restaurant, I saw groups of people, as is typical in Chinese restaurants, gathered around large round tables eating and talking. They understand the importance of conversation and shared meals.

Two of us, who had visited China, began telling stories and soon everyone was talking. After looking over the menu, most of us selected and ordered a side dish to share. Musical Mike, who spent a semester teaching at a Hong Kong university, insisted we order chicken feet, and offered to demonstrate how to eat them. When delivered, shanghai noodles, house fried rice, baby bok-choy sautéed with garlic and ginger, two different stir-fry dishes, the chicken feet, and steaming bowls of sticky rice filled the lazy Susan in the center of our table.

Musical Mike could be mistaken for an NFL linebacker, so when he picked up a chicken foot in his large hands and said, "Gently use your lips and front teeth to extract the skin and collagen from the bones," laughter erupted.

We ate and ate, and then the three whole ducks we had ordered arrived. The wait staff skillfully carved the glistening deep brown birds tableside. The multiple plates of thinly sliced duck and duck skin, along with the requisite condiments of wheat pancakes, hoisin sauce and green scallions took their place on the lazy Susan. As it spun and moved back and forth between us, we ate and talked until we could eat no more. We opted for a dessert of hot tea and conversation to conclude a wonderful and delicious meal.

Everyone in the Carnivore Club had eaten at Indian restaurants, but when one of the members, Arsalan, who is culturally connected to Pakistan, suggested we gather at a northside Pakistani restaurant in his neighborhood, we quickly agreed. We all understood that having Arsalan as our cultural guide would lead to a great dining experience.

When we arrived and took our place in the buffet line, he proudly guided us along the lunch buffet selection, explaining each dish and recommending his favorites. In addition to the buffet, Dominic insisted we order one dish from the menu, the stewed lamb's brains. The sons-of-butchers, Mike and Mardy, supported the suggestion and soon we feasted on soft meat that tasted like the spicy sauce in which it had been cooked.

All the food, eaten with fluffy naan bread just pulled from the side of a tandoor oven, and flaky, buttery whole-wheat paratha bread, was flavorful and delicious. Because of the many common spices used in the dishes, our lunch tasted much like an Indian meal. As we sat there talking and eating meltingly soft and sweet gulab jamun for dessert, someone pointed out a cultural difference between Indian and Pakistani restaurants. One can order a beer, but not beef in an Indian restaurant. The reverse is true in a Pakistani restaurant. It would have been nice to have had a beer to wash down the brains.

A small Filipino restaurant, recommended by a university adjunct, only served a lunch-time buffet meal on Saturdays. It was small, maybe eight tables total. Shortly after we arrived, they began to bring out trays of hot food and position them in a warming table. We stood in line holding our empty plates and staring at mystery dishes, for we had no idea what the trays contained, and we did not have a waiter to ask. Since roasted whole pigs are an obsession in the Philippines, I did recognize small hunks of roasted pork with the crispy skin still attached. I put some on my plate, and then as I showed some hesitancy, a Filipino in line next to me, began to explain each dish. One, which he called a blood stew, turned out to be so tasty I went back for seconds. It contained pork offal simmered in a dark brown gravy flavored with garlic, chili, vinegar, and pig's blood.

Later, as I walked past him and his wife, we began to talk. He told me he had been born in the Philippines but currently lived in central Illinois. The two of them drove to Chicago and this restaurant to eat and be reminded of their cultural home, the Philippines. I explained that while serving in the U.S. Air Force, I was stationed in the Philippines. This led to a lengthy conversation. Before leaving their table, my new friend, who noticed the desserts being set on the buffet table, told me which ones I should try. Nothing like insider information. The mango float, a refrigerated dessert made of whipped cream, sweetened condensed milk, graham crackers and fresh mangoes was delicious.

Speaking of delicious, or I should say delicioso, we went to an Italian restaurant where I ate the best pizza of my life. That is a bold statement, but it is true. This pizzeria, Forno Rosso, imports their ingredient from Italy. Buffalo mozzarella, OO flour and San Marzano tomatoes. The pizzas are cooked in a blazing hot wood-fired oven and are ready to eat in about three minutes.

Our good friend Mike, who started the carnivore club, had called ahead to ensure there would be enough seating available for our large group. So, when we arrived, the hostess showed us to an empty back room and seated us, all by ourselves, at a large rectangular table positioned in front of a large window. The deep room provide a dark background while we sat flooded in daylight. Mike, who was seated across from me, and facing the window, was illuminated by the glorious light.

I pulled out my cellphone and said, "Hey Mike, the light is really making you look great; give me a smile."

I showed Mike the photo and he said, "Hey, that is pretty good, send it to me."

We ordered and ate at least five different pizzas that day, but the one that was out of this world was the tartuffo, or truffle pizza. It was a mushroom pie that had a white sauce, canned porcini mushrooms, a little black truffle paste, crumbled Italian sausage and buffalo mozzarella spread across the pizza dough. As the wait staff set the finished tartuffo pie on our table, the truffle aroma wafting from the bubbling surface was other worldly, and it tasted even better.

The photo of Mike, taken in this pizzeria, became very meaningful not long after our gathering. Mike had not been feeling well, and just a few months after sharing pizza together, he received a medical diagnosis that resulted in his untimely death. The carnivore club members were all shocked and deeply saddened by the loss of our good friend. We continue to meet for lunch, and Mike is with us in spirit. Sitting on our table is that same photo of Mike, framed by Mark, still illuminated in light.

The Carnivore Club food experiences have been wonderful and yet they are secondary to the camaraderie and friendships we have developed over the years. Our conversations over lunch are more meaningful than the food, except for the tartuffo pizza mentioned above! This really is a men's club that allows us to gather to do what men often fail to do, share stories about the ups and downs of life, and occasionally, even share our feelings. With each outing, we have grown closer together and cemented our bond using food as the reason to gather. Both the food and the shared conversations are nourishing. Our dear friend Mike, who brought us together, continues to touch us and make a difference in our lives.

CHORIZO AND EGG TACOS

Ingredients

½ stick of Mexican style Chorizo
4 eggs
6 corn tortillas
4 oz cheddar cheese, shredded
1 green onion, finely chopped
4 sprigs of cilantro, chopped

Preparation

Remove the chorizo from the plastic casing and sauté in a non-stick skillet for 5-6 minutes over medium heat. Use a paper towel to soak up some, but not all of the grease. Break the eggs into a bowl and beat until well combined. Season the eggs with salt and black pepper. Add them to the skillet and scramble. Remove them from the heat while the eggs are still moist. They will finish cooking in the warm pan.

Heat the tortillas in a dry skillet, turning once.

To serve, fill the tortillas with some of the egg mixture and garnish with cheese, cilantro, and onions.

20

THE START AND THE END

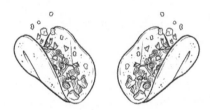

Aexican grocery store, owned by my friend Raul's uncle, opened about five blocks from my home when I was fifteen years old. Raul was then hired to staff the store during his summer vacation. That store, like all ethnic grocery stores, was a cultural education center. As I visited Raul and investigated the stores offerings, it became my port of entry to the foods of the world. My global travels had begun.

I still remember the earthy, toasted corn smell of the still warm corn tortillas that a truck delivered daily. Oh, and the pungent, floral, dried fruit smell of a wide variety of dried chilies sitting in open trays. Their colors ranged from deep reds to almost black. And conchas, those not-so-sweet, light airy pastries with the crisscross cookie dough top, that because of my insatiable sweet tooth, called out, "eat me," every time I entered the store.

Then one day, I boldly purchased some chorizo sausage. Following the advice of my friend Raul, I fried it up, and then drained some of the rendered pork fat before scrambling two eggs in the red spicy pork meat. I wrapped the hot steaming mixture in one of those fresh corn tortillas and bit into something more flavorful than anything I had ever eaten. The meals of meat, potatoes, and canned vegetables that my mother normally prepared suddenly faced extinction.

That Mexican food store changed my life. From that point forward I sought out, ate, and cooked the foods of the world. Doing that has enriched not only my life, but the lives of those around me.

My love of Mexican food has lasted a lifetime. About ten years ago, a small storefront Mexican restaurant opened in a strip mall near my home. It quickly became my go to place. As a regular customer, the owner always greeted me with a warm hello and a broad smile when I walked up to the counter. I would ask how business and life were going for him, and he would ask the same of me.

A few months after the 2016 presidential election, Sandy and I returned home from five weeks of travels. We were hungry and needed to buy some groceries, so I suggested we visit our favorite Mexican place, eat, and then go to the grocery store.

Because I knew Mexicans had been derided during the election campaign, when I approached the counter to place my order, I asked, "So how are you doing since the election?"

With downcast eyes, the owner responded, "I am doing okay, taking it day by day." Clearly his body language and tone of voice did not support his verbal response.

Since we had been traveling and I did not have any cash I asked, "Can I use a credit card?"

"No, I am sorry. But please, just order and eat. The next time you are driving by you can pay me," he replied.

"Are you sure?" I asked.

"Yes, what would you like?" he responded.

We ordered and ate delicious chicken enchiladas with salsa verde. Then, after we finished and were about to walk out the door, I shouted, "I will be right back."

Looking up from the counter, he quickly responded, "No, no, you can pay me later."

Sandy and I drove to a nearby pharmacy where I withdrew some cash from an ATM, and I then purchased a fifth of Patron silver tequila. I drove back to the restaurant and while Sandy waited in the car, I entered and approached the counter. I set down a twenty-dollar bill, to cover the cost of our meals, and the bottle of tequila. The owner and another restaurant employee looked down at the counter, and then at me. The owner asked, "What is this?"

"The money is for the delicious meal you prepared for us, and the tequila is a gift," I responded.

I continued slowly and emotionally, "It is a gift to let you know I care about you. I am so happy you are here preparing wonderful food that I really enjoy."

Then, both of them looked at me while their eyes filled with tears. My gift allowed these two hard working men to release the pent-up sadness they felt. I had to turn and walk away for tears were welling up in my eyes, and men are not supposed to cry.

As I opened the car door and sat down, Sandy asked, "How did it go?"

"Okay, they know we care about them," I said.

So now, it is up to you. Start your journey. Decide what type of "Bumping and Snacking" experiences will help you grow and better understand yourself and others.

With understanding comes acceptance.

Everyone wants to be accepted.

Everyone.

ABOUT THE AUTHOR

Robert B. Hafey lives in Homer Glen, Illinois. Writing *Bumping & Snacking* allowed him to weave his love of food, cooking, and photography along with his view of the world and its people, into his travel experiences. He loves to hear from his readers. Contact him through Facebook.

His other published books include:

Boomhood – A Baby Boomer's Free-Range Childhood: This memoir appeals to all baby boomers because it contains common childhood experiences that they all identify with, like getting their first car. National events like the Kennedy assassination and the Vietnam War, along with cultural revolutions like rock and roll music and the hippie movement are all included.

Lean Safety – Transforming Your Safety Culture with Lean Management: This groundbreaking book, the first book to combine the topic of safety and continuous improvement, transformed how people view industrial safety.

Lean Safety Gemba Walks – A Methodology for Workforce Engagement and Culture Change: This practical guide to redirecting the safety culture of a business has been a game changer in industry.

Made in the USA
Coppell, TX
28 February 2021